The Rise of Neoconservatism

The Rise of Neoconservatism

Intellectuals and Foreign Affairs

1945–1994

John Ehrman

Yale University Press ▪ New Haven and London

Designed by Rebecca Gibb.
Set in Univers and Linotype Centennial types by Marathon Typography
Service, Inc.
Printed in the United States of America by Edwards Brothers, Ann
Arbor, Michigan.

Library of Congress Cataloging-in-Publication Data
Ehrman, John, 1959–
The rise of neoconservatism : intellectuals and foreign affairs,
1945–1994 / John Ehrman.
p.   cm.
Includes bibliographical references and index.
ISBN 0-300-06025-4 (alk. paper)
1. United States—Foreign relations—1945–1989.   2. United
States—Foreign relations—1989–   3. Conservatism—United
States—History—20th century.   4. Liberalism—United States—
History—20th century.   I. Title.
E744.E36   1995
327.73'009'045—dc20   94-28386 CIP

A catalogue record for this book is available from the British Library.
The paper in this book meets the guidelines for permanence and dura-
bility of the Committee on Production Guidelines and Book Longevity of
the Council on Library Resources.

10   9   8   7   6   5   4   3   2

Contents

Preface

This book is about the ideas and impact on American foreign policy of a small but influential group of cold war liberals who became known as the neoconservatives. Neoconservatives are a diverse group. Contrary to what the label implies, some are liberal on social issues and favor governmental intervention in economic affairs; others are social and cultural conservatives who are reluctant to interfere with markets. Some advocate an aggressively interventionist foreign policy, whereas others urge caution and restraint in the use of American power. Tying both groups together, however, is their common identity as activist intellectuals, as well as a deep anti-Communist commitment.

The neoconservatives were originally part of the broad anti-Communist coalition that dominated American liberalism from the late 1940s until the late 1960s. The core of this book is the story of how they maintained their hard-line anti-Communism, gradually broke with what they viewed as a dangerous turn to the left during the 1970s by liberalism and the Democratic party, and regained their influence as part of President Ronald Reagan's conservative coalition during the 1980s. In addition, I seek to illustrate the problems of intellectuals when they move beyond their customary arenas of abstract ideas and small magazines and try to operate in the real world of party politics, where principle often must give way to compromise or expediency.

In telling this tale, I will make three main points. The first is that the neoconservatives of the 1970s and 1980s were still representative of the cold war liberalism—often called the vital center—that developed after World War II. Second, I argue that the neoconservatives' anti-Communism was accompanied by a belief in the superiority of American democratic values. Their view of democracy, or what they often referred to as liberal democracy, was essentially that developed by Protestant theologian Reinhold Niebuhr in his books *Moral Man and Immoral Society* (1932) and *The Children of Light and the Children of Darkness* (1945). According to Niebuhr, because human behavior in groups tends toward tyranny, reason and rationality are poor guides to political action and "moral and constitutional checks" are necessary restraints. Consequently, while they saw the American constitutional system as a model which other peoples could aspire to follow, the neoconservatives remained reluctant to try to impose it on other countries. Third, I will show how these strains of thought worked together in the 1980s, when many neoconservatives held office under President Reagan, to reinforce the administration's anti-Communist outlook while also moving it toward a policy of actively assisting foreign governments or groups trying to develop democratic institutions of their own.[1]

My second purpose in telling the neoconservatives' story is to try to correct some of the misconceptions about them. Neoconservatism is often explained glibly or dismissed as a demonstration of intellectuals' crankiness. Fred Barnes, for example, wrote in 1992 that "neocons defected from the Democratic party in droves in the late 1970s and early 1980s. Their chief gripe: Democrats were accommodating in the face of Soviet expansionism and supportive of social permissivism." Such simplistic comments display a lack of awareness of the differences among neoconservatives and the circumstances under which they left the Democratic party. At the same time, Barnes's comment is typical of how neoconservatives are often portrayed, by their sympathizers and opponents alike. A group that contains liberals, conservatives, politicians, and literary intellectuals is not so easily defined or described. Much of what follows is my attempt to illustrate the differences among neoconservatives, to account for their successes and failures, and to understand their place in both modern American liberalism and the conservative movement.[2]

My focus is on the political migration of the neoconservatives from liberal Democrats to Republicans and what caused it. The framework is chronological, and each chapter explains the evolution of neoconservative thinking and political activity during a given period. To illustrate the major developments and differences among neoconservatives without cluttering the text with the stories and writings of numerous minor figures, I concentrate on the careers and thinking of the most important intellectual and political figures, including Norman Podhoretz, Jeane Kirkpatrick, Daniel Patrick Moynihan, and Robert W. Tucker. I hope that this approach makes a complicated tale more readily comprehensible.

Acknowledgments

I am indebted to all the people who helped me during the researching, writing, and revising of this book. At George Washington University, Leo Ribuffo provided encouragement, numerous suggestions, and invaluable guidance. Ed Berkowitz told me to be sure to tell a good story, a remark I always remembered when I was having trouble organizing my thoughts. William Becker, Peter Hill, Charles Herber, and Howard Gillette all asked probing questions and made points that helped me sharpen my thinking. Dan Barthell helped with computer searches. At the University of Wisconsin, Glen Jeansonne closely read an early version. He, too, provided many helpful ideas and encouragement.

I am also grateful to people on both coasts for their assistance. In Washington, Jed Snyder offered suggestions and put me in touch with Walter Slocombe and Robert Hunter, both of whom took time to talk to me. Irving Kristol, Elliott Abrams, Richard Perle, and Charles Horner were all generous with their time, and I owe a special debt to Jay Lefkowitz. In New York, Stephanie Neuman, Bill Bode, and David

Sidorsky treated me to a stimulating day at Columbia University. Midge Decter devoted several hours to answering my questions. In California, the staff of the Hoover Institution's archives were uniformly gracious and helpful.

Charles Grench and his assistants at Yale University Press not only provided invaluable assistance, but were also indulgent toward a first-time author.

My greatest debt of all is to my wife, Diane. Through our courtship and first five years of marriage she has endured classes, reading lists, language examinations, time alone while I was writing and revising, and editorial chores. It is for her patience, fortitude, and love that I dedicate this to her.

1

The Liberal
Foreign
Policy
Consensus
and After,
1948–1976

Liberal foreign policy thinking shifted several times between 1945 and 1976, often against a backdrop of rapid social and political change in the United States. In the period stretching from the end of World War II to the collapse of South Vietnam, American domestic life and politics changed dramatically, driven by such forces as vigorous economic growth, the rise of the civil rights movement, and the maturing of the baby boom generation. During this time, liberal intellectuals were often in the forefront of change, criticizing the status quo and calling for innovative solutions to social ills. Until the political upheavals of the late 1960s, however, liberals were comfortable with America's role in the world. After a time of uncertainty following the end of World War II, they supported America's cold war policies and its position at the head of the Western anti-Communist alliance.

The post-World War II liberal consensus on foreign policy grew out of prewar battles among leftist intellectuals. During the 1930s, the intellectual left had been dominated by the Communists and their

Progressive allies. Their writings usually portrayed the Soviet Union as a bold social and economic experiment and, under Stalin's gifted leadership, a bulwark against Fascism. Liberal democracy, on the other hand, had lost the faith of many liberal intellectuals. It was not until the end of the decade, and then largely because of the shock of the Nazi-Soviet pact, that anti-totalitarian liberals broke free of Progressive and Communist domination. This proved to be a brief period, however. By the end of 1941, the German invasion of the Soviet Union and Hitler's declaration of war against the United States once more placed liberals, Progressives, and Communists on the same side. As before, the liberals' anti-totalitarian views were submerged in a sea of pro-Soviet and Progressive writings.

Between America's entry into World War II and the mid-1970s, liberal thinking on foreign policy changed sharply several more times in reaction to events abroad. At first, hopes for a peaceful world and continued Soviet-American cooperation in particular after the war were high: "The history of American-Soviet relations is a good portent for the future," noted the *New Republic* in August 1945. The development of the cold war showed such hopes to be unrealistic and liberals were soon embroiled in a debate over foreign policy. By late 1949, however, a consensus had been built around the argument advanced by liberal historian Arthur M. Schlesinger, Jr., in *The Vital Center* that "we must defend and strengthen free society" from Communist assaults, that it was a fantasy that "totalitarianism and democracy can live together," and that foreign policy must accordingly be based on containing Communism. Indeed, the term "vital center" became a shorthand for the liberal anti-Communism that emerged in the late 1940s. By the late 1960s, however, liberals were questioning the vital center's assumptions. Revisionist histories of the cold war, and the war in Vietnam in particular, steadily eroded both of these convictions and with them, the liberal foreign policy consensus. As early as mid-1966, John Kenneth Galbraith observed that the liberal anti-Communist consensus had passed on, and his point was proven many times over during the following ten years as liberal policy intellectuals debated the goals and course of American foreign policy.[1]

As in the 1940s, from about 1967 until 1976 liberals sought a new set of beliefs to guide foreign policy. Few were willing to return to the hard-line anti-Communism of vital center liberalism; the disagreement centered, instead, on how far to distance policy from it. More conservative liberals saw a technologically based, prosperous future that would obviate ideological conflicts. Others looked to international reforms that would reduce the amount of conflict in the world, and some, on the far left, saw the United States as an evil presence in the world and wanted to abandon an active role altogether. Not surprisingly, they were unable to forge a new consensus.

The post-World War II battle on the American intellectual left over relations with the Soviet Union was rooted in prewar factional infighting. During the 1930s there had been three main divisions among left-of-center intellectuals. The first, the Communists and their fellow travelers, owed their allegiance to the American Communist party and, through it, to the Soviet Union and its leader, Joseph Stalin. The second group, the Progressives, sought radical changes in American society and were willing to cooperate with the Communists and their organizations. The most prominent Progressive voices were the weekly magazines the *New Republic* and the *Nation*. The liberals comprised the third and most moderate group. They also championed social and economic reform, but their anti-totalitarian position made them more suspicious of cooperating with the Communists than were the Progressives. Because the liberals were not well organized, however, the Communists and Progressives were able to dominate the intellectual left. As philosopher Sidney Hook recalled 50 years later, "this picture of Communist influence, so strong that it amounted to domination of key areas of American cultural life . . . may appear incredible to those who were not involved at the time, but the evidence . . . [is] overwhelming."[2]

The Communists' strength was set in an atmosphere of doubt about the viability of American democracy. According to Edward Purcell, after World War I the rise of scientific naturalism and relativism had broken down traditional concepts of political ethics, while legal realism had attacked faith in the validity of law and constitutionalism. These developments undermined the idea that there existed higher, absolute laws and morality that validated the concept of constitutional democracy. The depression that began in 1929 reinforced these doubts and, in Purcell's words, led to "more . . . despair about democracy than any other period since the early nineteenth century," and left many to wonder if only dictatorships were "capable of meeting the problems of advanced industrial society."[3]

In this context, many intellectuals on the left focused their hopes on the USSR. Since the Bolshevik revolution, the Soviet experiment had provided radical and progressive intellectuals with an example of an alternative organization for politics and economics. Many had also visited the USSR in the 1920s and early 1930s and written favorable accounts of what they had seen. These, according to historian Alexander Bloom, "gave Communism in particular and radicalism in general a strong position among . . . intellectuals."[4]

The rise of Fascism in Europe during the 1930s reinforced the sympathy of Progressives and many liberals toward the Soviet Union. For most of the decade, and especially during the Spanish civil war (1936–1939), Moscow seemed to be the center of opposition to Hitler. "Indeed, from 1936 on," writes historian William L. O'Neill, "as sole supporter of the doomed Spanish Republic and leader of the Popular Fronts, it seemed to be the *only* antifascist power." This, in turn, led Progressives and many liberals to put aside any doubts raised by Stalin's purges and terror. In Hook's words, "hundreds of liberals, proud of the progressive American heritage they had invoked in criticizing injustices in the United States, Italy, Germany, and Spain, were prepared to turn their backs on it when questions were raised about justice in the Soviet Union."[5]

The Nazi-Soviet pact of August 1939, as well as the Nazi victories of 1939 and 1940, however, both eroded the Communists' domination of the left and strengthened the position of the anti-totalitarian liberals. Communism now appeared to be as great a threat to democracy as Fascism and, according to Purcell, the "threat of 'alien' totalitarian ideologies . . . led to a passionate reaffirmation of traditional political principles." Such prominent intellectuals as theologian Reinhold Niebuhr, journalist Walter Lippmann, and University of Chicago President Robert M. Hutchins spoke and wrote in favor of democratic theory. The anti-totalitarian liberals also began to organize. In May 1939 Hook, working with philosopher John Dewey, established the Committee for Cultural Freedom. According to the *New York Times,* the committee "emphasized opposition to the totalitarian ideas espoused in Soviet Russia as well as . . . Germany, Italy, Japan, and Spain." Niebuhr, who in March 1941 wrote that the moral cynicism of the Communists had become "practically identical" with that of the Nazis, founded a similar group, the Union for Democratic Action (UDA), the following month.[6]

By the end of 1941, however, the German invasion of Russia and the United States' entry into the war once again put liberals, Communists, and Progressives on the same side. In yet another reversal, the Soviet Union and Stalin quickly came to be portrayed as heroic allies, and this image was extended to show how similar Soviet ideals were to the democracies'. In early 1943, for example, Niebuhr revised his judgments to note that although "Communism uses dictatorship brutally . . . its moral cynicism is only provisional, and it is never morally nihilistic, as the Nazis are. It is, in fact, ultimately utopian in morals, just as is the liberal-democratic world." Ideally, noted Niebuhr, Soviet-American cooperation might even "lead to a wholesome exchange of political experience." Niebuhr was by no means alone in his favorable wartime appraisal of the USSR. One writer in the *New Republic* claimed that religious freedom had returned to Russia, and "all who wish to worship God are free to express their faith . . . today and will be in the future."[7]

Liberals and Progressives made similarly optimistic statements about their political vision for the postwar world. In fact, the Progressives set the tone for both groups' rhetoric. Once totalitarianism was defeated, noted the *New Republic* in February 1940, the world could turn to "the task of building a democratic, free, progressive and just civilization." Not to be outdone, the UDA declared in its founding statement that defeating Fascism would create an opportunity to change the "outworn capitalistic relations which have been allowed to continue to prevail in the democratic countries," and to bring an end to British imperialism. Led by Vice-President Henry A. Wallace, Progressives and liberals supported a set of ideals that anticipated extending New Deal-style reforms throughout the world, with "self-determination everywhere, an end to economic and political imperialism, and vast economic development programs to assure freedom from want."[8]

Progressives and liberals further expected that the Soviet Union and the United States would remain friendly after the war and cooperate to maintain world peace. "If there is to be peace in the world, it must be based on an agreement between Great Britain, Russia, China, the United States and the other United Nations. . . . The confidence of Russia in us is as vital as the confidence of the United Nations and ourselves in Russia," said former ambassador to the Soviet Union Joseph E. Davies in 1943. Niebuhr's wartime idea of Soviet-American ideological compatibility included postwar cooperation as well: "The possibility of achieving a stable world order, with Russia as one of the dominant nations of that order, is enhanced by the fact that Russia and the Western nations have a common interest in its establishment." Finally, there was a belief—apparently rooted in the perception that Stalin had become a democrat—that the Soviet leader would not fail to fulfill his people's hopes for peace. In fact, even entertaining doubts about the strength of the relationship was close to treason—"to play Hitler's game," according to Davies.[9]

If their plans were to fail, liberals and Progressives believed it would be the fault of the United States. In May 1942, the head of the UDA, Frank Kingdon, had urged Progressives and liberals to unite to sweep away isolationist members of Congress. The Soviets were believed to be aware that a Republican election victory "might easily give the reactionary and isolationist anti-Soviet groups the upper hand and thus undermine, if not destroy, the whole structure . . . of unity." The threat from the State Department was particularly acute because of the continued presence of "several of the Assistant Secretaries and many lesser persons, who are strongly reactionary."[10]

Even as these statements were made, however, awkward questions began to arise about the theoretical and political foundations on which they rested. One of the first and most significant shifts among liberals was Reinhold Niebuhr's. In early 1944, when he delivered the lectures that formed the basis for his book *The Children of Light and the Children of Darkness,* Niebuhr was again becoming less inclined to excuse dictatorships and more aware of the need to defend democracy: "Democracy has a more compelling justification and requires a more realistic vindication than is given it by the liberal culture with which it has been associated in modern history." Niebuhr worried that too much optimism about human nature was unrealistic and would ultimately undermine democracy; similarly, he fretted that the experiences of the 1930s and 1940s would lead to excessive pessimism and a loss of faith in democracy.[11]

Niebuhr still supported the ideal of a world community, but considered its chances for success quite slim. Man's limitations were a large part of the reason: "The task of building a world community is man's final necessity and possibility, but also his final impossibility. . . . It is an impossibility because man is . . . a finite creature, wedded to time and place, and incapable of building any structure or culture of civilization which does not have its foundations in a particular and dated locus." Niebuhr realized that world peace would still depend on British, Soviet, and American cooperation, but he was beginning to see that the Soviets would, at best, be difficult partners:

> Of these three, Russia will have the greatest difficulty in establishing inner moral checks upon its will-to-power . . . it is informed by a simple religion and culture which makes self-criticism difficult and self-righteousness inevitable. Its creed assumes the evil intentions of capitalistic powers and the innocency and virtue of a nation which stands on the other side of the revolution.[12]

Apart from his renewed suspicion of the USSR and the prospects for building a new world, Niebuhr's thinking posed an additional problem for liberal assumptions about postwar planning. Niebuhr's message was that a carefully prepared plan for the world was bound to fail, for the complex nature of international politics would "not yield to the approach of a too simple idealism." Instead, the task of achieving a world community had to be accomplished piecemeal, bearing in mind that it would be "the most difficult task mankind has ever faced," and that one generation could only "lay minimal foundations." Niebuhr wanted liberals to understand "the fragmentary and broken character of all historic achievements," so they would not reject a less-than-perfect world system. Such a pessimistic outlook undercut the liberal assumption that universal planning could be implemented effectively and quickly after the war.[13]

Niebuhr had not yet found his audience. Although he had a prominent public platform, his warnings were not within the liberal mainstream and, therefore, won few adherents. Despite growing unease over relations with Moscow in mid- and late 1945—particularly over East European issues—most liberals still believed "that American policy was the main barrier to friendship," according to historian Alonzo Hamby.[14]

After the war ended, Progressive intellectuals focused the blame for deteriorating relations on what they saw as Washington's generally aggressive posture toward the USSR and, specifically, its refusal to share atomic energy information. The *Nation* pointed out that American plans for the bases in the Pacific were bound to raise Soviet fears that the United States was planning for another war, but also noted that "the invention of the atomic bomb has also aggravated the mutual mistrust between Russia and the West." This was a comparatively moderate evaluation. During the fall of 1945, the *New Republic* printed a series of increasingly alarming editorials on relations with the USSR and the bomb. The tensions were caused by Washington's "refusal to share the atomic-bomb 'secret,'" the magazine argued in early November, and followed that two weeks later with the statement that sharing was necessary if the world was "to avert catastrophe." At the end of November, alluding to Secretary of State James Byrnes's comment that international controls on atomic energy could be established within sixty days, a *New Republic* editorial was headlined "Sixty Days to War or Peace!"[15]

Simultaneously, the Progressive journals found ways to excuse Soviet actions. The dominant theme of their regular contributors was that the Soviets posed no threat and acted as they did out of a justifiable concern for their security. "Stalin and his fellows have no intention of failing to justify the expectations of their people for a lasting peace and for security measures to prevent their own country from becoming a battleground if war should come again despite the efforts of the Soviet Union," wrote William Mandel in November 1945. In another case, Soviet misconduct was completely denied. Fears of Soviet domination of Poland were labeled a "fantasy" by one *New Republic* correspondent, who further claimed that "the trends in Poland are toward democracy." The United States was then faulted for making friendly relations contingent on conditions unacceptable to the Soviets which, editorialized the *New Republic* in April 1946, "merely strengthen[s] the obstacles to Soviet cooperation." The conclusion was invariably the same: "our faults in foreign affairs lie here, not in Moscow."[16]

By mid-1946, however, the Progressive journals had become marginalized, and their criticisms had virtually no impact on events. President Harry S Truman and his advisers were continually responding to new, and unprecedented, events and there is little reason to believe that they stopped to consider, or even cared about, what the *New Republic* said. Moreover, according to O'Neill, the Progressives "did not realize how demented [their analyses] seemed to others." The problem for liberals, if they were to have any influence over policy, was to break away from the Progressives and establish an independent and realistic voice. Their views would have to account for the world as it was, not as they hoped it would be.[17]

Although the origins of the vital center can be traced to 1944, when anti-Stalinist liberals resumed questioning the USSR's good intentions, its themes did not become apparent until 1946. It was then that the liberal-Progressive feud began to intensify, as the liberals responded to the accusations of Washington's responsibility for deteriorating relations with Moscow in January 1946. The liberal counterargument began with a straightforward statement of faith in the United States and its acts. In an article in the *New York Times Magazine,* publisher Arthur Hays Sulzberger rejected the idea that the United States was betraying liberal ideals. In fact, Sulzberger saw little reason to be disappointed with America's conduct in the world, citing the founding of the United Nations, economic and food aid, and the return of democracy to many areas of the world as "grounds for optimism." Sulzberger tied the crucial question of the Soviet Union to that of dictatorship in general. While he saw no reason not to try to be friendly toward Moscow, he was also cautious: "I do not believe that free people can afford to trust dictatorships whether they be of the right, or of the center, or of the left." Distrust of both left- and right-wing totalitarianism was to become one of the hallmarks of the vital center.[18]

Another major tenet of the developing vital center ideology, that Communism was the greatest threat to true liberalism, emerged in the spring and summer of 1946. Writing in *Life* magazine, journalists Joseph and Stewart Alsop decried confusion among America liberals caused, in their view, by the "idealized picture of the Soviet state," that liberals had formed during the war. Henry Wallace (now President Truman's secretary of commerce) earned the Alsops' special scorn for his "irresponsible" public dissensions from the Truman administration's policies. Liberal "self-delusion" about the Soviets as well as American Communists would sap the strength of liberalism, argued the Alsops, leaving it unable to fulfill its roles of bringing about needed social changes and organizing "a stable, prosperous, and . . . peaceful world," while leaving it vulnerable to a right-wing backlash. Consequently, Communism had to be fought both at home and abroad. In self-defense they urged a liberal program of support for the United Nations, foreign aid, and "firmness . . . to bring to a halt the process of Soviet expansion."[19]

The Alsops' theme caught on quickly, in large part because it drew on the liberals' prewar suspicions that the Progressives were fatally tolerant of totalitarianism. The prominent young Harvard historian Arthur M. Schlesinger, Jr., also writing in *Life,* repeated the claim that the Communist threat was greatest to the left and that "it is imperative for the American liberals, if they wish to avoid total bankruptcy, to get back to a sense of moral seriousness and of absolute devotion to the facts . . . when they are alert to the situation, liberals can lick the Communists." Schlesinger further asserted that American Communists were warped individuals, receiving from the party the "social, intellectual, even sexual fulfillment they cannot obtain in existing society." *Partisan Review,* long an anti-Stalinist bastion, was just as savage. It labeled the *New Republic* and the *Nation* a "fifth column," accused them of "appeasement," and claimed that they were "dragging down in their own ruin everyone else who genuinely desires the values that have been an essential part of traditional liberalism."[20]

The development of the vital center took another step forward in September and October 1946. Reinhold Niebuhr traveled to Europe in the late summer, departing with a still relatively moderate view of the USSR. From London, he wrote in the *Nation* that Soviet "truculence" was largely caused by insecurity, expressed some misgivings about not sharing atomic secrets, and advised that patience was the best course to follow toward Russia—"every resource must be exhausted." It was important, he argued, for the United States to walk a middle path and "neither play the militarist game of preaching war against Russia nor repeat the slogans of the fellow-travelers." Niebuhr went on to Germany, while at home Truman fired Wallace for his speech on September 12 criticizing the administration's foreign policy for being too harsh toward Moscow.[21]

Niebuhr's trip to Germany and his first-hand look at Europe changed his view of the USSR, and upon his return to the United States he joined the anti-Wallace chorus. Writing in *Life* in October as a member of "Henry Wallace's school of thought in domestic politics," Niebuhr echoed the Alsops' alarm over "the confusion in American liberalism, of which the Wallace speech is a symbol, [and which] must be recognized as catastrophic in the light of the European realities." These realities, Niebuhr pointed out, included constant Soviet pressure to expand, particularly in Germany, and "new demands" in response to "every gesture of trust." Political firmness and reconstruction aid were required to fight back, in Niebuhr's view, while true liberals must also "make our political and economic life more worthy of our faith and therefore more impregnable."[22]

Unlike his cautions in 1944, Niebuhr's article had a significant and immediate impact. After a year of disappointments and tensions with Russia, Niebuhr's firm tone, according to his biographer, Richard Fox, "rang true to an imposing array of liberals." In part this may have been because Niebuhr recognized the political problems created by liberals' anxieties about their own imperfections and their need to be reassured of the continued validity of their cause. "No culture or civilization is as good as it pretends," he had noted in *Life*, but "contradictions to its own professed faiths" could not be allowed to stand in the way of creating a policy to respond to an aggressive enemy. Addressing liberals' greatest area of insecurity, Niebuhr reassured them that their cause remained valid even if it, and they, were imperfect. As Irving Kristol would remark almost 50 years later, Niebuhr "gave me all the good reasons" to avoid falling into the trap of utopianism.[23]

The diverging attitudes on foreign policy soon led to an open split on the left. The major issue was which group could credibly claim to represent the liberal future. In December 1946, Wallace's supporters formed the Progressive Citizens of America (PCA), which sought to carry on the New Deal tradition and defend liberalism from the perceived threat of the right. On foreign affairs, consequently, the PCA was willing to try to reach an accommodation with the Soviets. According to historian Steven Gillon, the founding of the PCA was also "a clear challenge" to the Union for Democratic Action, which also claimed the mantle of the New Deal. The UDA had been plagued by financial problems, however, and by 1946 was close to collapse. A membership drive was planned and, by coincidence, the UDA held an organizational and expansion meeting in January 1947, a week after the PCA was founded. Led by Niebuhr and Schlesinger, and with such prominent anti-Communist liberals as Hubert Humphrey and Stewart Alsop in attendance, the UDA changed its name to Americans for Democratic Action (ADA) and affirmed its opposition to Communism and totalitarianism.[24]

In the winter of 1947 the PCA and ADA both claimed leadership of the liberals, but the ADA won out within the year as it became the group most representative of liberal views. It took about six months for the implications of the policy differences between the two groups to become clear. Wallace and the PCA opposed Truman's March 1947 request for aid to Greece and Turkey, but the ADA missed the chance to distinguish itself from the PCA, giving Truman only lukewarm support because of concerns about supporting the right-wing Greek government and the lack of a role for the still-young United Nations. That summer, however, the PCA also opposed the Marshall Plan, calling it "a clever disguise of traditional Truman anti-Communism," while the ADA gave the plan enthusiastic support. Most liberals supported the plan, for it promoted the type of economic aid to Europe that they had long sought as an alternative to purely anti-Soviet measures. In addition, liberals and the Truman administration alike could point to the Marshall Plan as a coherent policy proposal, while Wallace's supporters were left drifting, without a policy of their own to support.[25]

The triumph of the Marshall Plan and the ADA made Schlesinger and Niebuhr the leading liberal foreign policy theoreticians, and they spoke out and wrote frequently during 1947 and 1948, spreading the vital center message. Niebuhr continued to counsel a strong faith in democracy and liberalism: "To win the ideological battle against Communism it is not enough to point to the crass corruptions of the original dream of justice. . . . It is more important to make our cause so just that it will win the allegiance not of the comfortable but of the insecure and impoverished." For Schlesinger, too, the faith was strong—"a fighting faith," as he termed democracy in April 1948. Nor did Schlesinger see a need to apologize for the flaws of the democracy he defended: "We may still have a long way to go; but we are free to name the ultimate goals, to denounce the present abuses and to demand haste. That kind of freedom is increasingly precious in the world today." Schlesinger further supported strong measures to defend democracy. He endorsed the limited use of loyalty investigations, for example, to root out "that fanatical group which rejects all American interests in favor of those of the Soviet Union."[26]

Most important, Niebuhr and Schlesinger consistently advocated that foreign policy firmly resist Soviet expansionism. Writing in *Life* in the fall of 1948, Niebuhr examined the dilemma of how to face the Soviets without falling into the policy traps of peace at any price or preventive war. But facing the reality that "we cannot afford any more compromises," and that another war could be avoided only "if our nerves are steady," Niebuhr said bluntly that "we must be ready to risk war rather than yield to Russian pressure." Schlesinger, for his part, advocated extending Marshall Plan aid to cover military assistance, arguing that the Communist opposition to the plan "requires the military as well as the political and economic strengthening of free Europe." That Schlesinger's remarks appeared in the *New Republic* is itself an indication of how influential vital center thinking had become by late 1948.[27]

Another indicator of the vital center's gathering strength was the reception given to George Kennan's July 1947 article in *Foreign Affairs*, "The Sources of Soviet Conduct," signed "X." Kennan, a career diplomat and then director of the State Department's Policy Planning Staff, later wrote that he had based the article on what he had been saying and thinking for "at least two years," although his cables from the Moscow embassy in 1944 suggest even earlier origins. Regardless of its roots, however, the article was in perfect step with its times:

> The thoughtful observer of Russian-American relations will find no cause for complaint in the Kremlin's challenge to American society. He will rather experience a certain gratitude to a Providence which, by providing the American people with this implacable challenge, has made their

entire security as a nation dependent on their
pulling themselves together and accepting the
responsibilities of moral and political leadership
that history plainly intended them to bear.

Both Kennan and his article were quickly popularized. *Life* and
Reader's Digest printed excerpts (*Life* noted that Kennan almost certainly was the author), and the *New York Times Magazine* printed a
flattering profile of Kennan—"peculiarly well suited to a job that
combines the long point of view with hard-headed thinking"—and
printed his photograph on its cover in September.[28]

Schlesinger synthesized these themes in *The Vital Center,* which
was published in September 1949. The book gathered in one place
much of what had been said in the previous three years. Schlesinger
noted that the tensions of the times had produced an "age of anxiety" and drew on Niebuhr to justify faith in democracy: "Consistent
pessimism about man, far from promoting authoritarianism, alone
can inoculate the democratic faith against it." The Communists still
"presented an immediate political danger" to liberals. Schlesinger
embraced the United States' new world role, calling it a "world destiny," and continued to advocate containment as the way to protect
non-Communist countries. In the rest of the world, Schlesinger
wanted to stop Communism by combining trade, economic assistance,
and support for liberal nationalists. Moreover, just as Communism
was a threat at home and abroad, he sought to make domestic and
foreign liberalism inseparable: "We must commit ourselves to . . . the
struggle within the world against Communism and fascism; the struggle within our country against oppression and stagnation; the struggle
within ourselves against pride and corruption; nor can engagement
in one dimension exclude responsibility for another."[29]

The Vital Center quickly became the standard for mainstream liberal thinking. By reviewing the issues and restating the questions
and responses in one place, Schlesinger had done liberals a tremendous favor: they no longer had to grope for answers to their doubts.
His book contained little that was new or not already agreeable to
most liberals; consequently, the reviews were overwhelmingly favor-

able. *Commentary* praised "the precision, vitality, and emotional power of his restatement of commonly accepted views." The *New York Times* was succinct, calling *The Vital Center* "the best guide to our prospects for civilized survival we have seen in a long time." The *Nation* called it "a work of the first rank," and *Saturday Review* recommended it "because of the conviction with which [Schlesinger] reports the advent of a courageous mid-century generation equipped not merely with fears but a lucid and compelling faith."[30]

Schlesinger's timing was good. *The Vital Center* fit well with other liberal anti-Communist books of the time, including *The God That Failed,* a compendium of disillusioned intellectuals' experiences with Communism, and George Orwell's *1984.* Another indication of the strength of the vital center was the foundation the following year of the militantly anti-Communist Congress for Cultural Freedom, with a large number of American liberals prominent in its ranks.[31]

The vital center message and the liberal consensus built around it were strong enough to be adopted quickly into official foreign policy rhetoric. This, in turn, enabled liberals to maintain an audience in Washington for their analyses and policy suggestions, as well as a voice in the Democratic party and its positions. The most striking example of this trend was NSC-68, a document Truman requested in early 1950 as a review of foreign policy problems—which by then included the Communist victory in China, the Soviet development of the atomic bomb—and possible strategies for creating coherent policies. The document was drafted by a group headed by Paul Nitze, then head of the State Department's Policy Planning Staff, submitted to the president in April 1950, and approved by Truman in September. Nitze later characterized the draft as an effort to establish "a broad conception of national security." It was, in short, "the definitive statement of American national security policy."[32]

The group's policy proposals were not radically new. Historians have noted that they served to reinforce the existing policy of containment and that NSC-68's major initiative was a new emphasis on the military and increased defense spending. Previous policy papers, however, had been measured in tone and limited in ambitions; this caution was absent from NSC-68. Historian John Lewis Gaddis has commented that the purpose of NSC-68's rhetoric was to "shake" the bureaucracy and Congress into supporting its policy recommendations. The paper's wording also reflected the prevailing view of the high stakes of the cold war. Nitze recalls that the strategic recommendations, for example, were meant to solve the problem of getting "from where we are to where we want to be without being struck by disaster along the way."[33]

The rhetoric in NSC-68 reflected the new liberal assumptions. The first section of the document noted that "the people of the world yearn for relief from the anxiety arising from the risk of atomic war," and that the government and people "must now take new and fateful decisions" affecting the fate of civilization. In addition, the writers noted that "our free society finds itself mortally challenged by the Soviet system. No other value system is so wholly irreconcilable with ours, so implacable in its purpose to destroy ours . . . and no other has the support of a great and growing center of military power." Other passages reflected additional aspects of vital center ideology. Significantly, NSC-68 included the idea that freedom was a fighting faith and also echoed Schlesinger's commitment to the worldwide defense of freedom, claiming that the "assault on free institutions is world-wide now, and . . . a defeat of free institutions anywhere is a defeat everywhere."[34]

With the advent of NSC-68, liberal foreign policy ideology again coincided with the realities of government policy and the world situation. The change had been gradual and agonizing, for it had split the liberals and sent Wallace and his followers into political oblivion. The magnitude of the left's defeat also kept it from mounting an effective attack on liberal anti-Communism until well into the 1960s. For the victorious liberals, now known as cold war liberals, triumph meant that they would have a dominant voice in foreign policy for almost twenty years.

The vital center was successful as a unifying ideology for liberal internationalism as long as liberals had faith in its ideals and the ideals coincided with policy. Once the faith was undermined the liberal consensus quickly fell apart. Its disintegration is commonly blamed on the Vietnam war, which "utterly discredited cold war liberalism," in Alonzo Hamby's view. But Vietnam was only one factor. An equally important cause of the demise of the vital center was the attack on its intellectual foundations, which began well before President Lyndon Johnson escalated American involvement in Vietnam. Indeed, by the mid-1960s, the left had already articulated a case against the vital center, its assumptions about America's virtues, and the legitimacy of its global interests. These points made it difficult to restate old answers when questions arose about Johnson's ability to direct foreign policy.[35]

The revisionist assault began in the early 1950s and was led by historian William Appleman Williams, who had grown up in Henry Wallace's home state of Iowa and had become active in leftist politics while stationed by the navy in Corpus Christi, Texas, after World War II. After leaving the navy, Williams earned his master's and Ph.D. degrees in history at the University of Wisconsin and also briefly studied socialist economics in England. In his dissertation, published in 1952 as *American-Russian Relations, 1781–1947,* Williams began to develop the idea around which his writings would revolve, that American foreign policy was dominated by a search for access to foreign markets as an outlet for surplus domestic production which, in turn, had led to the creation of an informal empire. This idea had been put forward earlier by Charles Beard, but Williams brought the point up to date and, as John Lewis Gaddis points out, gave it its "most influential characterization." The belief that an expansionist foreign policy was the only alternative to revolution within the United States, wrote Williams, "supplied American empire builders with an overview and explanation of the world, and a reasonably specific program of action from 1893 to 1953," and provided guidance for the "crusaders for the Free World."[36]

Not surprisingly, Williams rejected the orthodox explanation of the origins of the cold war that emphasized Soviet culpability. Instead, he placed much of the blame on the United States, arguing in 1956 that American policymakers had known of the USSR's postwar weakness but chose to overstate the threat and institute containment in an effort to force the Soviets to conform to American expectations: "Abroad, therefore, they embarked on a program of forcing the Soviet Union to accept extreme terms of settlement. At home, meanwhile, they 'bombarded the American people,' in the words of one sober and ideologically impeccable student, 'with a "hate the enemy" campaign rarely seen in our history; never, certainly in peacetime.'" Williams believed that the results of the cold war policy had been disastrous; for example, the prosperity of the 1950s was chimerical because it was based on cold war spending. Furthermore, "prosperity at such a price may not lead to bankruptcy in the narrow economic sense, but it is likely to destroy the moral and intellectual integrity of society and bring about its physical devastation in a nuclear war." Nor was prosperity the only illusion Williams sought to dispel. He rejected, for example, the idea "that American society is based on the Vital Center, which includes everybody but the nobodies on the Right and Left."[37]

Williams presented his fully formed argument about American imperialism and the cold war in *The Tragedy of American Diplomacy,* published in 1959. The book's thesis centered on Williams's earlier contention that the search for markets was at the root of American foreign policy: "Formalized and symbolized by the Open Door Notes, the idea that America's imperial economic expansion was necessary, desirable, and possible was rapidly translated into specific policies and action." He also repeated his contention that this view lay at the heart of the cold war, for the United States had "rapidly embarked upon a program to force the Soviet Union to accept America's traditional conception of itself and the world." Williams absolved the Soviets of all blame, arguing that "Stalin's effort to solve Russia's problems of security and recovery short of widespread conflict with the United States was not matched by American leaders who acceded to power upon the death of Roosevelt."[38]

Williams believed that cold war policy had reached a dead end. The rest of the world, he suggested, was interested not in fighting the cold war but instead with solving its own problems. According to Williams, many people in the underdeveloped world were impressed by the achievements of Soviet and Chinese Communism and sought to follow these examples with revolutions of their own. In response, the United States "could resort to nuclear war or it could . . . [devise] new policies calculated to assist those revolutions to move immediately and visibly toward their goal of a better human life." Such policies would create, in Williams's phrase, "an open door for revolutions," and would help "other peoples achieve their aspirations in their own way."[39]

Williams used *The Tragedy of American Diplomacy* to develop further his criticisms of American society. Williams had already complained in the *Nation* about the "interminable" list of domestic problems the country was ignoring. Now in vague terms he outlined the need to stop seeing America's well-being in terms of overseas expansion and concentrate instead on "the central problem of reordering its own society so that it functions through such a balanced relationship with the rest of the world." Williams later termed this process one of "self-commitment" and denied that it was a form of isolationism, but acknowledged in the 1962 edition of his book that the process placed "limits upon America's freedom of action."[40]

Williams's achievement was to revive the progressive arguments that had been beaten down in the late 1940s. His tendency to blame the cold war on the United States and to gloss over the seriousness of international problems in favor of concentrating on domestic issues differed little from the Progressives' hopes for the postwar world. In addition, Williams's writings demonstrated that progressive ideas had survived the vital center's triumph and could still emerge from the left. Williams provided the fresh, articulate intellectual leadership they needed in order to return to prominence.

Williams had only a small audience at first. Reviews of *The Tragedy of American Diplomacy* were generally hostile, crediting Williams with an original interpretation but then condemning it. Williams was also harassed by the House Un-American Activities Committee in 1960 and 1961. But the major reason Williams failed to win many converts was that he was out of step with his times. Not only did the vital center consensus still hold in 1959, but some of its strongest days lay just ahead. In the 1960 presidential race, Richard Nixon and John F. Kennedy both sought to win votes by demonstrating their hard-line attitudes toward the cold war. In his inaugural address, Kennedy reaffirmed a strong commitment to the worldwide defense of liberty and followed up with civilian programs, including the Peace Corps, as well as with such military moves as increased defense spending. Schlesinger was among the ADA members appointed to positions in the Kennedy administration, giving the apostles of the vital center access to the highest levels of government.[41]

Williams and the revisionists rapidly gained strength, however, as the war in Vietnam escalated. A new generation of diplomatic historians emerged from the University of Wisconsin, including Walter LaFeber, Lloyd Gardner, and Thomas McCormick. Their works, influenced by Williams and Wisconsin's Progressive tradition, began to appear several years after *The Tragedy of American Diplomacy* and, in the mid-1960s, were joined by a growing number of other revisionist studies which emphasized American responsibility for the cold war. These works found a much more receptive audience than Williams's book had, political scientist Robert W. Tucker explained, because of "the substantial defection and growing disaffection of the intellectuals" over the war. Historian and social critic Christopher Lasch noted in early 1968 that Williams's radicalism had become more fashionable and his books were "beginning to pass into the mainstream of scholarly discourse." Lasch further pointed out that the view was spreading among radicals that foreign policy could not be changed until American society itself was altered.[42]

Questions also arose about the vital center because of growing doubts about the direction of foreign policy under Lyndon Johnson. These misgivings also came in advance of the emergence of Vietnam as the dominant foreign policy issue. Johnson's lack of preparation in foreign affairs was his greatest handicap, even more so than the inevitable comparisons with Kennedy. Less than six months into his administration the *New Republic* commented that Johnson "sometimes tends to talk as if most [non-Communist countries] did not possess the wheel until the United States graciously invented it." Johnson had organizational problems as well. Townsend Hoopes has recalled his experience on becoming deputy assistant secretary of defense for international security affairs in January 1965: "It was difficult to find out what was going on in foreign policy. . . . I felt the absence of an explicit framework of policy . . . there appeared to be a serious lack of . . . comprehensive assessment and long-range planning." Hoopes blamed Johnson's poor background in foreign relations and inability to make use of Kennedy's informal policymaking system for his administration's indirection and tendency to focus on immediate crises.[43]

Other contemporary analysts, while not always as harsh as Hoopes, were still quick to pick up on the post-Kennedy problems of foreign policy. One writer in *Commentary* pointed out that much of the blame lay with Kennedy, whose charisma "masked" problems; nonetheless, the spring of 1965 found America's international prestige "lower than at any time within recent memory." Vietnam was one problem, but the most serious one was termed the continuing "Achesonian" influence over policy which called for a hard-line, realpolitik approach to world affairs and undermined Washington's claim to moral superiority over Moscow.[44]

The lack of direction created an opening for challengers to the Johnson administration's policies. Senator J. William Fulbright (D-Arkansas) led one of the major assaults. Fulbright argued that world conditions had changed since the 1950s, that the Communists presented less of a threat, and that the United States was "clinging to old myths in the face of new realities." Most notably, Fulbright asserted that the United States had fallen victim to an "arrogance of power" which was manifesting itself in a foolish attempt to "remake" the rest of the world "in its own shining image." (The last point echoed William Appleman Williams's call for more tolerance of diversity in the world.) Fulbright was further disturbed by the president's growing power in foreign affairs, which came at the expense of Congress, as well as what he perceived to be a tendency toward overreaction to events overseas. Fulbright used his chairmanship of the Senate Foreign Relations Committee to question policy and to try to reduce the president's power to act without congressional approval. Although Fulbright had little success in affecting foreign policy—the Vietnam war, which became the dominant issue in foreign policy in 1965 and 1966, continued to escalate—his dissent showed that the Democratic consensus was deteriorating and that opposition to hard-line anti-Communism no longer carried a serious political penalty.[45]

The general foreign policy debate intensified after 1966. Participation was no longer confined to revisionists or liberal dissidents, but expanded to include the liberal intellectuals and moderate Republicans who "had long been committed to the same causes," in Robert W. Tucker's words. For the first time in 20 years the "scope, ideological temper, means, and purposes of American foreign policy" were open for discussion; John Kenneth Galbraith, one of the founders of the ADA, noted the end of "coalescence on the old and simple goal of anti-Communism." One indication of the debate's sudden growth was in the pages of *Foreign Affairs,* the most prestigious of the international affairs journals. Until 1967, it had been filled with articles addressing specific regional and functional problems without extensively questioning the foundations of American foreign policy. In the January 1967 issue, however, McGeorge Bundy, who had served as President Kennedy's national security adviser, wrote that "one can almost hear the nation asking where it is trying to go." Bundy argued that the international arena had become too complex for a foreign policy which saw the world in stark terms of black and white, or Communism and anti-Communism. But Bundy had little to offer as a new course. Even as he acknowledged the changes in the world, he returned to the vital center, writing that "we have a still more sweeping double duty: to carry on both these wide foreign activities and an active program of social progress at home."[46]

Bundy's outlook was rapidly becoming a minority view among liberal policy intellectuals, however. Historian Henry Steele Commager declared: "In the struggle against Communism . . . we have allowed ourselves to be maneuvered into the position of opposing revolution and what some of these people [in the underdeveloped world] think of as progress." Another historian, Theodore Draper, wrote of a "crisis" in American foreign policy, "of which the Cuban, the Dominican, and the Vietnam cases have been three incarnations." Not surprisingly, in September 1967 *Commentary* editor Norman Podhoretz was able to summarize the responses in his journal's symposium "Liberal Anti-Communism Revisited" by noting, "Virtually all seem to agree that the American effort to contain Communism by military means cannot be justified either politically or morally in the double context of a polycentric Communist world and an unstable underdeveloped world seething with nationalist aspirations."[47]

The presidential election of 1968 was the vital center's last gasp. Vice-President and Democratic candidate Hubert Humphrey represented the founding ethos of the ADA, commenting unapologetically in April 1968 that "we are the nation that has helped bind up the wounds of our former enemies . . . helped to liquidate Western colonialism and to contain Communist imperialism." But after his defeat the Democrats' party structure was left "abysmally weak," in historian Herbert Parmet's words, and the party reforms that followed served to weaken further the party while fragmenting power among various factions and individuals. The ADA, too, splintered and drifted steadily leftward, dropping its emphasis on anti-Communism in favor of "vague notions of world law as a means of ensuring peace," according to Steven Gillon, and advocating the reorientation of policy to serve the needs of underdeveloped countries. The lack of leadership and organizational discipline in both the ADA and the Democratic party allowed new ideas and proposals to come forward but also made it virtually impossible to create and sustain a consensus around any single set of beliefs.[48]

Richard Nixon's victory in 1968 freed liberals from responsibility for policy and allowed them to develop and debate alternatives. A new journal, *Foreign Policy,* was founded in late 1970 with the announced intention of providing a forum for debating "the revision of goals, the reconsideration of means, and the reformulation of the responsibilities of the United States." From 1968 until Jimmy Carter's election in 1976, a number of new ideas were put forward, in *Foreign Policy* and elsewhere, falling into three broad groups. Furthest left, and best represented by Richard J. Barnet, were those who adopted the revisionist framework not only to condemn existing policies but also the motives and social structure of the United States. The center, led by Stanley Hoffmann, struggled to find a constructive but less dominant role for the United States to play in what was perceived to be an emerging new world order. Finally, on the right, liberals led by Zbigniew Brzezinski sought to protect American interests in what they too believed was a changing world. During the eight years in which these factions struggled for dominance among liberals and Democrats, none was able to gain a lasting ascendency. Instead, the Democrats' views of the world and the United States' role in it became increasingly muddled.[49]

In *After 20 Years*, published in 1965, Richard J. Barnet, a mid-level State Department official under Kennedy, and his coauthor, Marcus Raskin, critiqued what they saw as outdated cold war policies. Barnet and Raskin argued that the Atlantic alliance had been used by the United States to fight the cold war rather than to build a community of nations or contribute to solving the world's problems. The focus on Europe and the NATO alliance, according to them, kept the United States from exploring the possibility with the Soviets of a European settlement and from paying much attention to the world outside of Europe. Barnet no longer saw the Soviets as a threat, writing that "it is now obvious that the Communist countries are seriously divided . . . that Soviet leaders temper ideology to fit changing political circumstances, and that the USSR is interested in some political accommodation with the West." For a new policy, Barnet and Raskin advocated the reunification of Germany as the beginning of a relaxation of tensions in Europe and between the superpowers. Work could then begin on building a "universal community" to deal with international problems, including overpopulation, starvation, and resources.[50]

By later standards, Barnet and Raskin's criticisms were mild.

After 20 Years saw Washington's policies as generally misguided, but not necessarily the result of any deep-seated evil in the American outlook. Nonetheless, the book illustrates how cold war revisionism and William Appleman Williams's call for an open door for revolution had given new life to World War II-era progressive hopes for a diverse and tolerant world. "It is quite clear that none of the existing economic and political ideologies or economic and political frameworks has the answer to the emerging problems of humanity," Barnet and Raskin wrote. "If there is an answer, that answer is the method of experimentation."[51]

On his own, Barnet became increasingly critical of the United States. In 1968 he published *Intervention and Revolution,* an analysis of American behavior in the Third World which even more strongly reflected the revisionist view. Barnet wrote that "there is a strong element of truth" in the belief that the United States "has committed herself against revolution and radical change in the underdeveloped world because independent governments would destroy the world economic and political system, which assures the United States its disproportionate share of economic and political power." Barnet argued that the United States used an imperial model to guide its relations with less developed countries, believing "that there is no way for a great country to relate to a small one other than as manipulator or exploiter."[52]

Barnet advocated a hands-off approach to revolutionary change in the Third World, claiming that American interference was dangerous and immoral. Local revolutions were of little danger to the United States, he believed, and "the danger of world war arises only if the United States is committed to resisting revolution," a commitment officials in Washington "have neither the capacity nor the right to make." In fact, he argued, revolution was a virtue. In China, Barnet claimed, "it is a fact that Communism has produced profound changes in a decade, whereas the process of modernization in a noncommunist country like India is mired in obsolete institutions, crippling traditions, and political malaise."[53]

Barnet continued to denigrate the United States and press his radical approach in the 1970s. He did not develop a coherent foreign policy theory or alternative approach but, instead, concentrated on condemning the United States and its motives. In 1971 he argued that the United States should be seen "not as the problem-solver of the world but as an integral part of the problem." The United States had to be prepared to sacrifice its interests for the Third World— "there is no objective, including the survival of the United States as a political entity, that merits destroying millions or jeopardizing the future of man"—and accept that "poor countries will, and many probably must, experiment with revolution to solve political and economic problems fast enough to permit survival for their people." In other articles Barnet ridiculed national security officials for playing needless games, continued to lament Washington's opposition to revolutions, praised the accomplishments of China, Cuba, and North Vietnam, and called for "a process of redefining American society." Finally, in his 1974 book *Global Reach* (written with Ronald E. Müller), he added multinational corporations to the list of the guilty, declaring that "the development track pursued by the global corporations in [the 1960s] contributed more to the exacerbation of world poverty, world unemployment, and world inequality than to their solution."[54]

Barnet's steadily growing advocacy of revolution and assault on American institutions caught on among some influential liberals, as evidenced by reviews of his books. Henry Kissinger denounced *After 20 Years* in the *New York Times Book Review,* but ten years later the *Book Review* gave *Global Reach* a sympathetic review. Although the *New Republic*'s review of *Global Reach* was more critical, it was almost three pages long, suggesting that Barnet's views were of some consequence. In addition, some impressive names appeared on Barnet's bandwagon. Writing in 1972, John Kenneth Galbraith echoed Barnet's criticism of bureaucrats who saw foreign policy as a game and further declared "how limited is our power to influence the inner life of other countries and, additionally, how slight is our need to do so."[55]

In the liberal center stood Stanley Hoffmann, an Austrian-born professor at Harvard University. Hoffmann shared the view that the vital center was worn out, noting in a book published in 1968 that

> for the United States, the outcome is a bitter kind
> of fragmentation of the international system. It
> must still man the barricades all over the globe,
> but in increasing isolation. Yet the only alterna-
> tives to its "guarding the whole world" seem to be,
> on the one hand, positive gains for its enemies,
> and on the other . . . letting the fate of each seg-
> ment of the system be determined by the hazards
> of local confrontations.

At the same time, Hoffmann explicitly rejected the idea of simply dropping "out of world affairs, as some people on the New Left seem to want." Hoffmann understood that the world would continue to have conflicts, regardless of American policy, and he sought to moderate them and their effects on the United States with "a more complex and balanced system of world order . . . which could be achieved by a better, more diversified distribution of power and by a multiplicity of institutions and methods for managing conflict."[56]

In his writings between 1969 and 1976, Hoffmann went beyond American foreign policy issues to address the theoretical and practical problems of developing an improved world order. On theoretical issues, Hoffmann devoted much of his energy to the basic task of demonstrating that traditional concepts of national power had become outmoded. The very concept of power had slipped beyond definition because of the "increasingly varied and rapidly shifting nature of its most salient ingredients." States even had trouble identifying their interests, owing to the "many alternatives, mysteries, and complexities" of the changing international system. Further, in Hoffmann's view, governments were facing a bewildering array of issues, including resource management, population growth, and international economic management, which called for cooperation. Hoffmann also examined the practical problem of defining ways for the United States to build what he called "a community against anarchy." He pointed out, for example, tactical and strategic choices to be made, such as how and when to intervene abroad, whether to concentrate on relations with other developed countries or with the Third World, and the need to secure domestic political backing for new policies.[57]

Hoffmann's thinking, though not completely formed in the early 1970s, was still very attractive to liberals. He did not pull all the strands together until his book *Primacy or World Order* was published in 1978. Until then, Hoffmann contented himself with describing problems, goals, and approaches in lengthy essays filled with impressive terminology. Yet his prose had a soothing quality. Hoffmann portrayed a new and safe world, with less emphasis on ideological competition, where cooperation would dominate and in which the United States would be able to act with restraint and usually avoid becoming involved in violent conflicts. Even Communist revolutions abroad were not to be feared:

> It is in our interest to play the game of diversity
> and to encourage their pursuit of their national
> interest as long as it is nonaggressive. . . . The
> best policy is one of prophylactic accommodation,
> which would aim at disconnecting the issue from
> the central balance, at trying to minimize the
> impact on the regional balance of power, and at
> preserving influence by keeping the maximum of
> cooperative contacts with the non-Communist part
> of the forces in power.

Hoffmann gave anxious liberals the comforting knowledge that the world had moved beyond the stage where containment was necessary and that events overseas which had once seemed dangerous to the United States no longer were.[58]

Hoffmann's centrist approach had a much greater impact on the policy elite than Barnet's writings. By the mid-1970s it had been incorporated into other analysts' articles in the major foreign policy journals. Richard Gardner, for example, wrote in *Foreign Affairs* of the benefits "at home and abroad [of] identifying our purposes more closely with those of the rest of mankind," and declared that "failure is simply not an acceptable alternative to decisive coalitions of nations." Hoffmann's world order theories were particularly important to the Carter administration's view of the world, an "unofficial philosophy," in the words of one scholar. In October 1976 Cyrus Vance, a lawyer and former secretary of the army and deputy secretary of defense under Lyndon Johnson who was soon to become Secretary of State, wrote in a memo to Carter that Soviet-American relations should not "so dominate our foreign policy that we neglect other important relationships and problems," and that policy should bring "a new sensitivity, awareness and priority to the vast complex of issues clustering around the relationships between the industrialized and the unindustrialized world."[59]

The theorist who remained closest to the vital center was Zbigniew Brzezinski. Brzezinski, born in Poland, was like Hoffmann, an Ivy League professor (at Columbia University), and he too saw a world in the process of transformation. In his 1971 book *Between Two Ages,* Brzezinski outlined the impact of changes he had been describing for several years. Calling the new era "technetronic," he described the emergence of "an age in which technology and electronics . . . are increasingly becoming the principal determinants of . . . the global outlook of society." In such a world ideology would decline in importance, for it was a relic from a time when the world was more mysterious, and the "basic orientation of new [Third World] elites will more and more respond to the intellectual impact of domestic changes in the more advanced world." Soviet-American competition would thus become less intense and the USSR might even come to participate in the new world because of its "own felt need for increased collaboration in the technological and scientific revolution." Finally, an active and engaged United States and the replacement of ideology and nationalism with a "global consciousness" would create a better environment for solving the problems of the world.[60]

Like Hoffmann, Brzezinski tried to envision a new world but provided little guidance on how to achieve it. His analyses were inconsistent, influenced on the one hand by the prevailing ideas and debates of the day, and on the other by the legacy of the vital center. Brzezinski, however, also remained strongly anti-Communist and aware that Moscow continued to threaten American interests. Consequently, Brzezinski did not build a unified or coherent body of writings. He began the decade with policy suggestions drawn from *Between Two Ages,* advocating in a February 1971 *Newsweek* column the same "community of developed nations" in Western Europe, North America, and Japan (later known as trilateralism) which he had proposed in the book as a way to approach the problems of the transition to the technetronic age. Yet just four months earlier, as *Between Two Ages* neared publication, Brzezinski had written in *Foreign Affairs* that Western Europe and the United States had the "most decent and the freest forms of self-government and social organization so far developed by man," whereas the USSR still sought a Europe "not directly subservient but necessarily sensitive to thinly veiled Soviet political influence," showing that a concern with ideological conflict was still present in Brzezinski's thinking.[61]

In the mid-1970s Brzezinski picked up on Hoffmann's ideas on complexity and interdependence and tried to incorporate them into his scheme for the developed states. The idea of interdependence was gaining "philosophical and political substance," he wrote in 1973, and American policy would have to "respond to the central concerns both of the power realists and of the planetary humanists," as the "long and gradual process" of building the community went on. Brzezinski still acknowledged the important role ideas and faith continued to play in national and world affairs—"It is essential to tackle head-on the pervasive mood of pessimism which dominates our centers of thought and learning." At the same time, however, he deplored an ideologically based foreign policy, calling it a "counterproductive . . . reinforcement to the . . . political-philosophical tendencies toward America's global isolation," instead of being "sympathetically sensitive" to the global shift toward equalitarian values not shared by the United States.[62]

Brzezinski's confused and confusing writings are indicative of the difficulties facing liberals who still held to vital center ideas in the mid-1970s. His writings showed a strong desire to hold the West together in the face of Soviet and Third World attacks. He further believed that the United States had to avoid becoming isolated so that it could continue to play a creative as well as a stabilizing role in world affairs. Yet Brzezinski also saw that new problems and conditions had arisen and believed that the vital center could not cope with all of them. Brzezinski tried to solve the problem by supplementing the vital center approach with a turn to technetronic and world order theories, but he was unable to come up with a consistent and coherent approach. Had he not become an early supporter of Jimmy Carter and then Carter's national security adviser, Brzezinski's theories probably never would have gained much influence.[63]

The latter half of the 1960s and the beginning of the 1970s had seen the vital center lose its cohesion and dominance over liberal thinking about foreign policy. Although three major approaches vied to be the replacement, none of them could provide a unifying theory that would appeal to a broad enough spectrum. Barnet's writings suffered from their underlying tone of anti-Americanism, whereas Hoffmann and Brzezinski both described worlds to come but provided vague or confusing guidance for coping with the world that was. But the splintering of the vital center did not mean that it had lost all of its adherents. In fact, many major liberal intellectuals still held to its tenets and were guided by Niebuhr's and Schlesinger's assumptions. As the liberal consensus collapsed, they sought to carry on the fight against Communism and for containment and democracy.

2

Liberalism's
Split:

The
Neoconservatives
Emerge,
1968–1975

Liberalism's political and social dominance during the 1960s meant that major upheavals would almost certainly fracture the liberal movement, and by 1968 there was no shortage of disturbances with great implications for liberal thinking. The civil rights movement had led to the rise of black militancy; the war in Vietnam contributed to the rise of campus militancy and protests which had been developing since 1964; and urban rioting had seemingly become a summer fixture. Unable to explain or cope with these events, the vital center consensus on domestic issues fell apart, just as it had on foreign policy.

The split in American liberalism led to the emergence of a new group of liberals. Mounting evidence of the failure of earlier reforms to make expected improvements in American society and the consequent social and political difficulties forced some liberal intellectuals to reconsider much of what they had believed earlier. Those who faced up to these developments frequently urged a turning away from what they viewed as the excesses of radicalism and the hubris of overly ambitious attempts at reform, but still looked for ways to improve society. These intellectuals confounded their colleagues, especially those on the left. The chastened liberals were seen as—or accused of—turning to the right, and at first were called "new conservatives." By about 1975, the label had changed to "neoconservative," which was itself a shorthand to describe a former liberal.[1]

The leading neoconservatives—Irving Kristol, Norman Podhoretz, Daniel Patrick Moynihan, and Nathan Glazer, to name a few—were veterans of the vital center and initially remained committed to its combination of reform at home and anti-Communism abroad. The neoconservatives were also social scientists, academics, and important figures in literary and cultural criticism. As intellectuals, they took their job of critical inquiry very seriously, seeking, in political scientist Mark Rozell's words, "a clear understanding of how a problem exists rather than how it can be 'solved.'" Their break with the liberalism of the early 1970s came in large part because they saw a threat to democracy, as well as themselves, from mounting social disorders, anti-Semitism, and—particularly in foreign affairs—what they viewed as the ascendency of wishful thinking. Or, as Nathan Glazer wrote in 1970, "Radicalism is so beset with error and confusion that our main task, if we are ever to mount a successful assault on our problems, must be to argue with it and to strip it ultimately of the pretension that it understands the causes of our ills and how to set them straight." Led by Podhoretz and Kristol, the neoconservatives used the pages of *Commentary* and the *Public Interest* to warn against the dangers posed by radicalism at home and Soviet expansionism abroad.[2]

The neoconservatives—who, as liberals, had been loyal Democrats—became increasingly isolated within the party. The Democrats' post-1968 reforms and the subsequent shifting of the party toward what the neoconservatives saw as ideas opposed to the interests of the United States and most Americans, deeply angered the neoconservatives. After George McGovern's defeat in 1972, they mounted a campaign to try to retake the party for their brand of liberalism, but by Christmas 1974 it was clear that they had failed and had become a relatively powerless faction.

Despite the confusion that prevailed among liberals during the 1960s, some still held to the tenets of the vital center. This was especially true for many of the New York intellectuals clustered around *Commentary*—which had been militantly anti-Communist during the 1950s—and the Congress for Cultural Freedom. In keeping with the views and terminology of Arthur M. Schlesinger, Jr., they remained committed to social reform and viewed themselves as genuine radicals. When he became the editor of *Commentary* in 1960, for example, Norman Podhoretz decided "to turn *Commentary*, as I myself had been turning, in the same leftward direction that I was confident the best energies of the sixties were also preparing to move." Such a shift, Podhoretz believed, would enable intellectuals "to assume the old . . . and much more comfortable role of critic once again." At the same time, however, this group continued to see liberal democracy in general, and American democracy in particular, as the best framework in which to develop and implement social reforms. As Nathan Glazer later recalled, "we valued the country, the role it had played in international affairs, its ability to handle complex domestic problems, its stability in the maintenance of democratic procedures, its capacity for change and correction."[3]

By the latter part of the 1960s, however, these liberals found that radicalism was running away from them. The rise of the New Left and its revolutionary rhetoric, set amid urban riots, campus upheavals, and a variety of other social disturbances, appalled them and, as Alexander Bloom has pointed out, "a large coalition of New Yorkers spoke out against it." New Left radicalism, wrote Irving Howe in late 1968, "insofar as it approximates a politics, mixes sentiments of anarchism with apologies for authoritarianism." Howe was not alone in viewing 1960s radicalism with a mixture of horror and contempt. Since the battles of the 1930s and 1940s these liberals had harshly and unforgivingly attacked anything which they saw as reflecting totalitarian thinking and had become acutely sensitive to ideas which they believed opposed or undermined liberal democracy. They took the New Left seriously, if only because as intellectuals they respected the power of ideas and words. Thus, when Irving Kristol argued in late 1968 that the ideologues of the New Left would "almost invariably end up by celebrating the virtues of a one-party dictatorship," he was not describing a trivial threat.[4]

Some of the reformist liberals believed that they were at least partially responsible for the rise of the radical threat. They laid much of the blame on the reforms that they had helped institute in the early and mid-1960s, but which had since failed to deliver on their promises. Many believed, in turn, that the roots of the failure lay in the flawed or incomplete theories on which the programs had been based. In the blunt words of sociologist and Kennedy administration appointee Daniel Patrick Moynihan, "the government did not know what it was doing." Kristol added a similar observation in 1968: "We have discovered in these past years that it just doesn't suffice to pass a law in order to solve minorities' problems." Furthermore, observed Kristol, "Somehow the money never seems to reach the people for whom it is intended—or, if it does, it never has the effect it was supposed to have."[5]

The perception of radicalism run amok and the knowledge of their own failures led many of these liberals to fear for the survival of the system and themselves. Inflated hopes unaccompanied by effective reforms had become "a recipe for violence," according to Aaron Wildavsky. This growing fear of violence was indicated by a 1967 article in Kristol's journal the *Public Interest*, which noted that the theories of Algerian revolutionary Frantz Fanon were being popularized in the United States, feeding "a tremendous market for pseudo-scientific writing concerning violence." American society, they feared, would be unable to defend itself because, according to Kristol, liberal failures and radical attacks meant that society's institutions were "being inexorably drained of their legitimacy."[6]

Responses to the question of how to cope with the situation demonstrated the divisions that were growing among liberals. Some began to advocate not only a clear rejection of radicalism as a way to avoid chaos and the disintegration of democracy in the United States, but also a broad reconsideration of their earlier assumptions. In September 1967, Daniel Patrick Moynihan told the Americans for Democratic Action that "liberals must see more clearly that their essential interest is in the stability of the social order," and that to protect order they "must seek out and make much more effective alliances with political conservatives." Moynihan further noted that the time had come to stop excusing urban violence and to look at its causes, which he believed had not been addressed by liberal programs. These remarks were so startling that they were front page news in the *New York Times* and moved columnist Tom Wicker to note acidly that Moynihan had become the "hero" of "those who find [law and order] . . . a convenient slogan to substitute for any effective action to achieve an approximate social justice in America."[7]

In addition to their implications for liberal democracy, the disorders of the late 1960s had some very personal dimensions for many Jewish vital center liberals. Most of the New York liberal community was Jewish, and its members were disturbed by what they saw as a sharp increase in black anti-Semitism. Black-Jewish relations, despite the two groups' alliance on civil rights, had long been rocky. Many blacks, for example, had seen Jewish merchants and landlords as exploiting ghetto populations. The tensions had increased with the success of the civil rights movement as blacks moved up the economic ladder into occupations dominated by Jews. In 1964 Nathan Glazer had observed that the "accidents of history have put the Jew just ahead of the Negro," and that the "well of ill-feeling [toward Jews] has moved upward to include a substantial part of the Negro leadership, mainly some of the newer leaders thrown up in the North by the civil rights revolution." On the other hand, hard evidence to back up these claims was scarce. A study published in May 1967 found that blacks were generally less anti-Semitic than whites, although they frequently did not distinguish Jews from whites in general. Black and Jewish intellectuals were aware of these realities; prominent blacks including Kenneth Clark and James Baldwin, as well as Podhoretz, had each addressed them in *Commentary* beginning, in the case of Clark, in 1946.[8]

In the superheated atmosphere of the times, however, these subtleties were ignored. The rise of black nationalism and other events of the late 1960s appeared to confirm Glazer's analysis, and urban rioting, which destroyed some Jewish-owned stores in ghetto areas, added to the feeling of being under attack. So did the 1968 New York City school strike, which pitted a black community against the heavily Jewish United Federation of Teachers. Furthermore, Jewish intellectuals had become less inclined to overlook or excuse what they viewed as instances of black anti-Semitism, especially when prominent or militant blacks were involved. James Baldwin wrote in the spring of 1967 that the Jew "is singled out by Negroes not because he acts differently from other white men, but because he doesn't." Earl Raab, a prominent Jewish leader, called such an argument "an exact and acute description of political anti-Semitism."[9]

The Jewish intellectuals' fears of black anti-Semitism and the New Left became intertwined in 1967 and 1968. One of the triggers was the stunning Israeli victory in the June 1967 war, in which it defeated the armed forces of Egypt, Syria, and Jordan. For American Jews it was a moment of great pride. But just two months after the war, in a move aimed at creating a vague kind of Third World solidarity, the Student Nonviolent Coordinating Committee (SNCC) charged Israel—"this illegal state"—with massacring and oppressing Arabs; claimed that the Rothschilds, who allegedly dominated European finance, had conspired with the British to create Israel; and published a cartoon showing Israeli Defense Minister Moshe Dayan with dollar signs on his epaulets. Ralph Featherstone, an SNCC official, declared that the intent had not been to attack all Jews, but "only Jewish oppressors," which included Israelis and Jewish shopowners in black ghettos. The resulting uproar was fed by black militant H. Rap Brown's comment a few days later that "we are not anti-Jewish. . . . We just don't think Zionist leaders in Israel have a right to that land."[10]

At the same time, the New Left's reaction to the June war provoked additional anxieties among many Jewish intellectuals. Comments by such prominent figures on the left as I. F. Stone and Noam Chomsky, who accused Israel of being an aggressor, were often cited as evidence that the New Left's views coincided with Soviet policies. Furthermore, wrote Robert Alter, the image of Israeli aggression was "all the more readily acceptable because it fits so neatly into a popular New Left mythology of world politics in which the nations are divided into sinister superpowers and innocent, freedom-loving peoples of the Third World. Israel, if not actually a tool of Western imperialism, is imagined as a beachhead of corrupt Western values." American Jews were also quick to note the similarities between the New Left's charges and the anti-Semitism of the far right. Citing the record of such fringe groups as the Liberty Lobby and the Minutemen, the executive director of the American Jewish Committee noted in December 1967 that "to this thunder from the right we can now add the thunder from the left." The fact that Stone, Chomsky, and other New Left critics of Israel were themselves Jewish added to the suspicion. Not only was the New Left a threat from without, but now there were quislings inside the Jewish intellectual community as well.[11]

Black militancy and the New Left also came together in the student rebellion at Columbia University in April 1968. By then student protests had become commonplace, and the Jewish intellectuals were taking a hard look at them. Nathan Glazer, who had been a professor at Berkeley when protests first began in 1964, commented, "Anyone who has experienced the concrete situation in American universities knows that the threat to free speech, free teaching, free research, comes from radical white students, from militant black students, and from their faculty defenders." Columbia, however, was particularly traumatic. It not only brought student uprisings to New York and the doorsteps of its intellectual community, but Columbia was also Norman Podhoretz's alma mater and the home of his friends Lionel and Diana Trilling, important vital center liberals in their own right.[12]

The Columbia uprising had racial overtones from the start. Columbia's physical expansion and evictions of Harlem residents from university-owned apartment buildings had led to poor relations between Columbia and the surrounding community. The university's plan to build a new gym in Morningside Park had made matters worse. Although Columbia planned to allow Harlem residents to use the gym, the administration had failed to consult with local black leaders about the gym's design or the terms on which it would be shared. As a result, the gym provided a concrete issue to link black students, many of whom were unhappy with their status at Columbia, with the predominantly white Columbia chapter of the Students for a Democratic Society (sɒs) when the latter began protesting Columbia's links to the Department of Defense. As one faculty member recalled, "When the black students—if only for one brief moment—joined with the white radical sɒs, they made direct action inevitable and at the same time virtually assured the success of the demonstration."13

The results were catastrophic. The black students soon separated from the sɒs, which they felt was not sufficiently militant, and each occupied different buildings. H. Rap Brown came to the campus and threatened that blacks were "preparing to come and deal with Columbia University at some point." Even the sɒs was taken aback. The *New Leader* reported that the white demonstrators had seen "the face of black power—a face that none of their liberal sympathies could soften into the slightest smile—and found it disturbing." After a week the New York police were called in, cleared the campus with their clubs, and Columbia shut down until the fall.14

The implications of the Columbia rebellion were immediately apparent. The *New Republic*'s analysis was that the stated issues were but pretexts: "The point of the game was power," and the sɒs had achieved its goal of showing that it could take control of a major university. If Columbia could be taken over by a small group of students, then no university was safe. Diana Trilling precisely defined the threat: "The Columbia uprising was . . . revolutionary. Its message was antiliberal. It was antiliberal in its lawlessness and its refusal of reasonable process . . . it communicated the contempt of a revolution for whatever is the embodiment of liberal commitment or suggestive of reform." Trilling saw an additional menace coming from the black students. "They were not cosseted middle-class boys playing violent games," she wrote. "For them the authority of the white world is an illegitimate authority." For remaining vital center liberals black militancy and the New Left were each disturbing enough by themselves; united, as they briefly had been at Columbia, they raised a terrible specter of disorder and destruction within one of liberalism's most important institutions.[15]

The effect of the assaults of the New Left and rising black anti-Semitism was to help bring together a group of "deradicalized" liberals who were ready to fight back against those they saw as their tormenters. Not surprisingly, this group was heavily Jewish and was centered in New York. Their anger and taste for intellectual combat—the latter a hallmark of the New York intellectuals—were further stoked by other intellectual and literary feuds at the time. The most notable was between *Commentary* and the *New York Review of Books*, which supported the New Left and published articles by Chomsky, Stone, and other radical sympathizers. Thus, by 1969, the former radicals had come to see not separate fights, but instead a unified battle that brought together all the issues which concerned them. Glazer summed up the conflict, saying that intellectuals

> have taught violence, justified violence, rational-
> ized violence. Anti-semitism is only a part of this
> whole syndrome, for if the members of the middle
> class do not deserve to hold on to their property, their
> positions, or even their lives, then certainly the Jews,
> the most middle-class of all, are going to be placed
> at the head of the column marked for liquidation.

All that the former radicals needed was a leader who could rally their energies and lead a sustained charge against their enemies.[16]

The war to defend moderate liberalism began in earnest in 1970. The fight was similar to the one between the Americans for Democratic Action and the Progressives 23 years earlier, in that both sides claimed to represent true liberalism and the best course for the future. At the same time, however, there would be no quick resolution to this quarrel. Instead, the fight dragged on, with neither side able to seize an issue or mobilize liberal opinion long enough to defeat the other as completely as the ADA had crushed the PCA.

The defense was led by Norman Podhoretz, a man as puzzling as he is important to neoconservatism. He is undeniably a man of great talent and ambition—an enfant terrible among New York literary critics during the 1950s and appointed editor of *Commentary* in 1960, when he was 30 years old. Biographies of Podhoretz often make it appear that his outspokenness was part of a clever strategy to rise within the intellectuals' ranks by drawing attention to himself. If so, this strategy has sometimes backfired. When he completed his autobiography, *Making It* (1967), for example, his frank depiction of his own and other intellectuals' ambitions raised a storm of criticism, much of it personal. Moreover, accusing Podhoretz of cynicism at best only partially explains his behavior. While Podhoretz undoubtedly has a talent for self-promotion, his passion and consistency leave no doubt that he is sincere in what he says.

Podhoretz's memoirs suggest that even in the 1950s he had sought to recreate for himself the excitement of the intellectual and political combat in New York during the 1930s and 1940s; having been born in 1930, he was too young to have argued with Stalinists, as Irving Kristol had during the thirties at the City College of New York, or to have participated in the fight against Henry Wallace. During the more placid 1950s ("bored with my own sensibly moderate liberal ideas"), he had looked to radicalism to provide passion. But even with *Commentary* as a platform, Podhoretz had not gone far from the liberal mainstream in the 1960s, if only because the country's general liberalism made the liberal center a very wide area. *Time* magazine, for example, printed a flattering profile of Podhoretz and *Commentary* in 1966 and noted that "Podhoretz is courted by politicians," including President Johnson. Despite his prominence among intellectuals as editor of *Commentary*, Podhoretz had not produced a body of writings that could make him as important a figure as Kristol or sociologist Daniel Bell, author of the influential book *The End of Ideology*.[17]

When the New Left ran off with the banner of radicalism, Podhoretz at last had his chance to become a general in the New York intellectuals' wars. He began his campaign in June 1970, when he "decided that the time had come to declare full-scale war" on the New Left. During the 1970s he would use *Commentary* and his skills as a polemicist in a continuous battle with the New Left and all of its manifestations. This is not to suggest that Podhoretz was an opportunist, seeking to take advantage of the situation for his own benefit. Instead, it was a fortunate set of circumstances which presented him with an important cause, one which he had long sought, in which he deeply believed, and to which he could devote his energies.

In June 1970 Podhoretz began writing a monthly column in *Commentary* called "Issues," using it to add his own comments to articles or themes discussed in each issue of the magazine. Topics included the war in Vietnam, refutations of liberal claims that liberty was under attack in the United States, and assaults on apocalyptic environmental predictions masquerading as scientific findings. He filled the remainder of *Commentary*'s pages with articles vigorously seeking to destroy the intellectual foundations of the New Left. The attack was carried out on all fronts as writers examined politics, education, social issues, the arts, and foreign affairs.

By the end of 1970 Podhoretz's assault had put liberal quarrels into the newspapers. In November, the *Wall Street Journal* discussed *Commentary*'s new tone in a long article on its editorial page, noting happily that "a pro-American type of intellectual is starting to speak up," calling Podhoretz (to his chagrin) an "improbable 'conservative,'" and approvingly quoting him on his conversion from skeptic to aggressor: "I always felt I was holding the line; now I'm on the offensive." The *Journal* further cited Nathan Glazer, Irving Kristol, and Midge Decter (Podhoretz's wife and a prominent writer and editor) as other examples of "deradicalized" intellectuals. Two days later the *New York Times*, focusing on Glazer as an example but also mentioning Podhoretz and Kristol, discussed changing ideological labels among the intellectuals and tried to puzzle out who among them was a liberal, a radical, a moderate conservative, or a conservative liberal.[18]

Commentary's targets on the left did not endure Podhoretz's attacks in silence. In early 1971, Eugene Goodheart wrote in the *Nation* that the fault lay not with the "radical conscience," but instead with Podhoretz's reactions, which he labeled the "new conservatism." Goodheart claimed that the offensive showed that Podhoretz was insensitive "to the fundamental fact that we are suffering a moral and political crisis of considerable magnitude and that this crisis has not been brought about merely by radical willfulness." He further argued that *Commentary*'s new conservatism served "to divert attention from the real evils to which radical consciousness had addressed itself." Others suggested that the new conservatism was motivated by an instinct for self-preservation among successful American Jews. In August 1971, Sol Stern, a self-described Jewish radical, wrote in the New Left magazine *Ramparts* that "*Commentary* has always been a bellwether for the thinking of the Jewish Establishment," and that its new attitudes reflected the interests of those "American Jews who have made it here and don't want anyone rocking the boat."[19]

As the New Left rapidly declined in the early 1970s, it became increasingly difficult for opponents of *Commentary*'s views, especially among more analytical leftists, to dismiss them completely. One of the first to offer a credible analysis was Peter Steinfels, who saw in the new conservatives "the conservatism of social scientists . . . they have come to serve as skeptical Brain Trusts to the government bureaucracies." Steinfels was sympathetic to the attack on the irrationality of the New Left and its "loose talk of fascism and genocide," but noted that Podhoretz himself was not rigorous "about accusations of Stalinism or anti-Semitism." Steinfels further noted the personal and institutional rivalries at work, particularly in the feud between *Commentary* and the *New York Review of Books*, as well as the sense of continuity with the liberal intellectuals' quarrels over McCarthyism and anti-Communism in the 1950s.[20]

By 1973, as the United States completed its withdrawal from Vietnam and the New Left became politically irrelevant, a fresh liberal analysis suggested that the new conservatives' victory was due largely to radicalism's own flaws. "What passed for the American left had grown mentally stale, dumb in fact. The New Left had no program to speak of, nor did it appear much interested in putting together a coherent critique of American life," wrote Joseph Epstein in *Dissent*. The New Left, he concluded, "went down to defeat by the new conservatives because they [the New Left] were woefully ignorant about the world as it is." By contrast, the new conservatives had emerged "extremely well-placed" in "government, in the academy, in journalism—in short, in all those modern institutions out of which influence can be radiated."[21]

The traditional right was at first suspicious of the new converts, but soon welcomed *Commentary* as an ally against the left. In December 1970, *National Review* approvingly noted Podhoretz's new attitudes, but was concerned that, like his earlier radicalism, it might not last: "The problem that arises in connection with these wanderings into and out of radicalism is that they tend to be excessively 'cultural'—that is, matters of mood and accident, traceable to, at best, fortuitous occurrences in the objective world. They are insufficiently rooted in serious political realities, in general principle, or coherent intellectual tradition." As *Commentary* continued to combat the New Left, *National Review* dropped some, but not all, of its reservations. An editorial in March 1971 applauded *Commentary*'s articles on "Revolutionism and the Jews," stating that printing them "would have been unthinkable in the pages of *Commentary* even a few years ago. But the journal has affected its *volte face* from support to disparagement of the radicals with remarkable skill." Even so, the turnabout was not yet complete, and the editorial concluded, "We will be delighted when the new realism manifested in these articles is applied by *Commentary* to the full range of national and international issues."[22]

As the label "new conservative" and the wariness of *National Review* indicate, the question of exactly where Podhoretz and his associates stood in the political spectrum of the early 1970s caused a great deal of confusion. By 1976 another label had been applied to them, "neoconservative," a term coined by Michael Harrington to describe right-wing socialists, but now meaning one who had been a liberal but had since moved to the right. Unfortunately, the term hid as much as it described. As sociologist Seymour Martin Lipset wrote in 1988, neoconservative "was invented as an invidious label to undermine political opponents, most of whom have been unhappy with being so described." Neoconservatives preferred to stress the breadth of their views and almost universally agreed with James Q. Wilson's remark that they share no "manifesto, credo, religion, flag, anthem or secret handshake." In fact, only Irving Kristol appears to have embraced the label, and then somewhat reluctantly. "I am, for better or worse, a 'neoconservative' intellectual," he wrote in 1976, although he claimed in 1979 to "have accepted the term, perhaps because, having been named Irving, I am relatively indifferent to baptismal caprice." Whatever his attitude toward the label, the lack of shared goals, ideology, and organization among neoconservatives led Kristol to conclude, "I do not think there really is such a thing as neoconservatism."[23]

Neoconservatives who continued to view themselves as liberals also shared Kristol's ambivalence toward their new label. In 1978, Daniel Bell commented that "those whose work decries those aspects of contemporary culture which make cheap claims to 'liberation,' often find themselves labeled as 'neo-conservative.'" Midge Decter wrote in 1976 that "I have no choice but to be a liberal" and defend the achievements of liberalism. She remarked in early 1991 that she eventually surrendered to the label of neoconservative simply as a way of avoiding arguments over who was a true liberal. Daniel Patrick Moynihan also saw neoconservatism as indistinguishable from being "a decent liberal." Both terms, he reportedly believed in 1976, meant "roughly the same thing: that a concern for the country's less favored citizens is tempered by the realization that, at least for now, capitalism seems to be a more efficient creator of wealth for all than socialism." In fact, Kristol stood out from other neoconservatives in the early 1970s for his unabashed conservatism. He openly supported Richard Nixon and by 1972 had become a Republican, switching party affiliation about a decade in advance of most other neoconservatives. Such differences among the neoconservatives lend a great deal of truth to Daniel Bell's quip that much of what is called neoconservatism is "just Irving."[24]

Being an anti-Communist liberal in the 1950s and 1960s did not always mean taking an active role as a foreign policy intellectual. Many of the future neoconservative intellectuals were comfortable with the foreign policy consensus and had little reason to develop individual views. Most of Midge Decter's writings from the 1960s were on the arts, family life, and related domestic issues. Daniel Patrick Moynihan, in a reflection of his interests and jobs, wrote widely on social and political issues, but not on foreign affairs, even though he had earned his Ph.D. at the Fletcher School of Law and Diplomacy. Others, however, were active in the liberal anti-Communist efforts of the 1950s and 1960s. Kristol was a co-founder of *Encounter*, the magazine of the Congress for Cultural Freedom, and Jeane Kirkpatrick's first book, *The Strategy of Deception* (1963), was an anthology of essays on "the characteristic instruments and procedures utilized by Communist parties in their efforts to come to power."[25]

In the foreign policy debate that followed the collapse of the vital center consensus, the new conservatives stood out for their continued adherence to the vital center idea of an activist, anti-Communist foreign policy. This posture was consistent with views much of the group had held since the 1930s. Irving Kristol has written about how he and his then-left-wing friends—including Glazer, Lipset, and Bell—argued constantly with Stalinist students at the City College of New York in the late 1930s. Kristol further recalls that the politics of the Trotskyists were "intertwined with an interest in, and deference to, the 'highbrow' in culture, philosophy, and the arts," especially as discussed in *Partisan Review*. As David Sidorsky, a philosophy professor at Columbia and friend of some of the neoconservatives, has noted, these debates showed an awareness of and strong interest in international issues on the part of the future neoconservatives. The exchanges also indicate an early suspicion of leftist totalitarianism and popular front politics, a suspicion which helped lead them into the postwar liberal consensus. Finally, the cultural aspects and background of foreign policy, as well as an appreciation of the importance of ideology in international politics, would remain a prime concern for the new conservatives of the 1970s.[26]

Younger members of the group came to similar views after World War II, often through the same debates that shaped the vital center. Midge Decter recalls reading Schlesinger, Niebuhr, and a number of books on the Soviet Union and subscribing wholeheartedly to the liberal anti-Communist, internationalist consensus. Norman Podhoretz, too, "maintained that liberal democracy was itself a value." Jeane Kirkpatrick, a student at Barnard College when Henry Wallace ran for president, was "ill at ease with the fashionable leftist reformism of the Wallaceites," and believed that Harry Truman was "the real thing," according to historian J. David Hoeveler. She, too, became a strong Democrat and continued to subscribe to strict anti-Communism after 1969. One of the youngest neoconservatives, Elliott Abrams (born in 1948), grew up in a liberal Democratic household in New York City and never deviated from the hard-line anti-Communist position.[27]

In addition to revisionism, these liberal internationalists faced a rising tide of isolationism in the late 1960s. Noting the reaction to Vietnam and disenchantment with containment policies, the popular press began to write of a "movement back to isolationism via pacifism," led by liberal intellectuals and backed by a feeling that "the inflation of American responsibility and commitments has involved the American people way beyond the reach of their vital interests and their real power." Despite the fact that the label "isolationism" was a broad one and that it triggered exaggerated fears of a return to the policies of the 1920s, the phenomenon was not entirely a figment of editors' imaginations. One poll in 1969 found that more than half of Americans favored a major reduction in overseas commitments, and other data, summarized in an article in *Foreign Affairs*, indicated that those under 30—an ominous portent for the future—were "disillusioned about what good America [could] do abroad." To combat this, the article could only make the weak suggestion that "A new internationalism based on a peaceful response to human needs is the only effective response that the new generation of isolationists will heed." By its nature, however, such a version of internationalism looked toward the utopian goals and easy road to peace that Niebuhr and vital center liberalism had specifically rejected twenty years earlier.[28]

Irving Kristol led the attack against such thinking. As liberal intellectuals searched for a new policy approach that would avoid what they saw as past mistakes, Kristol impugned both their motives and their goal. The role of intellectuals in foreign policy, he argued in 1967, is to provide "intellectual and moral guidance." Without naming individuals, Kristol asserted that intellectuals had abandoned their sense of responsibility and, "bemused by dreams of power without responsibility," simply vilified the United States and its policies. In Kristol's view, despite "much fancy rhetoric, pro and con, about 'the purpose of American foreign policy,'" liberal intellectuals had little or nothing to offer as an alternative to previous policies.[29]

Kristol founded his defense of a continued activist anti-Communist foreign policy on an updated version of Niebuhr's view of the world and great power responsibilities. Kristol had no doubt that the United States would continue to hold a leading role in the world. "The United States is not going to cease being an imperial power," he wrote in 1967, and he reiterated the point in mid-1968: "The world *does* rely on American power." Such a role, Kristol acknowledged, would not always be a comfortable one, for in it "one is always forced to compromise one's values." Nor did Kristol see any hope of escaping from world leadership, even if it were desirable to do so:

> To dodge or disclaim these responsibilities is one form of the abuse of power. If, after Vietnam, the nations of the world become persuaded that we cannot be counted upon to do the kind of "policeman's" work the world's foremost power has hitherto performed, throughout most of history, we shall unquestionably witness an alarming upsurge in national delinquency and international disorder everywhere. Nor shall we remain unaffected, in our chrome-plated American fortress.[30]

At the same time, Kristol realized that world politics were dynamic and he did not deny the inevitability of change. Rather, he sought gradual, conservative changes that would avoid massive upheavals. He argued, for example, that containment was a policy for just such changes, "a relatively conservative doctrine, since it insists that the pattern of world power change gradually, subtly, as unobtrusively as possible." It was for this reason that Kristol supported Hubert Humphrey's candidacy in 1968. Foreign policy, Kristol admitted, would have to be changed, if only to keep up with changes in the United States and the world. But change would have to come gradually if the country were to avoid "a dangerous reaction whose political consequences could be disastrous for the future of American liberalism." In Kristol's view, Humphrey stood for "the principle of continuity amidst change." Above all, however, Kristol argued against pursuing utopian goals. "We certainly do have it in our power to make improvements in the human estate," he wrote in late 1971, in words reminiscent of Niebuhr's *Children of the Light*, "but to think we have it in our power to change people so as to make the human estate radically better than it is . . . [is an] arrogant assumption. . . . [B]y acting upon this assumption we shall surely end up making our world worse than it need have been."[31]

Despite his intellectual strengths and skills as a essayist, Kristol was not well suited to the role of chief neoconservative theorist for international politics. International affairs, as a branch of political science, was dominated by professors, and their work was characterized by occasional scholarly articles, long books, and, at least in appearance, in-depth research. Kristol's talents, on the other hand, lay in an ability to write quickly and clearly on a variety of topics, and were better suited to borrowing, explaining, and popularizing ideas rather than coming up with new concepts. The development of the basis of neoconservative replies to theorists like Stanley Hoffmann, then, did not fall to Kristol but to two academics, Robert W. Tucker and Walter Laqueur.[32]

Tucker was a professor of political science at Johns Hopkins University. By the early 1970s he had written several books on international relations theory, as well as closely argued commentaries on current foreign policy debates. Two of these commentaries, *Nation or Empire?* (1968) and *The Radical Left and American Foreign Policy* (1971), displayed an unusual talent not just for picking apart others' arguments but also for seeing what parts of otherwise flawed analyses could be set aside and put to good use in other contexts. Commenting on cold war revisionism, for example, Tucker noted that its monocausational aspects made it a poor guide to the present but, "if nothing else, the radical critique has forced us to acknowledge the extent to which an obsessive self-interest has been central in American foreign policy."[33]

Nor did Tucker shy away from cutting to the core of matters, posing difficult questions, and dismissing shallow or glib answers. In *Nation or Empire?* he noted that critics of American policy often focused on the issue of style, which they saw as the "failure of political intelligence, an incapacity to see the world for what it is . . . an unwillingness to accept and adjust to the 'real world' with its never-ending conflict and strife." As a result, Tucker pointed out, these critics tended to focus on the easy issues of form while failing to address the difficult questions of national interest, which were what really drove policy: "Yet however important the matter of style, the critical issue of policy remains one of interest and commitment . . . a change in style may still leave unchanged the substance of policy."[34]

Tucker argued that the basic issue was whether the United States should be an empire, refusing to "distinguish between the security of the imperial state and the security of the greater [world] community," or a nation, content to refrain from interventions abroad. From 1968 to 1972, Tucker chose the more modest course of nation, arguing that the rest of the world did not necessarily wish to be like the United States. In particular, he wrote, "the course of wisdom is to accept this outcome and, at the same time, to abandon the conviction that America can only regenerate herself by regenerating the world."[35]

Tucker explored the implications of this argument most completely in his 1972 book *A New Isolationism: Threat or Promise?*

Tucker's was not the reflexive isolationism of the unhappy young. He denied that the "new isolationism" sought a withdrawal from the world and instead claimed that it "is not to be identified with the absence of all significant relationships but, rather, with the absence of certain relationships . . . the refusal to enter into alliances and to undertake military interventions." Tucker argued that strategic and economic realities had changed enough since the 1940s to allow such a "redefining [of] America's relationship to the world." Nuclear weapons, for example, provided "a surfeit of deterrent power," and although the United States was heavily involved in the world economy, he denied that it had become economically dependent on the rest of the world and rejected the argument that "military withdrawal would jeopardize these interests." Tucker believed, therefore, that an isolationist policy could be followed with a reasonable degree of safety ("The risks a new isolationism entails, then, are not risks to America's core security"), but he did not expect isolationism to be cost free: "The price of a new isolationism is that America would have to abandon its aspirations to an order that has become synonymous with the nation's vision of its role in history. The price of isolationism today is to be found above all in the prospect of a world in which American influence, though still considerable, would markedly decline."[36]

The 1973 Middle East war and subsequent oil embargo, however, graphically demonstrated the practical limits and consequences of isolationism and had a great impact on Tucker. He admitted overestimating the willingness of other states to protect their security interests, including access to oil. But he pointed out that isolation had not been meant as a guise for weakness and inaction:

> Even the few among us who have argued for a
> radical contraction of America's interests and
> commitments have done so on the assumption that
> the consequences of an American withdrawal
> would not be a world in which America's political
> and economic frontiers were coterminous with her
> territorial frontiers, and in which societies that

share our culture, institutions, and values might
very possibly disappear.

Tucker made this point in an article in *Commentary*, "Oil: The Issue
of American Intervention," in which he explored, and came close to
advocating, military intervention to secure American control of some
of the oil fields in the Persian Gulf.[37]

In the course of the article, Tucker brought up two ideas that
would become prominent in neoconservative thinking later in the
decade. The first was that the use of force should still be considered
an option for protecting national interests: "This apparent absence of
force as an element in the crisis seems astonishing. At least it must
seem astonishing to those who assume *some* continuity with the past
. . . it is clearly the absence of the credible threat of force which ren-
ders plausible the expectation that the interests placed in jeopardy by
present oil prices will not be preserved in the future." Tucker's second
contribution to neoconservative thinking in this article was the idea
that the foreign policy elite had lost its will. Because of Vietnam, he
wrote, "there is the pervasive and still growing conviction among the
foreign-policy elites . . . that force has . . . lost its legitimacy." The
elite explained its refusal to intervene, according to Tucker, because
it feared adverse public reaction as well as a Soviet countermove,
but this was just camouflage. "When men do not wish to undertake a
certain course of action, they will find any number of reasons for not
doing so," he claimed.[38]

Tucker continued to explore these ideas in *Commentary*. Tucker's
explanation revolved around what he viewed as a growing ideology of
egalitarianism, which was marked, he noted, by Third World
demands for equality with the developed states. This meant that "the
powerful are not to employ their power," that there would be "discrimination on behalf of the materially disadvantaged," and that the
state would be "the exclusive guardian of the interests of, and sole
dispenser of justice to, the human beings who comprise it." Tucker
claimed that Western liberal elites, including prominent figures like
John Kenneth Galbraith, went along with this because they believed
that interdependence made it in their self-interest to acquiesce. They

feared that, in a supposedly interdependent world, the weak could "transmit misery in the form of chaos and war." Their fear was backed up by a misguided sense of moral obligation toward the less fortunate.[39]

Tucker saw such a world as dangerously unstable. There was, in his view, "a growing disjunction between power and order . . . in which the principal holders of power . . . may no longer be the principal creators and guarantors of order." At the same time the "need for order" would increase as the demand for equality created "relationships . . . and claims which, if not somehow resolved, may lead to chaos." As a result, the changing system would be prone to disorder, in Tucker's view, for, he asked, "how will . . . conflicts be resolved if the traditional means for resolving them [i.e., force] are to be neither employed nor meaningfully threatened?" The 1973 war and oil embargo were only the first hint of what lay ahead: "The oil crisis is not a manifestation of interdependence in the sense that proponents of interdependence have in mind. . . . Instead, it is the latest manifestation . . . of an egalitarianism which . . . is likely to result first in chaos."[40]

Walter Laqueur, the other major theorist for the neoconservatives, had fled Nazi Germany as a youth. By the early 1970s he had become a prolific and respected historian and writer on Middle East affairs and international politics. During the first half of the decade his policy-oriented articles concentrated on two major themes, liberal illusions and the dangers present in the world situation.

Laqueur believed that many of the writings of such liberal theorists as Stanley Hoffmann were based on fallacies. The idea, for example, that the Soviets were gaining a stake in the status quo—a point made by Brzezinski—was, in Laqueur's words, an example of the "escapism which these days pervades political thinking in the United States and Western Europe alike." Instead, Laqueur argued, the Soviets were "purposeful and dynamic, out to win the global struggle rather than to preserve the status quo." Laqueur attacked other examples of what he saw as wishful thinking, and he considered the findings of cold war revisionists a poor base for evaluating policy. Even if the United States had "acted but with all the wisdom of gods," Laqueur believed that the cold war would probably have still come about, if only because no combination of western concessions or guarantees could have overcome the Soviets' postwar "state-of-siege psychology." By 1975, Laqueur had included many of the hopes of Soviet-American détente, European unity, and global economic cooperation on his list of "hopes and expectations widely voiced in recent years [that] were much less firmly rooted in reality than appeared at the time."[41]

Laqueur further argued against the view that a new world order was emerging. In articles written between 1972 and 1975, Laqueur consistently attacked the idea that economics were replacing military and political strength as the key to national power as one of the "misconceptions of the state of the world that are truly fundamental." The idea of a multipolar, interdependent world was, therefore, for him, an illusion. Europe was living on "borrowed time, incapable of mustering sufficient strength to overcome national particularism," and, referring to Japan, he declared that there was no "real ground for supposing that new superpowers have emerged."[42]

Moreover, the kind of American retreat advocated by Richard J. Barnet and others on the far left was, to Laqueur, further foolishness. At the root of his criticism lay a continuing belief in the threat of Soviet expansionism. "The only certain result of a greening-of-America policy," he noted, "would be the emergence of Russia as the dominant power in Europe and some other parts of the world." Laqueur did not doubt that the Soviets would try to fill any vacuum left by retreating American power: "While America is in retreat, the Soviet Union still has a globalist policy. As the U.S. opts for disengagement, the Soviet Union increases its commitments." America could not survive alone "once the lights go out in the rest of the world," in Laqueur's view. Even if the United States somehow survived in isolation, it would not be able to cure its domestic problems, as the left believed: "A confident, dynamic country can play an active part in world affairs and at the same time cope with its internal problems. A people adrift, lacking purpose and conviction, cannot do either."[43]

Laqueur saw the world not only as a dangerous place but also as one heading for disaster. Although he had decried excessive pessimism in 1972, by 1974 he had come to see "much reason" to expect "a major international upheaval such as the world has not experienced since World War II." Laqueur believed that the economic difficulties of the times, in particular those related to the increased price of oil and expected food shortages, would worsen domestic and international tensions in the Third World and Europe. Laqueur's pessimism was marked by certainty—"when the collapse comes," he wrote of India and Southeast Asia, while Europe's political progress was "in full retreat." Laqueur placed little hope in the abilities of the institutions of a multipolar world to stave off disaster: "It is quite unrealistic to expect the United Nations, the World Bank, OECD [Organization for Economic Cooperation and Development], or the International Monetary Fund to take effective action . . . to combat world inflation, to solve the problem of raw materials, and to cope with the emergency facing the have-not nations." Again, as the world situation continued to worsen, Laqueur expected the Soviet Union to "try to expand its spheres of influence in Europe, the Middle East, and possibly also in Southeast Asia . . . the essence of Soviet policy will not consist in refraining from seizing an advantage over the United States wherever possible."[44]

Despite their differences, Tucker and Laqueur performed two important services for the neoconservatives. First, they provided a specific framework for viewing the world. Although this approach continued to assign a primary role to the Communist threat, as had the vital center, it provided an updated view of the world in which Communism was joined by the new threats of Western political weakness, confusion among elites, and Third World attacks on the developed states. These were all themes which would become prominent in neoconservative writings later in the 1970s.

Tucker and Laqueur's second contribution was to provide the neoconservatives with an updated, explicit link between foreign and domestic politics. Just as the vital center had seen support for liberalism at home and abroad as inseparable, the neoconservatives would see leftist attacks on American foreign policy as part of the assault on democracy at home. Thereafter, the battle against the New Left would take place on both fronts—"domestic policy was foreign policy, and vice versa," in the words of Midge Decter. Tucker and Laqueur also saw the consequences of a leftist triumph in apocalyptic terms—the end of democracy in the United States and a Communist triumph abroad. This view, which left no room for compromise, set the tone for much of what the neoconservatives would write during the 1970s and 1980s.[45]

The Democratic party had been weakening steadily in the second half of the 1960s. Herbert Parmet has found that under Lyndon Johnson, funding and patronage decisions were made in the White House, which undermined the party's organization, while the cumulative impact of war, black militancy, and inflation helped to fragment the party's coalition. When Hubert Humphrey assumed control of the party in 1968, according to Penn Kemble (then the national secretary of the Socialist Party, USA, and later a Democratic activist), "the staff and budget had been drastically reduced, the youth arm virtually disbanded, and confusion and incompetency given free rein." After the disaster of the 1968 Chicago convention—which is usually remembered for the riots that surrounded it—and Humphrey's defeat, the Democrats embarked on a series of reforms, later known as the McGovern reforms. They were intended to make the party more of a participatory democracy, replace traditional bosses, and stress social action. This approach was usually referred to as the New Politics.[46]

Some Democrats quickly concluded that the reform process was leading the party in the wrong direction, and *Commentary* provided a platform for their protests. In October 1969, journalist William Pfaff wrote that "America's New Politics . . . today is being conducted as if our problems were matters of election-year tactics, whereas what are involved are fundamental questions affecting the political organization of industrial society." A year later, as the reform process went on and the Democrats faced the elections of 1970, Penn Kemble wrote of some of the New Politics' threats to the party, chief of which was the dominance of intellectuals over traditional politicians and their methods:

> To the extent that any force in American politics embodies the interests of the new intelligentsia, this does—or at least is attempting to. . . .
>
> The strategy of the New Politics movement has been to concentrate on its own favorites, regardless of their importance to the larger political picture, and in a manner completely independent of—and occasionally in conflict with—the other major liberal blocs.

Kemble's warnings went unheeded, however, and in the wake of George McGovern's defeat in the 1972 presidential election, he and Joshua Muravchik (later a major neoconservative intellectual) looked back bitterly on what they saw as the left's hijacking of the party. The reform commission "exceeded its mandate," they argued, and rewrote the rules so that McGovern would be nominated with "no more than 25 per cent of the total votes cast in primaries," while Senator Henry Jackson—a Washington Democrat, strict anti-Communist liberal, choice of the neoconservatives, and "the candidate whose stands on issues most clearly resembled the attitudes of the Democratic electorate"—was forced to drop out of the race. In sum, Kemble and Muravchik believed, the party was "in a shambles" because "a conception of democratic participation which is far more concerned with the demands of the political activist than it is with the needs of the ordinary citizen has gained such favor among liberals and Democrats."[47]

Regardless of any role he had in taking the Democratic party away from their beliefs, the neoconservatives felt only scorn for McGovern. To Podhoretz, McGovern's followers were "ideologues . . . hostile to the feelings and beliefs of the majority of the American people." Jeane Kirkpatrick analyzed McGovern's defeat in her first article in *Commentary* (another indication of the magazine's role as a refuge for anti-Communist liberals), attributing it to "an inability to establish identification with traditional American cultural values." Thus, Kirkpatrick believed, "as the candidate of one cultural class, he became the enemy of another. McGovern came to be perceived by millions of Americans as a man who had gone over to the enemy."[48]

Seymour Martin Lipset and Earl Raab provided a similar analysis, based on polling and voting results. The American people were not resistant to change, they argued, but they rejected McGovern because he was perceived as a threat "to the social order itself." Lipset and Raab, too, saw the alienation among traditional Democrats that McGovern had triggered. McGovern's followers, they wrote, were factionalists who "also had qualities generally associated with extremism: they were ideological, moralistic, and evangelistic. These are characteristics which a coalition party, containing sharply diverse factions, cannot afford to harbor or encourage."[49]

Another indication of the seriousness of the tensions between the neoconservatives and the party's dominant factions was the issue of foreign policy. Other than his opposition to the Vietnam war, McGovern had little to say about foreign affairs except for vaguely reassuring platitudes such as "we should begin to place less emphasis on alliances and arms in our pursuit of security and begin to concentrate more on building a better international system for maintaining peace and controlling the weapons of war." During the 1972 campaign McGovern waited until June, when he was all but nominated, to assemble a group of foreign affairs advisers. The group included Stanley Hoffmann and Richard Holbrook, the editor of *Foreign Policy*, showing a strong bias toward world order theory and away from containment. This was confirmed in October, when McGovern released the major foreign policy statement of his campaign, which claimed that "forces beyond our control will have the most to do with shaping the political arrangements of the future." McGovern further emphasized the importance of cooperation with the Soviet Union to build "a future that is not based on outdated stereotypes of military confrontation and power politics," and stressed putting America's own house in order, claiming that "at the bottom of it all must lie a just and prosperous domestic society." Coupled with the McGovern campaign slogan "Come Home, America," the foreign policy platform represented to the neoconservatives the triumph of isolationism among the Democrats, "the fondest wish of all Movement radicals," in Norman Podhoretz's words.[50]

Even before McGovern's defeat in November, a group of neoconservatives sought to take the Democratic party back to the reformist, anti-Communist policies of the vital center. Decter, Podhoretz, and Ben Wattenberg (a Humphrey speechwriter, political analyst, and former aide to Jackson) began looking for a way to overthrow the New Politics forces in the party in favor of Humphrey and Jackson supporters. They saw that McGovern was "going to be such an electoral disaster," Decter recalled, that his defeat would provide an "opportunity to recapture and revivify . . . the Democratic party and take control of it again, take it back to the good old days of Harry S Truman."[51]

After the election they founded the Coalition for a Democratic Majority to unite Humphrey and Jackson supporters and, in Wattenberg's words, "fight this battle for the soul of the Democratic party at the level of ideas and issues." Wattenberg and Decter were joined on the organizing committee by Max Kampelman (a former aide to Humphrey), Jeane Kirkpatrick, and Penn Kemble (who was made executive director of the coalition). Lending their names as sponsors were Daniel Bell, Nathan Glazer, Seymour Martin Lipset, Michael Novak, Podhoretz, Richard Pipes (a Harvard professor and Jackson supporter), and labor leader Albert Shanker. In December, the coalition took out an advertisement in the *New York Times* to announce its founding and declare that the election results were "A clear signal to the Democratic Party to return to the great tradition through which it had come to represent the wishes and hopes of a majority of the American people—the tradition of Franklin D. Roosevelt, Harry S Truman, Adlai Stevenson, John F. Kennedy, Lyndon B. Johnson, and Hubert H. Humphrey." The statement went on to denounce the New Politics for "its contempt for the very people and institutions on which the Democratic Party has built its electoral strength," and proclaim the need for "a sober but spirited assumption of America's share of responsibility" abroad and the belief "that without democratic order there can be no justice."[52]

The coalition was ultimately ineffective. It issued a number of position papers and foreign policy analyses, but its major goal was to roll back the reforms, particularly for delegate selection, which the coalition's founders blamed for enabling the New Politics forces to gain control of the party. At the Democrats' December 1974 midterm convention in Kansas City, however, the party approved "a document that institutionalized the major McGovern guidelines," as the *New Republic* reported, leaving the coalition with little choice "but slip quietly away." As Decter put it, "the New Politics people walked all over us," and Richard Perle (another of Jackson's aides) recalled that the coalition's only real achievement was to keep the Jackson supporters together as a coherent group.[53]

Their experiences with the Coalition for a Democratic Majority provided valuable lessons for its founders. For many, it had been their first experience in organizational politics. Midge Decter, for example, had never been active in a political organization before the coalition, and she and many of her liberal intellectual associates had no experience translating their ideas into actions. "We never thought of that as being our end of the world," Decter remembered. "We wrote and debated and argued and criticized and that's what we did. That's the kind of people we were." They learned the limits of compromise and the need for members of a group to agree strongly on their central purpose.[54]

Decter also blamed much of the coalition's failure on Humphrey supporters—"broken down liberals," she called them—who wanted to reconcile the party's factions rather than eject the McGovernites and New Politics supporters. The necessity of having a candidate to provide a focus for efforts and to attract supporters also became clear. Despite many of the members' preference for Senator Jackson, Decter recalls that he was reluctant to become the coalition's candidate and thus be openly identified with it, thereby leaving the coalition without a rallying point. As she later put it, "if you are going to be . . . a partisan political organization, you need a candidate. And if you don't have one, all you are is a lot of hot air."[55]

By the end of 1974, the neoconservatives appeared to have reached a political dead end. As guardians of vital center liberalism, they had become a minority faction within the Democratic party, unable to do more than protest the party's leftward drift. In the era of détente, and given the prevailing view among liberals that the United States should shy away from the use of force abroad, their anti-Communist internationalism and suspicions of the Soviet Union seemed dated and discredited. In addition, their movement lacked an effective organization and leadership. Most important, there was no proof that their approach would bring political success. No politician associated with the neoconservatives had caught the public imagination, and there was no reason to believe that their activist approach to foreign policy would be popular. This bleak outlook began to brighten considerably in the spring of 1975, however, when Daniel Patrick Moynihan stepped forward and became the first successful neoconservative politician.

3

The
Intellectual
in Politics:
Daniel Patrick
Moynihan,
1975–1978

Daniel Patrick Moynihan was the first neoconservative to bridge the gap between the worlds of intellectual abstraction and day-to-day politics. For 25 years he shifted back and forth between the academic and political spheres. A social scientist specializing in urban and ethnic affairs, he also served a governor of New York and four presidents, applying social science techniques to problems ranging from auto safety to black family stability to easing India's debt to the United States. In each case he sought liberal approaches that could make concrete improvements to an existing situation, which was what he saw to be the point of government. As often as not, he failed—sometimes spectacularly—because the substance of his intellectual approach was often distorted and attacked in the political arena. But over two decades, Moynihan's basic approach never varied.[1]

Moynihan held to the tenets of vital center liberalism. As a college student he opposed Wallace and supported Truman, and went on to become prominent in the Americans for Democratic Action. Moynihan's liberalism was chastened during the 1960s, and he came to have a more cautious view of social change, but he did not abandon his commitment to reform. Nor did Moynihan ever vary from strict anti-Communism. During the 1970s he adopted the skepticism of the Third World and its claims that marked neoconservative thinking on international politics, although he came to this view by a route of his own.

Moynihan was an ambitious man, although he did not openly proclaim it, the way his close friend Norman Podhoretz did in his book *Making It* (1967). Moynihan never stayed at one level for very long, serving first a governor, then a cabinet member, and then a president, before receiving two ambassadorial appointments. He climbed impressively in the academic world as well, going from Syracuse University to Wesleyan and then to Harvard, where he moved from the post of professor of education to the more prestigious government department. Such drive is not unusual in a bright boy who grew up on the edge of poverty, but in Moynihan's case it also helps explain why he kept returning to politics despite repeated setbacks, rather than sitting comfortably in a tenured academic position.

Moynihan also had a certain amount of luck during his career. In the spring of 1975, when he returned to prominence as ambassador to the United Nations, South Vietnam had just fallen to the Communists and the national mood was gloomy and uncertain. The situation was tailor-made for Moynihan's rhetorical and intellectual talents, and he took advantage of it to remake his political image. His popularity was so great, in fact, that he was able to go on from his ambassadorship to a successful career in the U.S. Senate.

Daniel Patrick Moynihan was born on March 16, 1927, in Tulsa, Oklahoma. His father, John, was a newspaper reporter and advertising copywriter who earned a good living in the early 1930s. Moynihan's mother, Margaret, did not have to work and had charge accounts at department stores in New York City, where John had found work in late 1927. John was a philanderer, gambler, and drinker, however, and he deserted his family in the fall of 1937, plunging them from a comfortable, middle-class existence to a life on the edge of poverty. Margaret's situation was precarious but not desperate; she and her children (by then Pat had a brother and a sister) lived in a series of small, dingy Manhattan apartments, but they were never homeless. The children stayed in school and, as an adolescent, Pat Moynihan worked at various part-time jobs. In 1940, his mother married again, this time to a man of moderate wealth, and the family moved to rural Westchester County. By late 1941, however, the marriage had failed and Margaret and her children were back in a Manhattan apartment, while Pat attended high school and worked. Wartime prosperity made life a little easier; Margaret worked in a defense plant and Pat worked as a stevedore on the New York docks after he was graduated from high school in 1943. That fall he entered the City College of New York, where he completed one year before entering the navy's officer training program.[2]

Moynihan spent three years in the navy, two of them on college campuses. From June 1944 to June 1945, he was at Middlebury College in Vermont, attending classes and drilling. From there he went to Tufts University, near Boston, where he did the same. In June 1946 he went on active duty for a year. Moynihan returned to Tufts after his discharge and received his B.A. in 1948. He earned an M.A. from Tufts' Fletcher School in 1949 and began working on his Ph.D. Moynihan then went on to the London School of Economics on a Fulbright scholarship, where he acquired a taste for English clothes and mannerisms but did little serious studying. He traveled in Europe after his scholarship ended, spent some time on naval reserve duty, and returned home in early 1953 to resume working on his doctorate.[3]

Moynihan first became involved in politics when he returned to the United States in 1953. He worked on Robert Wagner's campaign for mayor of New York and then got a job with the International Rescue Committee, a private organization that aided refugees. In the fall of 1954 he joined Averell Harriman's gubernatorial campaign, and then spent four years in Albany as an assistant to Governor Harriman. Moynihan appears not to have had a sponsor helping him in Harriman's office, but rather gained increasing responsibility as his outgoing personality and obvious ability won him recognition. After Harriman lost his bid for reelection to Nelson Rockefeller in 1958 Moynihan was hired by Syracuse University, where he worked on Harriman's papers and his Ph.D. (finally completed in 1960). In the meantime, he campaigned for John F. Kennedy in 1960, was again noticed as an able young man, and was rewarded with an appointment as special assistant to Secretary of Labor Arthur Goldberg.

Surprisingly for a graduate of the Fletcher School, Moynihan seems to have had little interest in foreign affairs during the 1950s and early 1960s. He had failed the foreign service exam in 1949 and is not known to have pursued a job in any other foreign affairs-related area. Moreover, except for his brief stint with the International Rescue Committee, his jobs after he returned from Europe were in state and local politics. Moynihan's first published articles were also purely domestic in focus, covering auto safety and New York State Democratic politics, for example. Similarly, his jobs at Syracuse and with Secretary Goldberg were removed from foreign topics.[4]

Moynihan fit easily into the liberal postwar consensus. According to his biographer, he was "a strong supporter of Harry Truman and an equally strong opponent of Henry Wallace," whose party, he wrote to a friend, was "under the Communist Party aegis." In the 1960s, he became a member of the national board of the Americans for Democratic Action. He developed a passion for government, what he viewed as the process of identifying problems, analyzing them, and devising workable solutions. Moynihan was very talented at this social science approach, which he saw as separate from the political process of local organizing, dealing, and compromising.[5]

Moynihan made clear his conception of government in his first article for *Commentary*, in June 1961, in which he commented on the futility of many of the New York Democrats' activities. In fact, argued Moynihan, the party's regulars were dinosaurs, as exemplified by Tammany leader Carmine De Sapio: "De Sapio is incomparably the most able politician the New York Democrats have produced since Farley. He is just that, a politician. . . . He is not the least interested in government, only in politics. It is simply too bad that he should have come to power in a world in which this was no longer good enough." Under Harriman, Moynihan applied his talents to such diverse activities as reforming the system which tracked progress on New York state agencies' reports—a job which also kept Moynihan abreast of many developments within the state government—and the chairmanship of the Governor's Traffic Safety Policy Coordinating Committee, where he became an early advocate for safety in auto design.[6]

Moynihan's analytical approach was well suited to the dominant liberal intellectual trends of the era. He did not espouse a formal or rigid ideology. Instead, his was a practical, step-by-step liberalism that was satisfied with gradual progress and did not seek sudden or vast improvements in the human condition. Unfortunately for Moynihan, this approach made him a relatively poor politician. When he came up against others who did not share his analytical approach or who were wedded to a more ideological outlook, Moynihan tended to come out the loser. It was just such an incident that first brought him to national attention.

In 1965, Moynihan wrote a report on the condition of black families in the United States, "The Negro Family: The Case for National Action." At the time, he was assistant secretary of labor, a post he had assumed in 1963, and which made him responsible for the Office of Policy Planning and Research. This put him in charge of the "development of information from which the effectiveness of the Department's activities could be assessed and with the development of programmatic ideas and policy goals." From his post, Moynihan reported to the secretary of labor, which freed his work from the "long review process typical of government reports [and ensured] that it received high-level distribution." Moynihan had already given some thought to the subject of the black family before 1965, mainly as an outgrowth of his government work on poverty programs, his collaboration with Nathan Glazer on *Beyond the Melting Pot* (1963), and his attendance at a 1964 conference on the Negro in America. He decided to write the report in November 1964, recalling later, "I felt

I had to write a paper about the Negro family to explain to [optimists] how there was a problem more difficult than they knew and also to explain some of the issues of unemployment and housing in terms that would be new enough and shocking enough that they would say, 'Well, we can't let this sort of thing go on. We've got to do something about it.'" With two assistants, Moynihan collected data, developed his arguments, and wrote the report, which was approved by Secretary Willard Wirtz in March 1965 and sent to the White House in May.[7]

"The Negro Family" sought to demonstrate that for blacks to progress from securing their civil rights to achieving true equality with whites required "the establishment of a stable Negro family structure." Moynihan argued that blacks were falling behind most other Americans in terms of income and living standards because of "the deterioration of the Negro family," and he used a large amount of statistical evidence and stark wording about divorce, illegitimate births, and welfare dependency to show that the "family structure of lower class Negroes is highly unstable . . . approaching complete breakdown." The roots of the problem, according to Moynihan, stretched back to slavery, but also included rapid urbanization and high unemployment; moreover, a vicious cycle was at work, as family instability and poor education deprived children of opportunities, making it difficult for young blacks to break out of poverty. Moynihan wrote that the matriarchal structure of the black family was also contributing to the failure of black children, who were increasingly ill-prepared for life and were thus "withdrawing from American society" in large numbers, further tightening what he called the "tangle of pathology." In his conclusion, Moynihan stated, "The policy of the United States is to bring the Negro American to full and equal sharing in the responsibilities and rewards of citizenship. To this end, the programs of the Federal government bearing on this objective shall be designed to have the effect, directly or indirectly, of enhancing the stability and resources of the Negro American family."[8]

As a result of its dramatic language and high-ranking authorship, the Moynihan Report, as the document became known, was brought to

President Johnson's attention. Moynihan's timing was good, for the administration was already considering policies to pursue following the enactment of the 1965 civil rights bill. Moynihan and White House speechwriter Richard N. Goodwin were then asked to draft Johnson's June 4 commencement address at Howard University, and they drew heavily on the report. Johnson's speech declared, for example, that the "breakdown of the Negro family structure" was the "most important" problem facing blacks and that "unless we work to strengthen the family," no other black gains would "be enough to cut completely the circle of despair and deprivation." Planning began for a White House conference in the spring of 1966 on civil rights, the idea for which had come out of Moynihan's report and Johnson's speech, although Moynihan left the government in July 1965 to run for president of the New York City Council.[9]

The Moynihan Report and its contents gradually became public knowledge during the summer and fall of 1965. The report was finally released to the press in August, after leaks of its contents had already circulated, fortuitously coinciding with the Watts riot in Los Angeles. The riot helped focus attention on the report (it was "all the rage," according to the *New Republic*), making its contention that without help for black families "there will be no social peace in the United States for generations," seem prophetic. But rather than receiving praise, Moynihan and his report were soon at the center of a storm of controversy and criticism. Civil rights leaders condemned it for diverting attention from what they viewed as the real sources of black problems. Whitney Young, Jr., wrote, "Family instability has been presented in the press and elsewhere as being the cause of Negro failure to achieve equality. This is a gross distortion. It is instead the result of patterns of discrimination which deny to Negro citizens the same chance to hold a job and earn a decent living that the white American has." Perhaps the harshest critique came from Harvard psychologist William Ryan, writing in the *Nation*. Ryan attacked the report's statistical evidence and methodology which, he claimed, led to "inexact conclusions from weak and insufficient data," called the report "smug," Moynihan inept, and accused him of subscribing to a "new ideology" that saw blacks as "savages." In the face of these reactions, the Johnson administration backed away from its endorsement of the report, "which was not even among [the 1966 White House] conference's official working papers," and allowed the issue to drop.[10]

Moynihan made no public comments about the controversy in 1965 or 1966. His candidacy for the New York City Council ended with a primary loss, and he then spent the 1965–1966 academic year at Wesleyan University, in Connecticut. In the fall of 1966, Moynihan became the director of MIT and Harvard's Joint Center for Urban Studies, succeeding his friend James Q. Wilson, and also received an appointment as a professor of education at Harvard. With the report controversy largely over and having found a secure job, Moynihan published a reply to his critics in February 1967.

Moynihan portrayed the entire affair as a tragedy, with blacks as the losers. He gave two major causes for the debacle. This first was a lack of vision by civil rights leaders and liberals. The time between President Kennedy's assassination in November 1963 and the escalation of the Vietnam War in late 1965 had been one of national willingness to try new social policies and of enough prosperity to finance them, according to Moynihan. Johnson's Howard University speech, in Moynihan's view, was a commitment to further civil rights efforts, to taking on increasingly difficult tasks—such as black family stability—as segregation ended. But there had been little consensus behind Johnson's plans—"the civil rights movement had no program for going beyond the traditional and relatively easy issues of segregation and discrimination," wrote Moynihan—and the family issue was so sensitive that liberals preferred simply to avoid it. Moreover, a significant liberal faction would not allow the matter to be addressed.[11]

Moynihan argued that the second cause of the failure was closed-mindedness among liberals. He argued that the liberal movement harbored some of its greatest enemies, ideologues who would oppose any plan, however well thought out and presented, that challenged their views of the world. The "liberal Left," he claimed, contained a core "of intense, purposeful, powerful, and dedicated persons," but they were quite different from most of the people they claimed to represent who had, "on the whole, quite conventional views and expectations." Thus, in Moynihan's view, "The reaction of the liberal Left to the issue of the Negro family was decisive. . . . They would have none of it. No one was going to talk about their poor people that way." Furthermore, "The insistence . . . of the liberal Left that the issue . . . not be made a matter of public concern resulted directly in its not being made a matter of public action." For Moynihan the lesson was plain. "The liberal Left," he wrote, "can be as rigid and destructive as any force in American life."[12]

Moynihan's experience with "The Negro Family" was a turning point. He had been a strong sixties liberal, enthusiastically supporting Kennedy and then Johnson's programs. But now Moynihan saw that not all liberals shared his pragmatic and intellectually honest approach, and this came home to Moynihan in starkly personal terms. Until 1966, much of Moynihan's writings and politics had dealt with large abstractions—impersonal auto companies, the black community—but had not been on a personal level, let alone one filled with invective. Moynihan had seen for the first time what such attacks could do to an individual and his ideas, no matter how well intended they were.

The Moynihan of 1967 was a neoconservative in all but name. His commentary on the report's critics as well as his September speech to the Americans for Democratic Action (ADA) showed how much tougher his outlook and lower his expectations had become. Norman Podhoretz later recalled that Moynihan still wanted to "preserve and defend" the welfare state. At the same time, in his ADA speech Moynihan talked not just of stability but also of the lessons liberals needed to draw from reform's failures. "We have got to become a great deal more rigorous in the assessment not only of the reality of problems, but of the nature of proposed solutions," he said. Liberals had also to "overcome the curious condescension that takes the form of defending and explaining away anything, however outrageous, which Negroes, individually or collectively, might do."[13]

Moynihan was also considerably more famous than he had been when he went to Washington in 1961, which must have given him a great deal of satisfaction. In November 1967 he was the subject of an article in *Life*, which noted that the "most important side effect of the [Moynihan] Report was that a lot of people remembered it and they remembered its author." In mid-1966 *The New York Times Magazine* profiled him during the controversy over the report, the first of seven flattering profiles the magazine would run between then and late 1990. Also in 1967, Moynihan was on the cover of *Time* ("currently the most controversial of urban affairs analysts.") Moynihan may have been out of the government and less optimistic about the effectiveness of its programs, but he was now someone whose views were listened to and with whom others would have to reckon.[14]

From the time of the ADA speech until 1971, Moynihan expanded on his theme that growing instability posed a significant threat to the American political system and to liberalism. He did not take the apocalyptic view that American democracy was on the verge of collapse; in Moynihan's view, Johnson's forced retirement in 1968 meant that the system still functioned. Rather, the threat was that liberal failures would lead "toward a conservative Republican President and a conservative-to-reactionary Congress: a regime marked by . . . hostility to social change at home." Presumably, such a combination would lead to rigid policies that would, in turn, exacerbate existing tensions. To prevent this, as well as to help restore political stability, Moynihan continually argued that liberals had to learn from their mistakes, including the tendency to be "too much interested in ideas, especially if they are new, and too little interested in administration."[15]

Moynihan placed a great deal of the responsibility for the deterioration of stability, and its restoration, on intellectuals. In addition, his articles showed the continuing influence of the vital center on his thinking. "The times are tragic and will be surmounted only, I should think, by men capable of accepting that fact. Our politicians have been better about this than have our professors," he wrote in September 1970. A year before he had condemned intellectuals for failing to educate the public about the true nature of social problems: "Much of the intense difficulty of our time . . . arises from a massive misstatement of our problems. Intellectuals, if this view is correct, have done their work badly." The core of the problem, Moynihan claimed, was the "imbalance between the intellectual-literary-media resources liberals have in this country as against conservatives. . . . A problem in America is that we don't have a conservative class. . . . This is not healthy."[16]

In this atmosphere of apparent crisis, Moynihan returned to the federal government to work for Richard Nixon. He had supported Robert Kennedy in the spring of 1968 ("He gives us the hope that we will pick up where his brother left us," Moynihan wrote in *Commentary*) and, although he hardly campaigned for Humphrey, his biographer reports that he was angered by Nixon's electoral victory. Soon after the election, Leonard Garment, Nixon's law partner and a relatively liberal Republican, suggested an appointment for Moynihan. Nixon reportedly hesitated over hiring a Kennedy liberal, but Garment persisted and Nixon was willing to give Moynihan's views a hearing, which he apparently found congenial. In December 1968 Moynihan was appointed assistant to the president for urban affairs and made secretary of a new body of cabinet members, the Urban Affairs Council.[17]

Moynihan's precise reasons for accepting the position are not clear, but having had a taste of influence in Washington followed by three years of academic life, he undoubtedly looked forward to having the attention of another president. Several writers have attributed to Moynihan a desire to try to move the conservative Nixon in the direction of liberal social reforms as a way to bolster domestic stability, to make Nixon an American Disraeli. This view gains credibility from Moynihan's previous thoughts about the desirability of a liberal-conservative alliance. Moynihan also gained an opportunity to put his ideas for reform into action, and to work to keep urban and poverty programs from being abolished. He planned to stay with the administration for two years, and began working in a cramped White House office immediately after Nixon's inauguration.[18]

Moynihan's major project was welfare reform. During the 1960s, welfare rolls and costs had expanded tremendously as had the percentage of the rolls comprised of broken families. This situation was tailor-made for Moynihan, presenting an opportunity to institute reforms based on recent social science research as well as to resume his attack on the problem of family instability among the poor. Moynihan developed, and Nixon endorsed and sent to Congress, the Family Assistance Plan, which proposed abolishing Aid to Families with Dependent Children and substituting a negative income tax-based plan to provide, under a complicated formula, a guaranteed annual income of $1,600 for a family of four. Moynihan claimed, in a memo to Nixon, that the plan would "abolish poverty for dependent children and the working poor," and that the cost would be modest. The plan was indeed radical in that it would have done away with the major welfare program of the day, placed money directly in the hands of the poor, and created a national welfare standard. Nixon unveiled the plan publicly in August 1969, and the House of Representatives passed it on April 16, 1970, but after much debate and controversy, it died in the Senate in January 1971.[19]

Moynihan's efforts to improve government had once again suffered a political defeat and he drew what he believed to be the appropriate lessons. The Family Assistance Plan had been opposed by many liberals who believed that its benefits were too low; conservatives worried about the plan's costs and the possibility that some of the working poor not then receiving welfare could become eligible for benefits. (According to Nathan Glazer, research since the early 1970s strongly suggests that the plan would have cost much more than expected and would not have solved the problem of family breakups.) At the time, however, Moynihan focused his ire on his liberal Democratic opponents, whom he believed saw welfare as their policy turf. He made his point in language similar to that he had used to condemn the "liberal Left" in 1967, that "with few exceptions all the major programs enacted in the middle third of the twentieth century were Democratic programs, welfare included. Any assertion that a major program had failed, any proposal to eliminate one and substitute another, was perforce a criticism of the Democratic record." Compounding this, in Moynihan's views, was the liberals' hatred of Richard Nixon:

> To a degree that could be obsessive, liberal
> Democrats had defined their belief and measured
> their worth in terms specifically opposed to that of
> Nixon. Now he had performed the ultimate per-
> fidy. In triumph—as *president*—*Nixon* had pro-
> posed a measure of which even the most liberal
> Democrats had scarcely dared to dream . . . of a
> sudden, they found themselves behind. Behind
> *Richard Nixon!*

Liberals, as Moynihan once again drew the lesson, could not be trusted to take a realistic approach to reform, that is, to evaluate proposals on their merits and accept incremental improvements over the status quo. As Moynihan summarized liberal opposition to the Family Assistance Plan, they "preferred nothing to something they regarded as less than perfect."[20]

As the plan bogged down in Congress, Moynihan became em-broiled once again in racial politics. In early 1970 he sent Nixon a memo reviewing the position of blacks in America. The memo noted that the "American Negro is making extraordinary progress . . . [but] there would seem to be countercurrents that pose a serious threat to the welfare of blacks and the stability of society." Moynihan went on to note black gains in income and education, but also the contin-uing deterioration of the black family and resultant growth in crime and social alienation: "This social alienation among the black lower classes is matched and probably enhanced by a virulent form of anti-white feeling among portions of the large and prosperous black mid-dle class. It would be difficult to overestimate the degree to which young, well-educated blacks detest white America."[21]

Moynihan's analysis broke no new ground and his recommenda-tions were modest as well: that the administration develop a more coherent strategy for dealing with black problems, conduct further research on crime, and cultivate the politically moderate black working class. But the memo was to be remembered for another recommendation, that the administration work to tone down racial passions so that true progress could continue: "The time may have come when the issue of race could benefit from a period of 'benign neglect.' The subject has been too much talked about. The forum has been too much taken over to hysterics, paranoids and boodlers on all sides. We may need a period in which Negro progress continues and racial rhetoric fades."[22]

The benign neglect memo, as it became known, was leaked to the press and appeared in the *New York Times* on March 1, 1970. Reaction focused on Moynihan's suggestion for a period of benign neglect, which was usually quoted out of context and then twisted in meaning to indicate that he did not care about blacks. The *Times* called the memo "a sad document," and said that it was "cold comfort for Negroes and whites alike who have watched the low—not to say disappearing—profile of the administration in several areas of civil rights." Moynihan also lost some of his old allies. Social psychologist Kenneth Clark, who had supported Moynihan during the controversy over "The Negro Family," "now turned against him, believing Moynihan a racist and regretting ever having defended him."[23]

The memo reflected Moynihan's continuing limitations as a politician. He had realized that the sensitivity of the topic and the possibility of a leak meant that he had to select his words with care. "I had written 700 memos arguing the case for a liberal social policy," he later said, "particularly in the case of blacks, and nothing else had leaked." When a leak finally came, the subtleties of Moynihan's elaborate phraseology were quickly lost in the political and personal uproar. Moynihan had also outsmarted himself; when the memo was leaked the reaction did everything but cool racial passions. The incident was another lesson to Moynihan that his efforts could be quickly and easily undone by those interested only in politics.[24]

Moynihan returned to Harvard as planned at the end of 1970 and pondered another lesson of his second stint in Washington, which was that the press was as much of a problem for government as were doctrinaire liberals. His analysis, "The Presidency & the Press," appeared in *Commentary* in March 1971, and argued that the "political consequence of the rising social status of journalism is that the press grows more and more influenced by attitudes genuinely hostile to American society and American government." In an argument clearly based on Schumpeter, Moynihan concluded that journalists had become part of a "culture of disparagement," and gave little thought "to just how much elitist criticism is good for a democracy." Moynihan also took a look at the practice of leaking—a "traffic in stolen goods," as he called it—and condemned the media's willingness to print leaks without looking deeper into the story: "What the press *never* does is say who the leaker is and why he wants the story leaked. Yet, more often than not, this is the more important story: that is to say, what policy wins if the one being disclosed loses, what individual, what bureau, and so on." Moynihan concluded that little could be done to put a stop to the irresponsibility of the press, although it could be fought. "Misrepresentations of government performance must never be allowed to go unchallenged," he wrote. "Misinformation gets into the bloodstream and has consequences," one of which would be "pervasive dissatisfaction with the performance of the national government."[25]

Moynihan played little role in the remainder of Nixon's first term. In the fall of 1971 he served as a public member of the United States delegation to the United Nations General Assembly, but gained little notice. Although a Democrat, he made no efforts on behalf of George McGovern during the 1972 presidential campaign. (He also refused Leonard Garment's invitation to join Democrats for Nixon.) In fact, Moynihan was probably pleased by Nixon's reelection. McGovern and his supporters had many of the illusions about reform that Moynihan had shed and now sought to refute, and their reforming zeal ran counter to Moynihan's desire to slow reform in order to encourage social stability. Furthermore, they represented the strain of self-righteous liberalism that had so savagely attacked him over racial issues.[26]

After his reelection, Nixon asked Moynihan to become ambassador to India. According to his biographer, Moynihan believed that it was his opposition to the United States' tilt toward Pakistan in the 1971 Indo-Pakistani war—expressed directly to Nixon—that led the president to offer him the post. Moynihan accepted, was confirmed by the Senate, and arrived in New Delhi in February 1973. His assignment was to improve Indian-U.S. relations, which were still poor as a result of the tilt and a legacy of Indian distrust of the United States. Seeking a practical, concrete way to improve the relationship, Moynihan focused on settling India's rupee debt to the United States. As a result of large amounts of food aid provided to India at concessional prices in the 1950s and 1960s, New Delhi owed Washington billions of dollars worth of rupees, a debt which was continually growing because of interest, and which on paper was putting much of India's money supply into Washington's hands. Moynihan spent 1973 working with the Indians and flying back and forth between Washington and New Delhi, finally reaching a settlement in December. Under its terms United States was to repatriate the rupees to India by spending them on aid programs and embassy expenses.[27]

At the time Moynihan claimed that India would be his last public job. Moynihan later wrote that he saw the rupee settlement as the realistic limit for improving relations at the time, and he saw little prospect for a job in Washington after he left New Delhi: "There's very little success in politics. I'm not a failure, but I would bring liabilities of the past—just or unjust—with which a wise President would be advised not to encumber himself." Moynihan saw his immediate future in a return to Harvard rather than to government. He spent much of 1974 traveling in India and studying the "impact of Western ideas on the East." Moynihan's interests were shifting and he claimed to be interested in pursuing research on the "problems of legitimacy in government, the problems of maintaining legitimacy in a culture that's questioning and in some fundamental ways an adversary culture," questions which were of concern not just to Moynihan but to many other neoconservatives. But, given his ambitious nature, the prospect of returning to a purely academic life probably held less appeal than ever. In fact, while he was in India

Moynihan had already begun working on the issues which would return him to public view and more prominence than ever.[28]

Moynihan's brief service at the United Nations in 1971 had a lasting impact on his thinking. He had been assigned to the Third Committee, which was responsible for social, humanitarian, and cultural affairs, and was considering the quadrennial *Report on the World Social Situation*. The report used the presence or absence of dissent as a measure of a country's well-being, and equated a large amount of dissent with poor social conditions. "The result was a totalitarian tract," Moynihan later wrote. "Czechoslovakia came out as just about top country." In his fight against the report, Moynihan first developed many of the points that would characterize his thinking and writing between 1974 and 1978. In an interview with the *New York Times*, he lamented American diplomats' inability to defend against ideological attacks. "I don't think we're very good at ideological argument. . . . We have a lot of experience about how you run a decent country, but surprisingly little experience at describing the process. This is a weakness of our foreign policy." He was also clear about the necessity of standing firm against the argument that totalitarian societies had some good points: "I will not split the difference between a totalitarian society and an open one, or suggest that there is good to be said on both sides."[29]

After the United Nations, his tour in India gave Moynihan time to think about the fate of democracy in the Third World. Although India was still democratic throughout his time there—Prime Minister Indira Gandhi did not seize dictatorial power until mid-1975—Moynihan was disturbed by what he saw. Gandhi, he recalled noting at the time, "was running the economy into an ever more rigid state socialism. The consequent economic decline was creating ever growing opposition. . . . As the opposition grew, the day of suppression grew nearer . . . [when] she would destroy the Indian democracy." Moynihan also visited China on his way home in early 1975 and saw that, while a successful society in some respects, "there was no trace of personal freedom and no foreseeable likelihood of its appearance."[30]

For the third time, Moynihan wrote down what he believed to be the lessons of his observations. In February 1974, while still ambassador, he spoke at the Woodrow Wilson International Center for Scholars, asking "Was Woodrow Wilson Right?" In Moynihan's interpretation, Wilson stood for a "quest for legitimacy in the world order . . . of the natural goodness of man prevailing through the Holy Ghost of Reason." Fulfilling this vision meant accepting the "duty to defend and, where possible, to advance democratic principles in the world at large," for "democracy in one country was not enough simply because it would not last."[31]

For Moynihan in 1974 there was no question that Wilson had been correct and that his vision still applied to the United States, whose own freedom was tied to that of others more than ever before. As immigration made the ethnic composition of the United States increasingly similar to that of the larger world, Moynihan argued:

> There will be no struggle for personal liberty (or national independence or national survival) anywhere in Europe, in Asia, in Africa, in Latin America which will not affect American politics. In that circumstance, I would argue that there is only one course likely to make the internal strains of consequent conflicts endurable, and that is for the United States deliberately and consistently to bring its influence to bear on behalf of those regimes which promise the largest degree of personal and national liberty.

Yet Moynihan saw disturbingly little inclination on the part of the elites in the democratic countries to carry on the fight. There was, he said, echoing Niebuhr, "a crisis of faith," at a time when the "political elites of most of the world are poisonously anti-American."[32]

Moynihan had begun looking for a way to fight these trends while he was still in New Delhi. He later recalled becoming "more and more absorbed by the seeming inability of American representatives to deal with ideological argument or even to recognize it." On one occasion when the United States fought back, in August 1973, Moynihan took the highly unusual step of sending a congratulatory cable to United Nations Ambassador John Scali for his denunciation of Cuban meddling over the status of Puerto Rico. Moynihan noted in the cable his "concern not only at the emergence of an anti-democratic bias at the United Nations," but also what he saw as the continuing passivity of American diplomats. Furthermore, wrote Moynihan, states making unfounded accusations against the United States should pay a price: "Something specifically bad should happen to each one of them, and when it has happened they should be told that Americans take the honor of their democracy most seriously."[33]

Moynihan placed much of the blame for America's poor performance on liberal world order theorists, citing their "great delusion" that the "North-South agenda somehow avoided the sterile ideological conflicts of the previous and presumably past era." Moynihan spent December 1974 writing a summary and analysis of all of these points. At the end of the month he sent his paper to Norman Podhoretz (with whom he had become close friends), "as it was clear that only he could edit it, and, such was the time, that probably only he would publish it." Podhoretz printed the paper, entitled "The United States in Opposition," in the March 1975 issue of *Commentary*.[34]

In "The United States in Opposition," Moynihan discussed what he saw as the roots of the Third World's anti-American ideology. Its origins lay, he argued, in the "general corpus of British socialist opinion as it developed in the period roughly 1890–1950," and was marked by "a suspicion of, almost a bias against, economic development," and an anti-Americanism stimulated as much by British "aristocratical disdain," as by dislike of American capitalism. These ideas spread through the British empire, according to Moynihan, as well as the other European powers, and were joined by two additional concepts: that the colonial areas were entitled to their independence, and that they had suffered economic exploitation and discrimination. Thus, the new nations saw themselves as aggrieved parties who were owed reparations from the developed world. As Moynihan put it, "there were scores to be settled." In the meantime, the Third World's

Fabian-based policies had turned a large number of countries into impoverished police states.[35]

Moynihan reiterated in the article his contention that the United States had been unsuccessful in dealing with this ideology. What he termed "a massive failure of American diplomacy," had come about because the United States had not "seen the ideology as distinctive," and thus had failed "to perceive that skill and intelligence were required to deal with it successfully." To support this point, Moynihan cited the 1971 *World Social Situation* report and other UN conferences and publications which had made wild accusations against the West and against whose promulgation American diplomats did nothing. But despite its diplomatic failures, Moynihan cautioned that the United States had to remain an active participant in the United Nations system. Citing atomic energy issues as an example, he pointed out that "world society and world organization have evolved to the point where palpable interests are disposed in international forums without precedent," which made it counter to the United States' own interests simply to walk away from the UN.[36]

Moynihan advocated that the United States adopt a parliamentary outlook toward the UN and go into opposition. The Communist and Third World bloc made the United States and its democratic friends a minority within the body, but the democracies were still dedicated to the institution and its original, liberal goals. The United States, Moynihan declared, should stay and defend its liberal policies against the anti-capitalist, anti-democratic assault of the Third World and Communists:

> It is the peculiar function of "radical" political
> demands, such as those most recently heard in the
> international forums, that they bring about an
> exceptional deprecation of the achievements of
> liberal processes. . . . But the truth is that interna-
> tional liberalism and its processes have enormous
> recent achievements to their credit. It is time for
> the United States to start saying so.

In action, this meant that Third World claims for reparations were to be denied. Their poverty "is of their own making and no one else's, and no claim on anyone else arises in consequence." The United States would also have put an end to thirty years' worth of habits which had "created patterns of appeasement so profound as to seem wholly normal," stop "apologiz[ing] for an imperfect democracy," and proclaim the American case: "Those nations which have put liberty ahead of equality have ended up doing better by equality than those with the reverse priority. This is so, and being so, it is something to be shouted to the heavens in the years now upon us. *This is our case.* We *are* of the liberty party, and it might surprise us what energies might be released were we to unfurl those banners."[37]

The article put Moynihan into the public eye once more, and at just the right moment. Podhoretz held a press conference on February 26, 1975, to release the article, a first for *Commentary*, and Moynihan was soon being interviewed on national television. Secretary of State Henry Kissinger read the article and liked it. More important, Moynihan was proposing a new course of action just as Kissinger was to suffer one of his greatest defeats. In early March, South Vietnam began to collapse. On March 26, Kissinger offered Moynihan the job of ambassador to the United Nations. Moynihan met with President Gerald R. Ford and accepted the offer on April 12, just three weeks before the *New Republic* editorialized that the "Vietnam debacle should occasion a reassessment of both the purposes and limits of our power; if the Bicentennial helps us focus the contrast between our idealism and our crimes so much the better."[38]

Moynihan's goal at the United Nations was to fight a battle of ideas and restore the liberal internationalists' nerve. In effect, he was battling against the attitudes represented by the *New Republic*'s editorial. Even if the liberal elite had lost its self-confidence and the widespread antagonism of the Third World toward American democracy indicated that "history has simply not been with us," it was still the duty of true liberals—those who still held to the faith of the vital center—to take up the defense of the country: "It is on the Democratic Left that we are most likely to find both informed and unintimidated advocates of a vigorous American role in world affairs, and equally unashamed partisans of American performance."[39]

To make his case, Moynihan planned to use the simple strategy of exposing lies and rebutting accusations. At his confirmation hearings he told the senators that, "we are in a propaganda war. We have to respond with a comparable level of effort to that which is directed against us." This, in turn, meant that unfounded accusations against the United States would not be tolerated: "It seems to me that the first object of American policy with respect to this kind of . . . accusation is to see that it is not made, and when it is made, the second object should be to see that it is stopped, and if that can't be, then the third necessity of responding comes into play." As a possible response, Moynihan cited cutting aid to offending governments. The point, as he put it, was to make clear to Third World countries seeking American assistance that they "can't have it both ways." Moynihan was confirmed by the Senate and sworn in at the end of June. For his staff he recruited Leonard Garment, with whom he had become close friends in the Nixon White House, and Suzanne Weaver, a faculty member at Yale and one of his former students. Norman Podhoretz hovered in the background as an unofficial adviser and writer.[40]

Moynihan's appointment presented a unique opportunity. The United Nations ambassadorship gave him a much more prominent position than that of New Delhi, and hence a way to return to public attention. Given the behavior he could expect from the Soviet bloc and the Third World, Moynihan also had the chance to score easy— and domestically popular—debating points against America's opponents. In addition, Moynihan would be dealing almost exclusively in foreign issues and he could draw on his past experiences to avoid domestic political traps. In sum, he had an excellent chance to remake his public image.

Moynihan's unusually eventful eight-month tenure as ambassador to the United Nations began with two victories. In August, the Decolonization Committee began preparing to debate a Cuban resolution supporting Puerto Rican self-determination and independence, by now a routine issue. Moynihan told Kissinger that a defeat on Puerto Rico so soon after the defeat of South Vietnam would be "intolerable." Countries sitting on the committee were informed that Puerto Rico was a functioning democracy in which voters had rejected independence and were further told that voting for the resolution would be viewed by the United States as an "unfriendly act." The resolution was defeated. In September, the Seventh Special Session of the General Assembly convened to consider issues surrounding international economic cooperation. The Third World bloc was using the session to demand more aid from the developed countries and a price fixing arrangement for natural resources. Moynihan and his staff rewrote the draft resolution, eliminating its radical anti-Western rhetoric and calling instead for the use of monetary and technical methods to help create greater opportunities for poor countries to help themselves. After strenuous negotiations, Moynihan's moderate resolution was passed. Moynihan was satisfied that his tactics were working; accurate information and threats had stopped one blatantly unfriendly resolution while nimble writing and negotiation had transformed another into a more reasonable, realistic plan.[41]

Moynihan suffered his greatest defeat as ambassador in November, however, when the General Assembly passed a resolution declaring Zionism to be a form of racism. Despite American maneuvers and diplomacy, the resolution had been slowly progressing for several months and was approved November 10. By then, all Moynihan could do was make a vigorous denunciation of it. The night before the vote, Moynihan, with Podhoretz and Weaver, prepared his speech in reply to the resolution. "This is a lie," he told the General Assembly, and went on to detail its linguistic perversions. "I am here making one point, and one point only, which is that whatever else Zionism may be, it is not and cannot be 'a form of racism.'" The resolution, Moynihan argued, had implications far beyond Zionism. "Today we have drained the word 'racism' of its meaning," and "tomorrow, terms like 'national self-determination' and 'national honor' will be perverted in the same way to serve the purposes of conquest and exploitation. And when these claims begin to be made—as they already have begun to be made—it is the small nations of the world whose integrity will suffer." Not only would small states become more vulnerable, but so would individuals, argued Moynihan. Linguistic games could easily erase the individual's independence from the state, quickly putting an end to any protection of human rights.[42]

Moynihan did not confine his offensive to the floor of the United Nations. In early October, Ugandan dictator Idi Amin spoke to the General Assembly, making wild accusations against the United States and calling for the "extinction of Israel as a State." In a speech of his own in San Francisco a few weeks later, Moynihan called Amin a "racist murderer," and said that it was "no accident" that Amin was then head of the Organization of African Unity (OAU). A small international uproar followed, led by indignant Africans. (Amin, who was responsible for the murders of tens of thousands of Ugandans, was then the head of the OAU only because the job rotated among member states.) The State Department distanced itself from Moynihan's remarks, and *Newsweek* quoted one UN official as saying that Moynihan's usefulness at the organization was over. Moynihan, for his part, was content to assert that "I have said what had to be said," and saw the incident as confirming his belief that the State Department could not be relied upon to stand up to a petty tyrant.[43]

Moynihan also kept up a constant defense of liberal democracy and denounced any attempts to attack it. The day after the San Francisco speech, Moynihan said in New York that the Zionism resolution was part of "a general assault by the majority of the nations in the world on the principles of liberal democracy." But he saw no reason to despair: "Out of the decline of the West there will, I sense, emerge a rise in spirits. We have shortened our lines. We are under attack. There is nothing in the least in the culture that suggests we will not in the end defend ourselves successfully."[44]

At home, Moynihan's political and personal campaigns were stunningly successful. His bandwagon began rolling in the fall of 1975, when his combative tactics got the attention of the newspapers and newsweeklies. *Newsweek*'s tone, for example, was one of cautious approval at first. An article in September described Moynihan's successes over Puerto Rico and the Seventh Special Session, but also brought up the benign neglect memo. It was his stand on the Zionism resolution, however, that completed Moynihan's rehabilitation. The resolution had been overwhelmingly unpopular in the United States, and Moynihan's strong oratory for once made him a hero. The *New York Times Magazine* published another profile in December, presenting him in an extremely flattering light. That same month the *Chicago Tribune* editorialized that Moynihan's "relentless harpooning of Third World idiocies," continued to be needed after years in which the "U.S. had always been a UN doormat, ignored or ridiculed except at bill-paying time," and had provided "a refreshing breeze that has done much to dispel the fetid stench in the UN." *National Review* declared him the "Man of the Year," and suggested that the Democrats nominate him for president. In January 1976, *Time* put Moynihan on its cover. Its story, too, recalled the Moynihan Report and benign neglect memo, but only after praising the "spirit of fight and daredeviltry that Moynihan has brought to the U.S.'s Turtle Bay headquarters." His major critics, according to *Time*, were merely "doctrinaire liberals."[45]

The media's praise reflected Moynihan's popularity with the general population. *Time* cited an opinion poll that found that 70 percent of Americans wanted him to continue speaking out, even if he sounded undiplomatic. Midge Decter recalls walking on the streets of New York with Moynihan while he was ambassador: "Wherever he went, people were saying 'You're great,' 'Right on,' 'Congratulations!' Taxis would literally stop . . . and the taxi driver would say, 'I just want to tell you you're great.' "[46]

The reasons for Moynihan's popularity—extraordinary for a UN ambassador—were several. For one, he provided the only bright spot in American diplomacy in 1975. Not only had Vietnam fallen, but by the end of the year Cuban forces, with Soviet support, were helping Communist guerrillas take over Angola. In this atmosphere of defeat, Moynihan's rhetoric provided a way to strike back and give national morale a boost. Moreover, it was hard to criticize him, for targets like Amin had no supporters in the United States who could counterattack, and Moynihan's defense of America was, if nothing else, patriotic.

Moynihan's major political problem while ambassador was his relationship with Henry Kissinger. When he took the job, Moynihan had no illusions about Kissinger's deviousness and willingness to undercut rivals. State Department Counselor Helmut Sonnenfeldt had given Moynihan a blunt warning of what to expect—"Henry does not lie because it is in his interest. He lies because it is in his nature." Moynihan hired Garment in large part as a counter to Kissinger. "No one knew Henry better than he. Knew every mood and every device, and most of the secrets. Perhaps *two* of us would be his equal." For his part, Kissinger had good reason to dislike Moynihan. In "The United States in Opposition," Moynihan had implicitly held the secretary of state responsible for the failings he listed and at the UN Moynihan's flamboyance and popularity overshadowed Kissinger, undoubtedly to Kissinger's annoyance.[47]

The result was a running battle in the press. As Eric Sevareid told Moynihan in an interview in May 1976, "My own impression was that from the moment you were on page one constantly your time there was finished, because I did not think that he [Kissinger] would be upstaged in his own theater." *Newsweek* inaccurately reported in November that Kissinger had rebuked Moynihan for his behavior at the UN, and Moynihan suspected that Kissinger was the source of the story. Also in November, the British ambassador to the UN publicly criticized Moynihan's conduct at the organization, stating that the "place . . . is not the OK Corral," and that "there is nothing whatsoever to be gained by ideological disputations of the most intense sort which one is probably going to lose anyway." Moynihan suspected that Kissinger was behind the attack, for he did not believe that the "British government for reasons of its own decided for the first time in history to publicly demolish a United States Ambassador." Moynihan decided to resign rather than be undercut, but stayed after President Ford, whose own popularity was sagging, gave him a public statement of support.[48]

Moynihan's turn in this semi-clandestine battle came in late January 1976, when he was able to make his case public by provoking a leak. He sent a cable to all American embassies claiming "considerable progress this year toward a basic foreign policy goal, that of breaking up the massive blocs of nations . . . which for so long have been arrayed against us," but castigating the State Department for being "reluctant to recognize these signs" because they had been achieved by unconventional means. The cable went on to detail several incidents which, according to Moynihan, showed "that governments are beginning to think that anti-American postures at the UN and elsewhere are not without cost and that the cost has to be calculated." He closed by repeating his claim of success and chiding Washington for its ignorance and lack of nerve:

> It appears to this mission that there is enough evidence in to make a general, interim assessment of our new posture at the United Nations. We like to think that we would be open to evidence of failure, and are aware that no one should accept our own assessment of success without some independent inquiry. But we do fear that there necessarily remains in the Department a large faction which has an interest in our performance being judged to have failed.[49]

The cable, dated January 23, was sent at a low level of classification and appeared in the *New York Times* January 28. Moynihan denied leaking it himself, and there is no evidence that he was the source, but given its subject, wide distribution, and low classification, he was probably confident that someone else would do it for him. As the *Times* dryly noted: "Two State Department officials said that the leaking of the cablegram could serve as a way of applying public pressure on Mr. Moynihan's critics, and particularly on Secretary Henry A. Kissinger to silence the critics in the State Department."[50]

Moynihan's victory was short-lived. On January 29, the *Times* reported Ford and Kissinger's statements of continued support, but went on to say: "The reaction from Mr. Kissinger and his department today ran counter to repeated private statements made in the past . . . by senior officials in the State Department . . . that Mr. Moynihan's outspoken style—what they have frequently characterized as demagoguery and a campaign for personal power—are seriously damaging United States interests in the United Nations." On January 30, James Reston wrote in the *Times* that Ford and Kissinger had supported him in public only out of political necessity. "Now Messrs. Ford and Kissinger support him in public and deplore him in private. Having put him in the job, they can neither tame nor repudiate him," claimed Reston. Moynihan saw that he had lost his support in the administration and resigned on February 2, to return to Harvard.[51]

Despite, or perhaps because of, the circumstances of his resignation, Moynihan returned to Cambridge in triumph. "The effect of the latest Moynihan flap," noted *Time*, "was . . . to strengthen once again his personal position with the public." At Harvard, he was trailed by a pack of reporters and photographers asking if he planned to run for the Senate that fall. But even without the media attention, Moynihan had good reason to be satisfied with his tenure in New York. He believed that his application of ideas to international politics had been a success, both in its effects on America's relations with the Third World and as a boost for the nation's self-confidence. This was a success which had eluded him in the Johnson and Nixon administrations. Personally, he had held his own against Kissinger, and was able to leave office as a hero rather than a pariah.[52]

Moynihan denied that he planned to run for the Senate when he left the United Nations. The previous fall, as his growing popularity triggered speculation about a run against the conservative Republican incumbent in New York, James Buckley, Moynihan had gone out of his way to deny any electoral ambitions: "I would consider it dishonorable to leave this post and run for any office," he told a national television audience. There is no evidence that Moynihan was being disingenuous, but given his success in New York, a run for office was an obvious and attractive option.[53]

Indeed, once he was back at Harvard Moynihan easily changed his mind. "There was some part of Pat that had always been drawn to electoral politics," recalled Midge Decter, and it did not take much urging to get him to run. "What he needed was not so much prodding [as] promises that he stood a chance . . . he needed promises of support from people," says Decter. Norman Podhoretz was a major voice urging Moynihan to run, and he and Decter helped arrange meetings with liberal Democrats and black leaders so that Moynihan could address their misgivings about his opinions of socialism and racial issues. It was at one of these gatherings, according to Decter, that civil rights leader Bayard Rustin told Moynihan that he had misunderstood Moynihan's intentions in the benign neglect memo and apologized for his attacks at the time. Rustin's apology showed how completely Moynihan had overcome the effects of his missteps under Johnson and Nixon. Moynihan had also seen his own electoral appeal that spring when he had campaigned for Henry Jackson, who was again running for president, and was easily elected as a Jackson delegate. With Podhoretz and Garment serving as advisers, Moynihan entered the race in New York on June 10, 1976.[54]

Moynihan's main opponent for the Democratic nomination was Representative Bella Abzug, who was from the left liberal wing of the party. The primary campaign was sometimes nasty, with Abzug trying to portray Moynihan as a product of the Nixon White House. Moynihan won a narrow victory, however, with 37 percent of the vote to Abzug's 36 percent. In the general election campaign, Moynihan and Buckley differed principally on social and domestic issues. Moynihan was the more liberal candidate, but his liberalism was clearly neoconservative. The *Chicago Tribune* noted that Moynihan's views left him "hardly a hero to many liberal Democrats. They disdain his anti-Communist foreign policies and his acerbic rejection of left-wing fashion." His basic stump speech, he recalled after the election, noted "that we faced unprecedented government problems which however had come about under the auspices of impeccably liberal governments in New York City and New York State." His remedy, too, was consistent with his social science approach and neo-

conservative attitudes: "We do not need more government in America, I said. We do need more national standards which is something
federalism can produce, and would be different from more government. We already have a huge amount of government, and the real
task is making it work." Moynihan beat Buckley by 574,000 votes,
almost 300,000 more than Jimmy Carter's plurality over Gerald Ford
in New York State, and became the first neoconservative intellectual
to be elected to public office.[55]

Moynihan arrived in the Senate as the favorite of the neoconservatives. "He was our horse," Midge Decter remembers, and was their
best hope for a future Democratic leader, now that Henry Jackson
had twice failed to win the presidential nomination. Jackson, too,
saw Moynihan as a future president, as what he had been unable to
become, according to one of Jackson's former aides, Charles Horner.
Jackson campaigned for Moynihan in the fall of 1976 and had helped
him raise money, according to Horner. Horner and Elliott Abrams,
another member of Jackson's staff, enthusiastically went to work on
Moynihan's Senate staff. As Horner put it in 1991, they "went to help
Pat" continue his ideological campaign.[56]

For his part, Moynihan sided firmly with Jackson on foreign policy
issues. His first speech in the Senate, for example, opposed President
Carter's nomination of Paul Warnke, a Washington lawyer and former assistant secretary of defense for international security affairs
during the Johnson administration, to be the chief negotiator for the
Strategic Arms Limitation Talks (SALT) with the Soviet Union. Warnke,
Moynihan declared, "was so shaken by the failure of American
strategic and military power in Vietnam that he came to feel it must
equally fail, that it must prove equally futile, in other circumstances
and other places," which was a "total misreading of the international
scene."[57]

In 1977 and 1978, Moynihan continued to speak out on the
themes he had pursued at the United Nations. He did not waver in
his conviction that democracy was under a worldwide siege, a theme
that would become prominent in neoconservative thinking during the
Carter years. By the mid-1970s, "Democratic regimes and values

were under totalitarian assault in every region of the world," he wrote in August 1977. "Israel is the democracy under attack just now," he told *Playboy* shortly after his election, "We don't know when it will be Canada, the United States or whoever. There aren't too many of us in the world and we've got to hang together." A major part of the attack, as he came to see it, was the subversion of language, as press reporting and official State Department statements made reference to "liberation forces" that were actually the "armed component of totalitarianism." Having seen his own words twisted and used against him, Moynihan wanted the truth about such groups to be stated plainly: "It is thus important that we convey the impression to the world that we understand the difference between national liberation and the progressive brutalization of politics which is being carried on by the Soviets in the name of national liberation."[58]

Another of Moynihan's major concerns was that the West's failure of nerve was leading to Soviet political dominance and military superiority. He made his views of the Soviet Union clear during the Warnke debate: "We face a determined and powerful foe who will exploit our weaknesses to advance interests adverse to ours and political beliefs we find abhorrent." Yet more than ever, he argued, the West was failing to stand up to the Soviets; the failure of nerve, he told Ben Wattenberg in April 1978, was affecting foreign policy "more so now than a few years ago when I originally sensed it." Moynihan continued to be especially irritated with those "former cold warriors . . . who . . . have decided that the country really is hopeless, that it has no capacity to resist the advance of totalitarianism, and that the best thing to do is to accommodate and to appease." He further believed that the USSR's confidence and dynamism were making it the leading force in world politics and "that dominance is clearly perceived in Western Europe, and it is beginning to be perceived here." These perceptions, according to Moynihan, were leading to such cautious actions that "this assumption about Soviet power is becoming an objective reality."[59]

Moynihan also castigated the Carter administration for what he saw as its cowardice and betrayals. In April 1978, for example, he noted that Secretary of State Cyrus Vance was leaving for Rhodesia, where black insurgents were fighting the white minority government: "He will seek to incorporate the Marxist guerrillas in the government of that new black-ruled country. . . . But why will the Secretary of State seek to bring into that government the Marxist guerrillas armed by the Soviets? The guerrillas say if we do not the Russians will send the Cubans and, of course, we will not resist it." The result, in Moynihan's view, was that "our foreign policy already portrays symptoms of a nation which knows it has been outmatched by the Soviet Union."[60]

Moynihan also spoke out strongly on human rights, an issue about which his feelings were almost proprietary. He had brought up the subject frequently at the UN, criticizing left- and right-wing dictatorships alike, and claimed credit for changing the "organizing principles that define our interests." But, Moynihan claimed, the Carter administration was fouling up its human rights campaign. The administration did not realize that human rights policy was a political weapon to be used in the battle against totalitarianism, and instead treated it as a "special kind of international social work." Quoting President Carter's statement that "Abraham Lincoln said that our nation could not exist half-slave and half-free . . . a peaceful world cannot long exist one-third rich and two-thirds hungry," Moynihan claimed that the effect of Carter's words was to "divert our attention from the central political struggle of our time—that between liberal democracy and totalitarian Communism—and focus instead on something else." Such policies, Moynihan pointed out, "will soothe the Soviet Union and only challenge Ecuador."[61]

From the time he jointed the Harriman campaign through his first two years in the Senate, Daniel Patrick Moynihan spent about two-thirds of his time in public jobs. Despite the ups and downs of his career, several consistencies stand out. First, apart from his academic and intellectual leanings, Moynihan had sharp political instincts. He had a knack for getting noticed and landing appointments. Second, he was skilled at identifying soon-to-be prominent issues and using them to advance himself. In each case—race and the black family, domestic political stability, and the external threat to democracy—he quickly identified the issue, advanced his views, and stuck with the theme for several years. Moreover, his scholarly training enabled him to put an academic gloss on his writings and speeches that set him apart from the average politician.

At the same time, however, Moynihan was usually his own worst enemy. His most spectacular failures, the Moynihan Report and the benign neglect memo, were caused by his addiction to elaborate and highly charged phrasemaking, as well as, in the latter case, a simple failure to protect his flanks in Washington politics. For all his talents, both academic and political, it took Moynihan two decades to develop into a consistently successful politician.

Moynihan's political goals were also largely unchanged. He always sought incremental improvements in the status quo and hoped to avoid any unforeseen consequences which would jeopardize past successes. He learned from the mistakes of past policies, especially those of the 1960s. This approach lay at the heart of the vital center and postwar liberalism, just as it formed the foundation of neoconservatism. Moynihan, therefore, is representative of neoconservatism's continuity with the vital center.

Moynihan also represented continuity in foreign policy thinking. The ideas he explored in India and defended at the United Nations— the superiority of liberal democracy and opposition to totalitarianism—were by no means his own creations. Moreover, his points could be abstract and easily questioned—did British socialism really explain the Third World's actions? Rightly or wrongly, however, he provided an intellectual underpinning for replies to Soviet and Third World attacks on the United States. Other liberals may have sought other ways to conduct international affairs, and some dismissed Moynihan's tactics as counterproductive grandstanding, but none had a more successful or popular strategy to offer, something which politician Moynihan had when it was needed.

Moynihan's consistency and success illustrate an important point about the vital center and neoconservatism. By 1975, alternative theories and some alterations in policy had been the rule for about eight years, yet their benefits were, at best, difficult to measure. Using ideas from the late 1940s Moynihan clarified the issues and led an unabashed crusade for liberal democracy. He was not indulging in xenophobia or cheap foreigner-bashing when he proclaimed the cause "of the liberty party." Furthermore, the popular response to his campaign easily explains why neoconservatives were so optimistic about Moynihan, seeing him as the man who could restore their style of liberalism to power. Ironically, just after their hopes climbed so high, the neoconservatives saw disaster looming.

4

Searching
for Truman,
1976–1980

The neoconservatives approached the 1976 presidential election as loyal, if wary, Democrats. On the positive side, they were able to bask in the reflected glory of Daniel Patrick Moynihan's popularity and the national attention focused on his senatorial campaign. At the same time, however, their influence in the national party remained limited. Henry Jackson, their choice for president, had been beaten by Jimmy Carter in the early primaries. Carter himself had been a relative unknown, a party outsider who captured the nomination through his own organization and loyalists—another demonstration of the changes brought about by the New Politics. When Carter won in November, he owed only limited debts to the conservative elements of the party, including the neoconservatives.

Carter had the misfortune to be president during a difficult period. At home, the United States faced serious economic problems, the most notable of which was a high rate of inflation. Abroad, Carter had several successes—including the Panama Canal treaties and the Egyptian-Israeli peace settlement—but they were overshadowed by the foreign policy disaster in Iran, the leftist revolution in Nicaragua, and the Soviet invasion of Afghanistan. These problems were not all of Carter's making, but combined with the nervous post-Vietnam atmosphere of the time and the Soviet Union's apparently increasing military strength, they left Carter open to charges of weakness and incompetence.[1]

In this context conflict between the Carter administration and the neoconservatives was virtually guaranteed to erupt. Well before the 1976 election the neoconservatives had been pushing for a strongly anti-Soviet, pro-Israel foreign policy to counter what they saw as renewed Soviet expansionism and to protect American interests in the Middle East. Moreover, they believed that the Soviets were engaged in a massive conventional and nuclear military buildup to provide the means for reducing American power, influence and, ultimately, independence. Carter, whose views on foreign affairs were often vague, hoped for a more cooperative relationship with Moscow, especially in arms control. For most of his term, Carter and his advisers (except for Zbigniew Brzezinski) did not see an expansionist threat, nor did they perceive the need for an aggressive anti-Communist policy. Realizing this in 1977, the neoconservatives turned violently against Carter and, with *Commentary* as their main platform, began an unceasing attack on him, his policies, and his advisers.

The break with Carter led to a sharp escalation of the conflicts that had been building within the Democratic party. Before 1977, neoconservatives had viewed party reformers and New Politics practitioners as a group distinct from the rest of the party, one that could be potentially isolated and driven out. The Carter administration's failure to pursue a strongly anti-Communist approach, however, forced them to reconsider their views. Led by Jeane Kirkpatrick, the neoconservatives came to the conclusion that party reformers held quasi-totalitarian views; their desire to reshape domestic politics was, according to this argument, no different from leftist revolutionaries' desires to remake mankind. Not only did this analysis explain the administration's reluctance to fight Communist totalitarianism, but it also suggested that the party might be too far gone to be saved.

Simultaneously, some neoconservatives were moving away from their traditional liberal views on social issues, inching toward a more classically liberal, laissez-faire view of society. Consequently, by 1980 the neoconservatives' commitment to the Democratic party had been greatly weakened.

Complicated arguments about totalitarianism were not the only factors driving a wedge between the neoconservatives and more liberal Democrats. Carter alienated many American Jews—and hence neoconservatives—with policies that suggested a weak commitment to Israel's security. In addition, Carter failed to support Jews against perceived anti-Semitic comments made by black leaders after he fired UN Ambassador Andrew Young in 1979. This, in turn, led many Jews to question their support for the Democrats. Finally, when it became clear that Moynihan would not challenge Carter for the nomination in 1980, as the neoconservatives had hoped, they found themselves without a credible figure within the party to turn to as a leader. All the while, the neoconservatives were gaining increasing press attention, which served to increase their own sense of importance and self-confidence. As a result, by early 1980 they no longer felt that they had to remain Democrats to survive politically.

Despite a last minute attempt by Carter to regain their support, the neoconservatives were effectively divorced from the Democratic party by February 1980. They had hoped to find a new Truman to rally around, a Democrat to promote their liberal ideas at home while fighting the cold war abroad. Not finding one, they embraced the Republican party and Ronald Reagan as the best alternative.

Jimmy Carter had virtually no exposure to foreign affairs before he became president. His education began in 1974, when Zbigniew Brzezinski started tutoring him. The two had met through the Trilateral Commission, a private group that sought to promote American, European, and Japanese political and economic cooperation. Brzezinski supplied Carter with papers, memos, and speechwriting assistance. "I was an eager student, and took full advantage of what Brzezinski had to offer," Carter later wrote. Carter acquired more foreign policy advisers as his campaign went on, including Cyrus Vance, but Brzezinski retained the greatest influence. Speaking to the Foreign Policy Association in June 1976, Carter echoed Brzezinski's technetronic and trilateral thinking when he declared that the "time has come for us to seek a partnership between North America, Western Europe and Japan. Our three regions share economic, political, and security concerns that make it logical that we should seek ever increasing unity and understanding."[2]

The speech in June was one of many examples of the vague, comfortable language that Carter used to describe his views on foreign affairs. Carter usually used simple language, trying to appeal to Americans' perceptions of themselves. "A nation's domestic and foreign policies should be derived from the same standards of ethics, honesty and morality which are characteristic of the individual citizens of the nation," he wrote in 1975. Political scientist Betty Glad has called Carter's style a form of populism in which "he traced recent problems in the United States to the government's loss of contact with the people and secrecy in decision-making." These views, concluded Glad, rested "on a simplistic moralism," and while Carter liked to back up his views on morality and politics with quotations from Reinhold Niebuhr, he admitted that he did not "deeply understand many of the philosophers" he cited.[3]

In addition to his rhetoric about morality, Carter also made the standard campaign pledges to show that he would be tough with the Soviets and would defend American allies. In March 1976, for example, he criticized Secretary of State Henry Kissinger for "giving up too much and asking for too little" in talks with Moscow and in June he urged "an unequivocal, constant commitment to . . . guarantee the right of Israel to exist in peace as a Jewish state."[4]

Fortunately for Carter, the 1976 presidential election did not turn on foreign issues. The campaign frequently was sidetracked by a number of other matters, such as Carter's religion, and media attention given to fumbles by Carter and President Ford that affected their images but had little to do with substance. Consequently, Carter did not have to provide detailed explanations of his foreign policy views.

By keeping his policy statements vague while emphasizing simple and uncontroversial ideas, Carter left it to his listeners to interpret his statements as they wished. As a result, the pundits tended to focus on what they wanted to hear and wrote accordingly.

The results were sometimes startling. On July 7, 1976, for example, Leslie Gelb wrote in the *New York Times* that Carter's foreign policy views placed him "in the liberal wing of the Democratic party." Carter, according to Gelb, had embraced liberal views and world order theories in 1972, when "he came to believe that the liberal wing of the party was dominant and would continue to be so." Henry Jackson would consider Carter's deemphasis of balance-of-power politics as "naive and unworkable." Just ten days later, however, journalist Tad Szulc wrote in the *New Republic* that Carter "will be a much tougher bargainer over such issues as SALT than a euphoric Nixon was in 1972. Scoop Jackson, who probably knows more about strategic weapons than anyone on the Hill, will be in Carter's corner when it comes to negotiating, ratifying, and enforcing SALT II."[5]

Because Carter's views were incomplete and inconsistent, many of the administration's views were articulated by high ranking foreign policy appointees. The views of some of these individuals were not always accurate reflections of Carter's beliefs. Nonetheless, statements from figures such as Vance, Carter's choice for secretary of state, Vance's adviser Marshall Shulman, arms control negotiator Paul Warnke, and UN Ambassador Andrew Young provide insights into the major currents of thought in the Carter administration. These views were often skeptical of traditional cold war assumptions.

Vance represented the moderate voice in the new administration. As a lawyer and longtime Washington insider, Vance's tendency was toward mediation and trying to solve common problems, not confrontation. He was by no means "soft" on the Soviet Union; his October 1976 memo to Carter outlining themes for a new administration's foreign policy noted that "in its dealings with the Soviet Union, the United States will keep itself strong, and will stand resolutely firm to protect key United States interests." Like Carter, Vance put a high priority on strategic arms negotiations with the Soviets, but he also wanted to give attention to other problems. At his confirmation hearings in January 1977, Vance told the senators, "I do not think that the preoccupation with these vitally important [Soviet] issues should so dominate our foreign policy that we neglect other critical issues which are growing increasingly important." These issues included the "control of nuclear arms and nuclear proliferation, economic development and the dignity of the developing world, energy, food, population, and conventional arms transfers." Others held these views as well. Leslie Gelb, the *New York Times* reporter who was appointed director of the State Department's Bureau of Politico-Military Affairs under Vance, had written shortly before the election that under Kissinger, "nuclear proliferation, North-South economic relations, Africa as a whole and relations with traditional allies were often ignored until they developed a 'Soviet dimension,' whether imagined or real."[6]

Marshall Shulman was another major administration figure who believed that Communist expansion and Third World revolutions no longer posed major threats to American security. In his case, this represented an acceptance of liberal world order theory. Shulman, then the director of Columbia University's Russian Institute and an adviser to Vance, explored the nature of Soviet-American competition in the context of world order theory in his January 1977 article, "On Learning to Live With Authoritarian Regimes." As part of the "effort to enlarge the international sense of community," he advocated taking a long-term approach of trying "to draw the Soviet Union, China, and other authoritarian regimes into constructive participation in that system, as they come to appreciate their self-interest in doing so." Already, Shulman noted, "a process of adjustment has begun on both sides to facilitate the meshing of . . . dissimilar institutions." Nowhere in the article did Shulman say that the USSR threatened American security. In fact, he believed that "the perceived necessity of competing with the methods of totalitarian states" was leading to the "degradation of democratic norms," and the failure to protect American values—two indications of the need for "a broader and more enlightened understanding of our real security interests."[7]

Paul Warnke, whose nomination as SALT negotiator was strongly opposed by Henry Jackson and Moynihan, took a revisionist stand when he dismissed the idea of a threat from Third World nationalism. "Our own internal situation is not so parlous or our world position so precarious that we are threatened when an alien people opts for a form of governmental organization that we find distasteful," he had written in early 1975. Warnke went even further, rejecting the maintenance of a military capability for intervention in the Third World. "The injection of American firepower into a local conflict is rarely compatible with our foreign policy interests," he argued. "For the most part, investment in such forces will buy us nothing but trouble." On the surface Warnke's summary statement—"we need not and cannot be the world's policeman,"—indicated that his views were compatible with Nixon and Kissinger's pullback from large-scale interventions in the early 1970s. Nixon and Kissinger, however, had sought to dampen regional instability and to safeguard American interests by working with local allies, such as the Shah of Iran or anti-Communist forces in Angola. Warnke, in contrast, feared earning the "lasting hostility of those whom we oppose," and praised the "commendable option of doing nothing at all" to oppose change in the Third World.[8]

Andrew Young was the furthest to the left of Carter's major foreign policy appointees. Young—a preacher, civil rights activist, and Georgia congressman—was another observer who viewed Carter as a representative of his own views. During the 1976 primaries Young saw Carter as the best candidate for avoiding the "resurgence of cold-war foreign policy" and the "very negative national mood in both domestic and foreign policy" which Young believed would have followed a Jackson victory. Young, far more than Warnke or Shulman, was prepared to embrace revolutionary regimes. "There's nothing wrong with their deciding to live under a socialist system," he said of Angola in 1977. Instead, said Young, "what I resent is our reacting emotionally to the presence of Communists." In Angola, moreover, Young believed that Cuba's intervention had been beneficial: "When the Cubans arrived, they filled a gap. They provided order where there was essentially an undisciplined guerrilla army that wasn't ready to govern. So I'm not trying to defend the Cuban presence, I'm just trying to get people to be rational about it." Finally, Young's declaration that morality consisted of "thinking through the alternatives and making a decision that is best for the largest number of people," rather than making attitudes toward Communism or the protection of American interests the litmus test, placed him firmly in the revisionist camp with Richard J. Barnet and William Appleman Williams.[9]

Despite the later accusations of the Republicans, dissident Democrats, and the neoconservatives, Jimmy Carter had several important foreign policy successes. The Panama Canal treaties, the Camp David accords, and the Israeli-Egyptian peace treaty were major achievements for American diplomacy. Moreover, Carter moved ahead with the deployment of a new generation of nuclear weapons in Western Europe. But on the all-important issues of standing up to the Soviets and Third World radicals, none of Carter's actions would ever satisfy the neoconservatives. Except for Brzezinski, the foreign policy makers of the new administration tended toward a more relaxed view of Soviet relations, minimizing what Carter himself labeled the "inordinate fear of Communism," and seeking what Raymond Garthoff has called "possibilities for the cooperative path." Unfortunately for Carter, however, the neoconservatives saw their fear of Communism as anything but inordinate and would not be satisfied with anything but a strongly anti-Soviet stand. Furthermore, the presence of such men as Young and Warnke would later be seen by the neoconservatives as proof that the left had taken over the administration and the Democratic party. Unlike 1972, the neoconservatives could not accuse the left of leading the party to defeat. Instead, they could charge it with something far more serious—leading the country to disaster.[10]

As the neoconservatives surveyed the political landscape in 1975 and 1976, they saw a growing crisis abroad. Unlike those Democrats who looked forward to the birth of a new world order and a consequent reordering of foreign policy priorities, they were more alarmed than ever about what they saw as the growing Soviet menace and America's weak response. The United States was, in their view, in full retreat abroad, lacking the will to defend even the most basic of its interests. "We have not for some time now been behaving like the most powerful country on earth, defeated [in Vietnam] or not," wrote Midge Decter as she deplored Washington's capitulation to the oil states and its eagerness to make deals with the Soviet Union. Others saw the retreat as institutionalized in Henry Kissinger's policies. "Appeasement [of the USSR] was built into détente," concluded Theodore Draper, although it was doomed to failure, if only because "appeasement cannot appease the unappeasable."[11]

Although détente had been a Republican policy, the neoconservatives abhorred the liberals' alternatives. Liberals, according to Norman Podhoretz, had been so traumatized by Vietnam that they had turned into isolationists, unwilling to defend the United States from the Soviet Union. "The new isolationism is for the moment most visible among liberals," he wrote in April 1976. Furthermore, in their attacks against presidential power, liberal isolationists had "first damaged the main institutional capability the United States possesses for conducting an overt fight against the spread of Communist power . . . then in their campaign against the CIA they helped reduce the main American institutional capability for conducting a covert fight."[12]

Isolationism was not the only charge levelled against liberals. Podhoretz condemned what he saw as the world order theorists' idea of "the declining capacity of the great powers to impose their will on other countries," and the view that "nobody was in charge" of the world. Walter Laqueur had anticipated this point when he refuted "Stanley Hoffmann's argument that the two superpowers are coming to control less and less of world politics." This view, according to Laqueur, "merely amounted to a rationalization of American weakness."[13]

The neoconservatives saw an additional threat from the liberal views of the mid-1970s. This was the possibility that liberals would cross the line separating passivity from outright betrayal. According to sociologist Peter Berger, for example, "a new intellectual-industrial complex" was forming, as intellectuals who admired Cuba and North Korea and who wanted to reduce American power combined with businessmen who saw such a rollback as a smart economic move. "The maintenance of American power in the world, previously perceived as an economic asset, is now coming to be seen as an economic liability," he wrote. In political terms, noted Berger, such a combination of self-righteousness and economics would create a powerful force, with "ominous results for the future of freedom." Also on the left, wrote Laqueur shortly after President Carter took office, intellectuals disillusioned with the Soviet Union as well as the United States were looking to Albania, Cuba, North Korea, and the largely repressive Third World for alternative political systems to provide "fresh hope for mankind."[14]

In contrast to America's confusion, the neoconservatives saw the Soviets as implacably determined. They held to the fundamental perception of Communism that had guided them for almost 30 years, and which Nathan Glazer summarized in mid-1976: "There is a major threat to democratic institutions and to the independence of nations coming . . . from Soviet Russia and communist China and the world movement over whose leadership they compete." Moreover, according to Glazer, the Communists would not be content with the status quo, for "Communism, while rarely adventurist, *is* expansionist." Nor could American policy escape from this reality. As Robert W. Tucker wrote in early 1977: "We have no alternative but to conclude that our relationship with the Soviet Union constitutes today, as it has since the close of World War II, the central problem for American foreign policy."[15]

The neoconservatives saw Communist expansion in the 1970s as not just a potential problem, but as an awful reality. Central to their concerns was the conviction that Soviet military power was steadily increasing, and that Moscow would use its new strength to make further conquests. Tucker referred to the "impressive and persistent growth of Soviet military power," and neither he nor any other neoconservative analyst showed any sympathy for attempts to play down the growth of Soviet military power. In the words of Edward Luttwak, a political scientist who wrote on strategic issues, "While the loudest American voices ceaselessly argue that mere numbers are meaningless, if not that military power is itself passé, the Russians are building missiles, bombers, and warships to acquire a worldwide strategic reach." Luttwak, too, reached the conclusion that it was "hard to deny that this growing strength signifies an expansionist intent."[16]

The neoconservatives pointed to Africa as the first example of how the Soviets would use their new power. As Angola prepared for independence from Portugal in 1975, the Soviets began shipping large quantities of arms, followed by advisers and Cuban combat troops, to the Communist side in Angola's developing civil war. By late 1976, the Communists appeared to have won, leading Bayard Rustin and Social Democratic activist Carl Gershman to comment, "The victory of the pro-Soviet forces in Angola not only increased Africa's vulnerability to a fate considerably worse than colonialism, but, to a degree not yet fully appreciated, it also weakened the security of the West." Rustin and Gershman placed much of the blame on liberals, who had resisted sending aid to the non-Communist faction out of fear of being drawn into another Vietnam. According to Rustin and Gershman's argument, this view was part of "a tissue of misconceptions and wishful thinking" which sought to prove that, because Angola was so far away, Soviet intervention did not threaten American interests. But Angola was not so remote; Rustin and Gershman noted its proximity to vital shipping lanes and sources of raw materials. The Angolan move, they believed, was part of Moscow's overall strategy of "subjecting the industrialized West and Japan to the hegemony of Soviet power."[17]

Another important theme in neoconservative writings in 1975 and 1976 was the belief that the United States could not survive as the sole democracy in the world once its allies and supporters had been taken over or neutralized by pro-Soviet forces. "Can freedom and traditional American values survive once the lights go out in the rest of the world?" asked Walter Laqueur in August 1975. They could not, answered Norman Podhoretz, for such a world would be "given over to barbarism and misery," and the United States could not survive in such an environment. For Nathan Glazer, the issue was straightforward. "For us the world is a safer and more congenial place with such [democratic] societies in it and would be a more dangerous and depressing place without them," he wrote. Thus, the United States, in Glazer's view, was obligated "to support the shrinking island of democracies in the world."[18]

The neoconservatives' growing pessimism was emphasized by their choice of metaphors for describing the world situation. Their articles frequently evoked the memory of French and British behavior in the 1930s, with the refusal to face up to the growing totalitarian threat, the reluctance to shore up the democracies' defenses, failed attempts at appeasement and, worst of all, the slide into a disastrous war. Norman Podhoretz was "struck very forcibly by certain resemblances between the United States today and Great Britain in the years after the first world war." One major similarity that Podhoretz noticed was "hostility to one's own country and . . . derision of the idea that it stands for anything worth defending." The neoconservatives called for strengthening the American military before it was too late, and, in a strange mixture of self-importance and self-pity, they compared the reception of their warnings with that given to Winston Churchill's. "There was not a day when Churchill was not accused of being a warmonger, a reckless man," wrote Laqueur, and Podhoretz noted that those sounding the alarm in the 1970s "are rewarded for their pains with accusations of hysteria, paranoia, servility toward the Pentagon, and worse."[19]

The memory of the 1930s was especially disturbing for the neoconservatives because so many of them were Jewish. For them the memory of the 1930s and World War II included the destruction of European Jewry; they feared, as a result of renewed Western weakness in the 1970s, the destruction of Israel and a repetition of the Holocaust. Podhoretz worried that the United States would try to appease the Arabs and the Third World by forcing Israel to trade land for empty promises of peace. "The United States has undertaken to do for the Arabs what the Arabs have been unable to do for themselves: force Israel to surrender the territories," he wrote. If Washington's cynicism facilitated such an outcome, he believed, it would be another Munich and the results would be just as terrible as they had been in 1938. In Podhoretz's view, the modern totalitarians would know that the answer to the question "If the United States will not defend a democratic country like Israel, whom will we defend?" was no one.[20]

At the same time that they warned of a return of the 1930s, however, the neoconservatives continued to refight the domestic political battles of the late 1940s. As with their comparisons of themselves with Churchill, this strategy allowed them to identify with past triumphs while lamenting that they were being ignored. The neoconservatives' denunciations of liberal blindness and unwillingness to fight for democracy, for example, were reminiscent of Schlesinger's charge that the progressive left was abandoning its responsibilities and "delivering free society to its totalitarian foe." But the neoconservatives were certain, as Schlesinger had been, that true liberals could still be rallied. As Peter Berger put it: "There continues to be a large segment of the American people that is highly susceptible to the old Wilsonian appeals to liberty and democracy. The popular response to Daniel P. Moynihan's speeches at the United Nations may be cited as evidence."[21]

Many of the neoconservatives in 1975 and 1976 looked to the past for inspiration. They recalled the triumphant vital center of 1948 and 1949 which, they noted, had created a successful foreign policy—what Podhoretz called "a bipartisan consensus in support of anti-Communist intervention"—and that still served as their guide to the world. But in the present the neoconservatives lacked a leader to rally behind, a new Churchill or Truman to give them hope. Indeed, as it quickly became clear to them that Jimmy Carter did not share their views, their frustration led them to undertake a savage and relentless campaign against him.[22]

The neoconservatives' criticisms of Carter began with his high level appointees. The new administration gave no major foreign policy appointments to the neoconservatives or members of the Coalition for a Democratic Majority. (One of the few neoconservative appointees was the chief negotiator for Micronesia's independence talks, leading to a bitter joke within the coalition that "they wouldn't give us Macronesia or Polynesia, only Micronesia.") The new administration turned instead to what Charles Horner later characterized as "the left-wing senators' staffers," including Anthony Lake (one of Henry Kissinger's aides who had quit to protest the 1970 invasion of Cambodia) and Robert Hunter (an aide to Massachusetts Senator Edward M. Kennedy).[23]

Seeing their enemies in charge, the neoconservatives began using their rhetorical talents to attack the new policymakers and their allies. As with any good propaganda, the criticisms were broad, with few names mentioned. Instead, the neoconservatives simplified the issues ("The basic issues are by no means difficult to grasp," claimed Walter Laqueur in 1980), and used labels and codewords in their blanket condemnations. Bayard Rustin and Carl Gershman, for example, wrote of the misperceptions of "American liberals," and political scientist Chalmers Johnson charged that "the list of political appointees to the Departments of State and Defense" showed that Carter had "turned over foreign policy to the 'New Politics' wing of the Democratic party," without naming any of the appointees of whom he spoke. In July 1980, Gershman provided one of the few instances of a neoconservative critic actually listing those in "the foreign policy establishment of Jimmy Carter." Vance, Marshall Shulman, Paul Warnke, Leslie Gelb, Anthony Lake, and Robert Hunter were among those he tallied.[24]

Andrew Young was one of the individuals most frequently attacked by name. Young's conciliatory posture toward the Third World and his comments about the Cuban troops in Angola made a neoconservative response virtually certain. Gershman became Young's most virulent critic: "It is Young's apparent lack of commitment to political freedom, and his ability to turn a blind eye to oppression if it is carried out by African and other Third World regimes in the name of a progressive ideology, that is the most troubling aspect of his thought and of his performance at the United Nations." Young was, concluded Gershman, "an advocate of U.S. acquiescence in a new system of tyranny."[25]

With the personnel issue as a point of departure, the neoconservatives launched a broad assault on the Carter administration's policies. In their attacks, the neoconservatives showed no mercy and took no prisoners; the administration was vigorously condemned on virtually every issue. Carter's policies, wrote Walter Laqueur, lacked "any clear concept . . . one faces vague trends and contradictory statements at frequent intervals." The result, according to Laqueur, was "growing complaints, most of them justified, about quick diplomatic successes that turn out to be spurious, about policies that show more consideration for America's enemies than for its allies, about a retreat from the high idealism of the early days to an aimless and inconsistent pragmatism." Robert W. Tucker built on this theme when he wrote in early 1980 that the administration continued to display "uncertainty in policy," largely because "the vision entertained of the world by the Carter Administration has not afforded much guidance for effectively coping with the problems it has had to confront." The result was "a pathology," manifested in "the refusal to confront reality (hence also . . . attempts, often ingenuous, to create a reality that responds to desire), in the voluntary concession of power and in the persuasion that all the while role and interests are being preserved."[26]

The neoconservative case against Carter did not rely solely on conceptual arguments. Specific criticisms abounded, including Gershman on Young, Moynihan on human rights policy, and Podhoretz on the failure to counter the Soviet menace. Many of these issues were best articulated in the long neoconservative campaign against the second strategic nuclear arms treaty with the Soviet Union, SALT II.

The neoconservatives came to oppose SALT II as a result of the so-called Team B report. In 1976, seeking an alternative analysis of Soviet strategic nuclear capabilities and intentions, Director of Central Intelligence George Bush commissioned a group of outside experts—called Team B, in contrast to the CIA's analysts, known as Team A—to review the available intelligence data and present their own conclusions. Team B included, among others, Paul Nitze and Richard Pipes, a Jackson Democrat. As Pipes later recalled, Team B

> concluded that the evidence indicated beyond rea-
> sonable doubt that the Soviet leadership did not
> subscribe to MAD [mutually assured destruction,
> the hostage theory that lay at the heart of the
> American view of nuclear deterrence] but
> regarded nuclear weapons as tools of war whose
> proper employment, in offensive as well as defen-
> sive modes, promised victory.[27]

Disturbed by Team B's findings, which confirmed his own long-standing doubts about the SALT process, Nitze started a new organization, the Committee on the Present Danger. Nitze later wrote that he wanted the committee to "help restore informed and objective discussion of national security issues." In its founding statement the committee declared its political independence and nonpartisan character, promising instead to "help promote a better understanding of the main problems confronting our foreign policy, based on a disciplined effort to gather the facts and a sustained discussion of their significance for our national security and survival."

There was, however, little doubt about the assumptions underlying the committee's research. "The Soviet Union has been enlarging and improving both its strategic and its conventional military forces far more rapidly than the United States and its allies," said the statement, and "Soviet expansionism threatens to destroy the world balance of forces on which the survival of freedom depends." Although the committee was not a strictly neoconservative organization (according to Nitze, 40 percent of its members were Republicans) its ranks contained prominent neoconservatives, including Podhoretz, Decter, Kirkpatrick, Rustin, Max Kampelman, and Seymour Martin Lipset.[28]

The committee soon began spreading its message with a steady stream of reports and statements. The Committee's shorter pieces appeared in such varied fora as the *New York Times*'s op-ed page and *U.S. News & World Report*. The message varied little. "Superiority in both strategic and conventional weapons could enable the Soviet Union to apply decisive pressure on the United States in conflict situations," argued one statement in April 1977. Nitze himself wrote in May 1978 that the Soviets believed "that preponderance at the strategic nuclear level can be exploited at lower levels in many forms of political pressure and violence." Another analysis warned:

> Soviet literature—not propaganda written for the
> West but Russians talking to Russians—tells us
> that the Soviets do *not* agree with the Americans
> that nuclear war is unthinkable and unwinnable
> . . . it tells us that they look at the world quite dif-
> ferently. . . . They believe the best deterrent is the
> capability to win and survive were deterrence to
> fail.

As the final shape of the SALT II treaty became apparent in 1979, it provided the committee with an identifiable target for its attacks. The treaty did not require cuts in strategic arsenals, specifically cuts which would have reduced what the committee saw as a dangerous Soviet advantage in missile throw weight. Therefore, warned Nitze, SALT II's terms "could result in forced accommodation to the Soviet Union leading to a situation of global retreat and Finlandization."[29]

Not surprisingly, the committee's arguments found a home in *Commentary*. The relationship was symbiotic. Podhoretz, Gershman, and most other neoconservatives were not familiar with much of the arcana of nuclear strategy and its associated technical issues. By opening the pages of *Commentary* to the committee they were able to take part in the campaign against SALT II without having to immerse themselves in the technical details of the issues. The committee, for its part, gained another platform for its arguments. Thus, in February 1979, Eugene Rostow (a committee member) presented the committee's familiar contention that "the Soviets are not interested in mutual deterrence and nuclear stalemate. To the Soviets, clear nuclear superiority is the ultimate weapon of coercive diplomacy." Six months later, Edward Luttwak argued that the treaty placed "no real control on the most important threat," and, in fact, was "a tool of [Soviet] policy."[30]

As their criticisms of the Carter administration imply, the neoconservatives advocated an alternative policy of strict, rigorous containment. They never wavered in their view that the Soviet Union's ultimate goal was the elimination of American power. Ben Wattenberg called this "old ideas in a new era" and argued, "there *are* Communists and their footprints are still menacing." As for the Soviets, Nitze insisted, "They believe the United States must of necessity oppose their basic aims. Therefore, the power and influence of the United States must be diminished by whatever prudent means come to hand." If the threat was unchanged after more than thirty years, so was the response. Richard Pipes stated the case for containment in terms very similar to those Kennan had used in his "X" article: "The ultimate purpose of Western counterstrategy should be to compel the Soviet Union to turn inward—from conquest to reform. Only by blunting its external drive can the Soviet regime be made to confront its citizenry and to give it an account of its policies."[31]

Walter Laqueur filled in the details, which served to adapt 1940s containment policies to the realities of 1980. He advocated moderating Soviet behavior by confronting Moscow "with equal strength and equal determination"; reforming NATO so that the Europeans would have more responsibilities within the alliance, thus forcing America's supporters "to stand up and be counted"; and the restoration of American military power and the will to use it to show the Third World that the United States was "an ally that can be relied upon, a power than cannot be abused with impunity." In this the neoconservatives were stretching containment to its limits, implying— but not explicitly arguing—that further Soviet attempts at expansion should be met with force and, possibly, an attempt to roll back previous Communist gains.[32]

In renewing the call for containment in the late 1970s, however, the neoconservatives had to face its less attractive side: Washington's record of alliances with Third World dictators. Wattenberg had acknowledged this regrettable necessity when he wrote that containment had meant "supporting other nations that were allied with us in resisting Soviet advances—even if those nations were not themselves democratic . . . using covert, undemocratic means to support undemocratic governments threatened by internal forces." For Laqueur the key political issue was how to build broad support for renewed containment. As he noted, "according to current mythology, the troubles of the U.S. in the Third World are rooted in its past association with and reliance on corrupt authoritarian regimes." This argument would have to be countered, and with an argument stronger than a simple appeal to memories of past glories.[33]

Even before Carter was elected, the neoconservatives had begun to discuss the practical differences between totalitarianism and authoritarianism, a distinction they borrowed from Hannah Arendt. In July 1976, Nathan Glazer declared that "there is something truly special about Communist governments which separates them from run-of-the-mill authoritarian regimes and military dictatorships." Glazer cited the thoroughness and permanence of Communist control over society as two things that made Communism unique. While Glazer conceded that it was at least theoretically possible for a Communist regime to evolve into a less rigid state, as Yugoslavia had, he was pessimistic about the likelihood. "Yugoslavia is indeed a maverick and . . . we should also remember that not a single other Communist state has followed its example," he concluded.[34]

Among political scientists, however, concern had begun to arise that the differences between authoritarianism and totalitarianism were being blurred by sloppy usage. "The word 'totalitarianism' has come to serve mainly as a stick with which to beat the Soviet Union," wrote British critic Maurice Cranston. Raymond Aron, the French political philosopher who was admired by many neoconservatives, worried that the Soviet Union was being portrayed as an ordinary country, "comparable with others in history; despotic, true . . . but despotic in the tradition of the ancient Asiatic (if not European) despotisms." What gave these concerns immediacy for the neoconservatives was Shulman's article, "On Learning to Live With Authoritarian Regimes," which had discussed the USSR under the category of authoritarian. In response, Walter Laqueur wrote: "It is hard to believe that this blurring of the enormous difference between authoritarian and totalitarian regimes was an accident, or that it was unconnected with the general drift of the Carter administration's position in world affairs."[35]

The neoconservatives quickly incorporated this view into their general attack on Carter. In fact, it became one of their most prominent themes. Carl Gershman, who noted in May 1978 that "the distinction between a society that is authoritarian or 'partly free' . . . and one that is totalitarian is not academic," used the idea to attack Andrew Young:

> Young's failure to distinguish sufficiently between
> democracy and totalitarianism also accounts for
> his inability to see any distinction between author-
> itarian and totalitarian societies. . . . He did not
> seem to understand that the right-wing regimes in
> these countries [Portugal, Greece, and Spain]
> could be replaced as quickly and as smoothly as
> they were precisely because they were *not* totali-
> tarian in the sense of controlling every aspect of
> human existence.

Peter Berger attacked Carter's human rights policy, whose "mechanical criteria fail to discriminate" between the occasional human rights violations of authoritarians and the "systemic assault" of totalitarianism. "Morally speaking," Berger wrote, "authoritarian regimes should be given a benefit of doubt that must be denied to totalitarianism."[36]

The neoconservative most often associated with the arguments over authoritarianism and totalitarianism was Jeane Kirkpatrick. Although originally from Oklahoma and not Jewish, Kirkpatrick was in other ways representative of neoconservatism: she came from a staunchly Democratic family, was an intellectual, and was a close friend and supporter of Hubert Humphrey. According to Allan Gerson, Kirkpatrick's counsel when she was Ronald Reagan's ambassador to the United Nations, she was first exposed to the authoritarian versus totalitarian issue as a graduate student at Columbia University: "She came into contact with such works as Hannah Arendt's recently published *The Origins of Totalitarianism*. She studied with . . . political refugees from war-torn Europe. . . . It was, as she put it, "all fresh." It would have been hard to have grown up in that climate and not developed an acute political consciousness."[37]

The idea that authoritarianism and totalitarianism were distinct from one another stayed with Kirkpatrick. In 1963 she wrote in the introduction to her anthology on Communist political tactics, that "the notion persists that Communists are somehow morally superior to other elites which use amoral means to gain power and impose repressive, minority dictatorships"—in other words, traditional authoritarian states. In her next book, on Argentine politics, Kirkpatrick was careful to point out that Peronist Argentina had not been a totalitarian state:

> There has been continuing discussion of whether Peron's Argentina was or attempted to be totalitarian. It seems to me clear that it lacked most of the distinguishing characteristics of totalitarian systems. . . . There was no official ideology. . . . There was no effort to establish total control of the political process. . . . There was no single mass party . . . with a monopoly of political functions. . . . There was not ubiquitous terror.

Finally, in the 1978 essay Kirkpatrick took pains to point out that totalitarianism was by no means synonymous with all forms of nondemocratic systems and that "such usage neither conforms to definitions of political scientists . . . nor permits distinctions to be made among types of nondemocratic governments."[38]

During the 1970s, however, Kirkpatrick stayed away from the question of authoritarianism and instead focused her research on domestic political issues, especially those involving the evolution of the democratic political system. Kirkpatrick's analyses, however, continued to be shaped by what she had learned about totalitarianism and modern dictators' attempts to change political systems by force. Her writings from this period show a growing distrust of attempts to manipulate political development through reform instead of allowing systems to evolve slowly on their own. At the conclusion of her 1974 study of women in state legislatures, for example, Kirkpatrick discussed various measures that could be taken to increase the political power of women. She rejected rigid prescriptions for increasing the number of female office holders, like quotas, in favor of the "continuation of existing trends toward gradual inclusion of women in power processes," although she conceded that true equality "in the near future [was] very unlikely."[39]

In addition, Kirkpatrick studied the effects of party and political reforms. In a 1978 essay, *Dismantling the Parties*, she gave a vivid example of the unintended effects of reform on American political parties, and particularly on the Democrats. Reforms intended to democratize the parties, she wrote, had actually handed intraparty power over to "public relations firms, professional campaign consultants, and candidate organizations." This, in turn, made it possible for an outsider like McGovern or Carter, "without standing as a national party leader [to] move through the nominating process to victory." Consequently, according to Kirkpatrick, neither party controlled its nominating process any longer and both were, in fact, in the hands of freelancing political professionals who served only the candidates who hired them, and were "fundamentally independent of party." The weakening of the parties to the point where they served only as easily manipulated organizing tools, Kirkpatrick argued, ran counter to the original goal of democratizing the parties and, furthermore, was bad because it had been "damaging to [the] institutions" of democracy. Moreover, she believed, it had provided an excellent illustration of the high hopes and poor thinking inherent in reform: "In party reform as in life, good intentions are never enough, and wishing does not make it so."[40]

During 1979, Kirkpatrick refined her views about the problems of reformism. Drawing on Schumpeter, she argued that the independent political professionals were, in her view, part of the "new class" of "intellectuals and semiintellectuals," who "shape debate, determine agendas, define standards, and propose and evaluate policies." In government, she noted, they were not elected officials who were accountable for their acts but, rather, were at the "second-level stratum surrounding, sustaining, and conditioning the highest officeholders." In politics, argued Kirkpatrick, the members of the new class sought power by promoting ideological, program-based approaches to issues, rather than by submitting to the will of the populace: "The desire that parties, candidates, and governments stand for programs not only reflects the intellectual's fascination with policy, but also manifests a broader belief that social institutions can and should conform to serve abstract principles."[41]

For Kirkpatrick, this analysis proved that new class activists posed a danger to liberal democracy. "Excessive faith in reason, equality, democracy, social engineering, [and] moral idealism produce their opposites: irrationalism, tyranny, force and immorality," she concluded in a 1978 article criticizing utopian approaches to politics. She believed that this outlook would lead the new class to take reformism to its logical conclusions—an attempt to reorder the world according to their views: "The political temptation of the new class lies in believing that their intelligence and exemplary motives equip them to reorder the institutions, the lives, and even the characters of almost everyone—this is the totalitarian temptation." The linkage of zealous reformism with totalitarianism, in turn, led Kirkpatrick to a conservative conclusion. Because "high levels of individual freedom and a significant degree of social and political equality already exist in this society," she argued, "liberals as well as conservatives [have] a vested interest in the status quo."[42]

It was in this context that Kirkpatrick wrote her most celebrated article, "Dictatorships and Double Standards." The article is most frequently remembered for its blistering criticism of Carter's foreign policy and its defense of American support for authoritarian governments facing revolutionary insurgencies. In fact Kirkpatrick's main theme was a reiteration of her view that democracy is the result of a process of political evolution. "Democratic governments," she wrote, "have come into being slowly, after extended prior experience with more limited forms of participation." Furthermore, she argued, attempts to put democracy into place overnight would, like many other reforms, soon backfire: "Hurried efforts to force complex and unfamiliar political practices on societies lacking the requisite political culture . . . not only fail to produce desired outcomes; if they are undertaken at a time when the traditional regime is under attack, they actually facilitate the job of the insurgents."[43]

Kirkpatrick wove together her convictions about the new class, reform, authoritarianism, and totalitarianism to arrive at her criticism of Carter's foreign policy. She believed that the administration held the erroneous belief that eliminating authoritarian regimes was desirable and that replacing them with democratic governments was easy. She accused the administration of believing, like party reformers at home, "that one can easily locate and impose democratic alternatives to incumbent autocracies." She continued, "it is this belief which induces the Carter administration to participate actively in the toppling of non-Communist autocracies while remaining passive in the face of Communist expansion." Carter himself, she believed, was "the kind of liberal most likely to confound revolution with idealism, change with progress, optimism with virtue." Thus, when Nicaragua's Anastasio Somoza and the Shah of Iran ("neither [of whom] sought to reform his society in the light of any abstract idea of social justice or political virtue," in Kirkpatrick's words) faced revolutionary attacks, American support turned into hostility and their regimes were actively undermined by Washington. In her view, the administration had forgotten that leftist revolutionaries—"armed intellectuals citing Marx"—were trying to establish totalitarian tyrannies. Moreover, charged Kirkpatrick, the administration was influenced by a deterministic outlook that saw revolutions as "manifestations of deep historical forces which cannot be controlled," and leading to the acceptance of leftist revolutions as something which "cannot be stopped or altered."[44]

Given these conditions, Kirkpatrick believed that the best chance for democratic change in authoritarian states facing armed challenges lay in active American support for their governments. Picking up on the neoconservative theme that totalitarian regimes could not evolve toward democracy, she argued that there was "a far greater likelihood of progressive liberalization and democratization" in Argentina, South Korea, and Taiwan than in China or North Korea. Building on what she saw as the lessons of reform and attempts at constitutional planning, Kirkpatrick suggested that the role of the United States should be to "encourage . . . liberalization and democratization, provided that the effort is not made at a time when the incumbent government is fighting for its life against violent adversaries, and that proposed reforms are aimed at producing gradual change rather than perfect democracy overnight."[45]

"Dictatorships and Double Standards" was a milestone in neoconservative thinking. First, it provided a coherent argument demonstrating that party reform, the New Politics, and liberal attitudes toward totalitarianism were not only linked but were also part of the left's assault on democracy. In effect, it turned the neoconservatives' gut feelings into theory. Second, it revealed how conservative the neoconservatives' views of foreign policy had become. Schlesinger had written that liberalism and democracy were "the instrument of change" in the world, and that "a little American efficiency, accompanied by a policy of support for native progressive movements, would go far to counter the appeal of the Russian revolutionary spirit in the underdeveloped areas." Although many neoconservatives still claimed to hold their original liberal anti-Communist views, they had become openly distrustful of any attempts to improve the world. Instead, they were happy to settle for just preserving it.[46]

Kirkpatrick was not the only neoconservative who was edging toward recognizably conservative views. Historian James A. Nuechterlein had noticed this trend in 1977, when he wrote that some neoconservatives "have moved to political positions difficult to distinguish from any other American conservatism." Some were exploring other implications of Kirkpatrick's developing emphasis on letting democracy evolve rather than be planned—a hands-off approach closer to that of Friedrich Hayek and Milton Friedman than to the Americans for Democratic Action of the 1940s and 1950s. Furthermore, in April 1978, *Commentary* asked if it was true that there was "an inescapable connection between capitalism and democracy," a view it acknowledged as once considered by many intellectuals to be "politically dangerous." Not many neoconservatives answered affirmatively (William Barrett and Peter Berger were two who did) and Gershman, Glazer, and Penn Kemble defended the Social Democratic ideal, but the very fact that Podhoretz had posed such a question showed how broadly receptive the neoconservatives had become to ideas once held only by traditional conservatives.[47]

The rightward drift continued through the remainder of Carter's presidency. In November 1979, Elliott Abrams wrote in the conservative *American Spectator:*

> Neoconservatives are less sanguine about the range of achievable goals, and lean to the view that the achievement of many of these lies in our hearts and not in our state. . . . They are, on "social issues," rather conservative. And believing that the growth of state power will solve few of our society's problems, while limiting our liberty and creating new and unintended, unforeseen problems, neoconservatives strongly oppose the growth of the state.

It would be an exaggeration to say that all neoconservatives became conservatives in the late 1970s. Rather, as a group they were continually and gradually reaching the conclusions toward which they had been moving since they discovered the virtues of traditional authority in 1970. This shedding of their liberal identity would ease their entry into the Reagan camp in 1980.[48]

Another major factor easing the shift of the neoconservatives away from the Democrats was the uneasiness that spread among American Jews during the Carter years. Carter had not been the first choice of Jews in 1976, most of whom preferred either the strongly pro-Israel Henry Jackson or liberal Representative Morris Udall. Moreover, Carter presented Jews with "a special set of perplexities," in editor and educator Milton Himmelfarb's words, many of which made them nervous. Himmelfarb's analysis of Jewish responses to Carter proved correct. "To them he is from a distant region, a strange faith, given to expressions of piety that are uncongenial to them," commented historian Martin Marty in *Moment*, a liberal Jewish magazine. Historian Melvin Urofsky noted that, for many Jews, "to proclaim openly one's religious fervor sets off alarm bells," and that "this type of religiosity has too often been linked with the Ku Klux Klan."[49]

For his part, Carter worked to soothe the Jews' anxieties, declaring during the campaign that"the survival of Israel is not just a political issue, it is a moral imperative. That is my deeply held belief." The Carter campaign made an intense effort to win over Jewish voters and, in return, the Jews gave Carter the benefit of the doubt and remained loyal, if guarded, Democrats. "Carter need not worry very much about his Jewish vote. I hope Jewish voters need not worry very much about him," concluded Milton Himmelfarb.[50]

The Jews' major concern was American policy toward Israel, and it was over this issue that Carter's standing among them began its rapid deterioration. Their worst fear, already articulated by Podhoretz in 1976, was that the United States would force Israel into a disadvantageous settlement with its Arab neighbors, one in which Tel Aviv would give up its buffer zones of occupied territory in return for vague Arab promises of peace. As Carter assumed office, it appeared that this policy was gaining support. George Ball, for example, who had served as under secretary of state in the Kennedy and Johnson administrations, argued in *Foreign Affairs* that the American stake in the Middle East was too great to let the Arab-Israeli situation, with its attendant risks of war, continue. Washington, he argued, had "to take a strong hand to save Israel from herself." Moreover, he believed that

> the parties will never come anywhere near agree-
> ment by the traditional processes of diplomatic
> haggling unless the United States first defines the
> terms of that agreement, relates them to estab-
> lished international principles, and makes clear
> that America's continued involvement in the area
> depends upon acceptance by both sides of the
> terms it prescribes.

The president, Ball added, would have to be prepared to "take the political heat from powerful and articulate pro-Israeli domestic groups."[51]

Although Ball's argument, appearing in such a prominent forum, was enough to make Jews nervous, Carter's own statements and actions added to their jitters. Speaking in Clinton, Mass., Carter said in March 1977 that one "ultimate requirement" for a Middle East settlement was that "there has to be a homeland for the Palestinian refugees who have suffered for many, many years." Moreover, in the fall of 1977 the United States brought the Soviet Union into the Middle East peace talks scheduled to begin in Geneva that Decem-ber—a role Moscow had until then been denied—and the two superpowers issued a joint statement that referred to the "legitimate rights of the Palestinian people." Rabbi Alexander M. Schindler, chairman of the Conference of Major American Jewish Organiza-tions, declared that the communique "on its face, represents an abandonment of America's historic commitment to the security and survival of Israel."[52]

In response, Israel's supporters began a campaign to support their argument that the Jewish state was an important strategic asset for the United States. In April 1977, Eugene Rostow—under secretary of state for political affairs from 1966 to 1969 and chairman of the Committee on the Present Danger's executive committee—called Israel "an indispensable ally" and "a bulwark whose presence and strength discourage imperial impulses on the part of Egypt, Syria, or Iraq." In addition, according to Rostow, successful Arab aggression against Israel would benefit Moscow, for the Arabs were not independent actors. "With every step down this path [of hostility toward Israel], Arab dependence on the Soviet Union is deepened and confirmed," he wrote. Political scientist Herbert Kampf echoed this view, writing in June 1977 that Israel was "the only reliable ally of the United States in this oil rich area," and "should the United States ever permit Israel to be overcome for the sake of relations with the Arabs, it will have unnecessarily lost an irreplaceable asset."[53]

The fear that Carter would tolerate a settlement unfavorable to Israel marked the beginning of the erosion of his support among American Jews. As it turned out, Egyptian President Anwar Sadat's trip to Jerusalem in November 1977 opened the way for a separate Egyptian-Israeli settlement and scuttled the Geneva conference. Many Jews, however, would not forget what the *New Republic* had called "an invitation to capitulation," and in December Leonard Fein cited a Harris poll indicating that "60 percent of the Jews gave Mr. Carter a negative rating" to support his conclusion that "the President and his people have abandoned Israel."[54]

In the spring of 1978, fresh trouble arose over a proposal to balance a sale of advanced weapons to Israel with similar sales to Saudi Arabia and Egypt. "In the American Jewish community, there is profound distrust of Carter's intentions in the Middle East," reported Morton Kondracke in the *New Republic*. Kondracke further noted that administration officials were aware of Israel's fear of a shift in the military balance but claimed "defiantly in some cases—that U.S. interests are not identical with Israeli interests." As a result of the administration's approach to military aid to the Middle East, reported *Newsweek*, "if another Presidential election were held today, some experts believe that disaffected Jews might turn the tide against Carter in crucial states such as New York, California, Illinois, and Michigan."[55]

It was an incident involving Andrew Young, however, which may have done the greatest damage to Carter's standing among the Jews. As ambassador to the United Nations, Young had become an important symbol to black Americans, both for his position within the administration and for his importance in world affairs. His outspoken style and revisionist leanings, however, had gotten him into trouble several times and worn down his domestic political support; in one instance he had provoked an uproar with a remark about "hundreds, maybe thousands of . . . political prisoners" in the United States. Finally, in August 1979 Young failed to inform the State Department of all the details of a meeting he had held in July with representatives of the Palestine Liberation Organization. Angered more by the apparent deception than by the meeting, Vance then demanded and received Young's resignation.[56]

Many blacks, however, blamed Jewish pressure for Young's firing and, in a continuation of their battle ten years earlier, leaders of the two groups traded charges over Young, the Middle East, and racism. A group of black leaders from the NAACP, Urban League, Congressional Black Caucus, and other major black organizations released a statement called "Black/Jewish Relations" which they described as "our declaration of independence" on the Middle East. The statement decried Israeli support for "the illegitimate and oppressive racial regimes in South Africa and Southern Rhodesia," and further noted that many American Jews had become "apologists for the racial status quo."[57]

In reply, the National Jewish Community Relations Advisory Council stated, "we can't work with those who resort to half truths, lies, and bigotry." Liberal Jewish writers shared this anger. "When you sit for photos with those who boast of the murderers of innocents, you imply that they are welcome in civilized company," wrote Leonard Fein, who went on to say, "so please, no sanctimonious sermons to us. If you need to declare your independence, find a different issue." Most upsetting for Jews, however, was Carter's silence during the affair. For six weeks, Carter said nothing to refute the charges of Jewish responsibility for Young's dismissal, leading writer Cynthia Ozick to comment in 1980 that "most Jews felt they had been made to walk the plank."[58]

Even after the Young incident died down, Carter was unable to improve his standing among the Jews. On March 1, 1980, apparently because of confusion within the administration, the United States voted in favor of a United Nations Security Council resolution condemning Israeli settlements in Jerusalem and the occupied Arab territories. This was the first time that the United States had voted against Israel on the settlement issue and, despite the administration's quick disavowal of the vote, "Arab states were pleased at what they took to be a major shift in U.S. policy," while Jews "were outraged," reported *Newsweek*. The *New Republic* called the vote "part of a consistent pattern of erratic behavior in diplomacy which betrays our allies, [and] encourages our enemies." The Jews vented their anger three weeks later in the New York Democratic primary, when they gave almost 80 percent of their votes to Senator Edward Kennedy, who was challenging Carter for the Democratic presidential nomination, providing much of the margin of Kennedy's victory over Carter. Moreover, one poll indicated that only one-third of Jewish primary voters believed that Carter was "a strong supporter" of Israel, according to the *New York Times*.[59]

Finally, Carter's brother, Billy, frequently lurked in the background. Billy Carter was a flamboyant alcoholic who attracted the attention the press often lavishes on "colorful" presidential relatives. During Jimmy Carter's term Billy became associated with the Libyan government and made such well-publicized statements as "the Jewish media tears up the Arabs," and declared that the Jews "can kiss my ass." Jimmy Carter was caught in the middle, trying to disavow Billy's antics without censuring his brother. "I know for a fact that he is not anti-Semitic and has never made a serious critical remark against Jews," said Carter, while refusing to make "any condemnation that I don't think is warranted." Not surprisingly, this waffling only increased Jewish unease. "No American Jew can ever be sure which Carter is actual," wrote Cynthia Ozick: "The overt decent Jekyll or the unproved, only suspected, hidden Hyde—the Hyde for whom there is no evidence beyond the fact that the same womb which gave the world Jimmy also brought forth Billy."[60]

For the neoconservatives, Carter's problems with the Jews appeared to provide a golden opportunity to build their influence within the Democratic party. As Jewish alarm began to grow, the neoconservatives were quick to point out to Carter the dangers inherent in alienating his pro-Israel constituency. In November 1977, for example, *Commentary* published an analysis by Seymour Martin Lipset and political scientist William Schneider of public opinion polls on the Middle East. Their findings showed "consistently . . . greater support for Israel among the better educated, the more affluent, and those in executive and professional positions, [suggesting] that Israel has strong backing among the elite sectors—those who are more active politically and presumably more influential." Furthermore, according to Lipset and Schneider, low support for Israel was tied to anti-Semitism, especially among blacks, further suggesting that a perceived anti-Israel position would cost Carter valuable political support while attracting only a relatively small number of marginal voters in return. Consequently, they concluded that "a confrontation with Israel . . . could have a devastating effect on the popularity and the chances for reelection of those responsible." To make sure that Carter got the message, Lipset and Podhoretz both told the *New York Times* "that they hoped the study would have an impact on Administration policy at a time when Mr. Carter is making Middle East initiatives of a controversial nature."[61]

Two years later, the neoconservatives used the flare-up over Young's resignation to try to consolidate Jewish support against the administration. Carl Gershman wrote, with some hyperbole, that "no episode in contemporary American history has been marked by a greater outpouring of animosity against Jews." Gershman claimed that the Young affair, anti-Semitism, and anti-democratic attitudes were closely linked. Not only were black leaders' charges against the Jews unfounded, according to Gershman, but also their support for Young, the Palestinians, and other Third World and anti-American causes, "Some black leaders [were trying] to precipitate a rupture with an earlier democratic orientation and to move a significant segment of the black leadership toward an ideological and political alignment with Third World radicalism." Gershman believed that Israel was a target because it "identifies with the democratic West and is prepared to resist the Soviet-backed forces in the Middle East," and that the ultimate objective was to "render America incapable of defending Israel or any other ally, or even itself." Thus, he concluded, as far as Jewish interests were concerned, "the Young affair . . . was actually about democracy and its enemies. And it is out of a commitment to democracy—the same democratic commitment that led Jews and others to support the civil rights movement—that it is necessary to oppose, and oppose resolutely, the political tendency which Andrew Young now leads."[62]

In line with this view, neoconservative writers urged Jews to distance themselves from liberals and the Democrats. In a *Commentary* symposium, "Liberalism & the Jews," Podhoretz asked a number of prominent American Jews (not all of them neoconservatives) for each one's "thinking as a Jew about liberalism." The responses, more so than any previous writings attacking McGovern or the influence of the New Left, showed how the neoconservatives had come to see liberals and the Democrats as almost hopeless. Midge Decter wrote that "Jews are losing their home in the Democratic party," because its brand of liberalism "is bad for the Jews not only because it endorses quotas, has come to extend its highly selective tolerance to anti-Semitism, and regards the PLO (as it once regarded the Vietcong) as a worthy instrument for national self-chastisement. It is above all bad for the Jews because it is bad for the country."

In a concise statement of the Jews' quandary, Nathan Glazer wrote that while "the ideal Jewish choice, of course, is the conservative Democrat," none could be found who had a realistic chance of victory. Other responses also reflected the neoconservatives' sense of alienation from the party. The Jews, in Elliott Abrams's view, were "floating, with the attachment to Democratic party liberalism broken." Joseph Shattan urged Jews to be wary and "not pay any attention to ideological or party labels," but instead "carefully scrutinize each candidate's key advisers, especially his foreign policy and energy advisers."[63]

The neoconservatives appeared, on the surface at least, to have good reason to believe that increasing numbers of Jews were coming to share their view of the Democrats. During Carter's term, for example, *Midstream* had printed articles with titles such as "The Theft of Liberalism—A Jewish Problem," and "The Institute for Policy Studies: Empire on the Left." Following the Young affair, Earl Raab worried about the emergence of a society "in which only groups were assigned rights and an individual's rights and identity were defined only through his membership in a group." In the fall of 1980, Raab took his argument to its neoconservative conclusion: "Such a society is emerging in America today, in the name of a more participatory democracy. The 'New Politics' encourages it, and the Democratic Party embraces it."[64]

The neoconservatives could also look beyond strictly Jewish publications for signs of widespread Jewish disenchantment with the Democrats and the growing influence of neoconservatism. In May 1978, at the time of the controversy over arms sales to Egypt and Saudi Arabia, a New York rally for Soviet Jews featured numerous anti-Carter signs, and Republican Senator Robert Packwood was cheered by the crowd as he denounced Carter's conversion to the State Department's "long standing and blatant" anti-Jewish views. In October 1979, a writer in the *New York Times* noted that "Mr. Young may be the best Republican vote-getter since Dwight D. Eisenhower." For their part, the Republicans were content to note that, with regard to Jewish voters, "if Carter is the Democratic nominee in 1980 we have gained by it." Other articles added to the impression that the Jewish community was catching up with its neoconservative vanguard. In 1978 Jeffrey Hart, a leading conservative academic, wrote in *National Review* of the increasing conservatism of Jewish intellectuals, and in 1979 journalist Peter Steinfels, then the executive editor of *Commonweal*, declared, "As it happens, such a conservative moment has arrived. Not just emerged, but *arrived*—taking center stage in American politics with a speed and a thoroughness that have left liberals stunned and disarmed." Or, as Podhoretz crowed in early 1980, "in the world of ideas generally, everyone agrees, whether happily or with alarm, that the most dynamic force in recent years has been the group known as the 'neoconservatives.' "[65]

Although it was undoubtedly significant, the neoconservatives probably overestimated the extent of anti-Democratic sentiment among Jews. In June 1979, sociologist Alan M. Fisher wrote that "the evidence of Jewish liberalism is extensive, persistent, and impressive." Even after the Young affair most Jews appear to have retained their attachment to the Democrats, if not to Carter. The *New Republic*, for example, reported in November 1979 on the warm reception given to Vice-President Walter Mondale by the Anti-Defamation League of B'nai B'rith—"several participants remarked that it was too bad such a good man was 'going down with a sinking ship.'" Most significant was the high Jewish vote for Kennedy in New York the following March. Although many of the votes were cast in protest against Carter, they were votes nonetheless—and for a candidate considerably more liberal than Carter on both domestic and foreign issues. Had the Jews been truly disgusted with liberals and Democrats, many more could have been expected to have stayed home on primary day.[66]

In fact, the neoconservatives shared this dilemma. They had been Democrats all their lives and still hoped to save the party. Moreover, they hesitated to become Republicans, for their attachment to the party had not, in Elliott Abrams's words, been "replaced by any real sympathy for the Republicans." Despite their discontent, through January 1980 they still sought a sign that the party would listen to them and that their influence would be restored. By February this ambivalent stance had changed, however, for it had become clear that the neoconservative position within the Democratic party was hopeless.[67]

One reason the neoconservatives had remained Democrats was their hope that Daniel Patrick Moynihan would somehow emerge as the savior of the party and their brand of liberalism, much as Harry Truman had three decades earlier. Their increasing dislike of Carter made Moynihan an ever more attractive figure in their eyes. As the Jews and neoconservatives became increasingly alarmed and angry with Carter over the Middle East, Moynihan kept up his assaults on anti-Semitism and the USSR, as well as his defense of Israel—a good strategy for a savvy politician with a large Jewish constituency. "I've been preoccupied with the success of the Soviet effort to delegitimate the State of Israel," he told an interviewer from *Moment* in August 1978. Moreover, he said, "The Israelis are a huge asset strategically, particularly if . . . the Iranians and the Saudis and the Egyptians and the Israelis all come to see their common interest. . . . That interest is to keep the independence of the region." A year later, in the fall of 1979, he wrote that "anti-Semitism has become a unifying global ideology of the totalitarian Left," adding that the "anti-Israel, anti-Zionist campaign is not uninformed bigotry, it is conscious politics. We are dealing here not with the primitive but with the sophisticated, with the world's most powerful propaganda apparatus—that of the Soviet Union."[68]

Not surprisingly, the neoconservatives looked to Moynihan's tenure at the United Nations as a golden age, particularly in comparison with Andrew Young's term. "Those eight months were rich in accomplishment," wrote historian Bernard Lewis in his review of *A Dangerous Place*. "During that brief period," wrote Edward Luttwak, "A new world view motivated our stance at the UN. If attacked, the United States would defend itself; if others proclaimed the virtues of the totalitarian order, the United States would speak out for democracy and liberty." Lewis noted the price of failing to carry on Moynihan's policies: "The corruption of the United Nations has continued and has been greatly worsened by the normalization of falsehood and intimidation."[69]

Moynihan also shared the neoconservatives' skepticism about the arms control process and the SALT II treaty. Writing about Team B in early 1978, Moynihan stated that "their notion, that the Soviets intend to surpass the United States in strategic arms and are in the process of doing so, has gone from heresy to respectability, if not orthodoxy." In August 1979 he made public his misgivings about the SALT II treaty itself. The problem, as Moynihan saw it, was that SALT "required American negotiators to reach agreement with the Soviet Union in an area where there is no agreement." That November, he published a long explanation of his view on the treaty and arms control in general, with two main themes. The first noted that neither the first nor the second SALT treaty had brought about arms reduction or even arms control—"There are no limitations of significance," he wrote. Because the Soviet Union sought nuclear superiority, the United States was forced to keep pace, building new and increasingly sophisticated nuclear weapons and acquiring along the way first-strike capabilities, thus obviating the strategy of mutually assured destruction: "Herein resides the final irony of the SALT process. Not only has it failed to prevent the Soviets from developing a first-strike capability; it now leads the United States to do so. The process has produced the one outcome it was designed to forestall. And so we see a policy in ruins." Moynihan's second point was a reiteration of the Committee on the Present Danger's contention that nuclear superiority mattered, and that the United States was in danger of becoming inferior to the Soviets: "Strategic superiority is the power to make other people do what you want them to do. Already, the Soviets, approaching a palpable strategic superiority, give signs that it is their intention to control our defense policy." Although the United States could live with this, noted Moynihan, it would lose much of its freedom of action: "Will anyone assert that in such circumstances we will not be living differently?" As both a warning of what he saw as the treaty's flaws and as a solution, Moynihan proposed amending it so that it would terminate on December 31, 1981, unless "significant and substantial reductions" were made in strategic nuclear weapons.[70]

It was in this context that talk of Moynihan running for president began. The idea appears to have first surfaced in the *New Republic* during the summer of 1978. "If there is not yet a Moynihan campaign, there is a Moynihan movement and a Moynihan logic," wrote Morton Kondracke. Kondracke identified Norman Podhoretz, Midge Decter, Jeane Kirkpatrick, and other leaders of the Coalition for a Democratic Majority as Moynihan's major supporters and argued that he would be attractive to Jewish, ethnic, Catholic, and Southern voters. Podhoretz, according to Kondracke, "understands all this, and he is pushing." The *New York Times* made a similar point six months later, noting that "the Moynihan-for-President talk stems from a conscious effort by those who share the neoconservative banner to put forward the most effective spokesman for their position."[71]

Talk of a Moynihan candidacy increased as Jimmy Carter's political woes mounted. In June 1979, William F. Buckley, Jr., called Moynihan "the outstanding representative of the Democratic right," and a Democrat "in the tradition of Dean Acheson [and] Harry Truman." If Carter chose not to run again, predicted Buckley, "Moynihan will campaign very hard for the nomination and will arrive at the convention as favorite son of the State of New York." The apparently serious prospect of a Moynihan candidacy so alarmed the editors of the *Nation* that they devoted most of an issue to a scathing "dissection of the man behind the image."[72]

Moynihan did little at first to discourage such speculation. In May 1979, he told a news conference that Senator Edward Kennedy's views were not those of most Democrats. In early August, he speculated that if Carter were "unhorsed in the early primaries and there is no clear choice from the party electorate," he would consider running as a favorite son candidate from New York. But Moynihan eventually dropped whatever favorite son ambitions he had and settled into an attitude of neutrality. He remained "cool" toward Carter, according to the *New York Times*, and said in January 1980 that he was a "neutral" in the Carter-Kennedy contest for the Democratic nomination.[73]

Moynihan's neutrality soon turned into equal criticism of both Kennedy and Carter. In January 1980 he called Kennedy's opposition to curtailing grain exports to the Soviet Union (one of Carter's steps responding to the December 1979 Soviet invasion of Afghanistan) "irresponsible." In early February, however, he observed that Carter's response had not been strong enough, either: "If President Carter deems the most recent Soviet outrages as something new and different, it is not evident that the American response is yet different from what it has been for three years." In March, as both candidates sought his endorsement for the New York primary, Moynihan felt that neither had "addressed himself sufficiently to the foreign and domestic problems of the country," according to the *New York Times*. In

May he announced that he would not be a delegate to the Democratic convention because he did not want to have to choose between "a leading colleague" and "the President of my party." In fact, Moynihan withheld his endorsement until August 17, when he finally backed Carter for the tepid reason that "I thought it the proper course to take."[74]

Moynihan's refusal to abandon Carter was another force weakening the neoconservatives' ties to the Democratic party. As a Democratic officeholder rather than an intellectual, Moynihan had to pay attention to his political prospects. "As a practicing politician, therefore, he was going to behave differently from these other people," recalled Charles Horner. "It's one thing for a writer, a Ben Wattenberg, a Norman Podhoretz or a Jeane Kirkpatrick to really write scathingly of the administration. It's another for [Moynihan] to do it," commented Elliott Abrams. As Abrams and Horner both recalled, Moynihan had to pay close attention to his reelection concerns—New York is a liberal state and Moynihan had not forgotten how narrowly he had beaten Bella Abzug in 1976—and so he had to be careful not to appear to be splitting or deserting the Democrats. Thus, whatever his personal beliefs, Moynihan was unable to continue drifting rightward with the other neoconservatives, gradually depriving them, in turn, of their most promising leader within the party. With no major figure to turn to, the neoconservatives had one less reason to remain loyal Democrats.[75]

The last straw came in late January 1980. According to Midge Decter, Carter decided to meet with the leaders of the Coalition for a Democratic Majority in order to court the support of conservative Democrats. A group from the coalition was invited to the White House, and the roster included most of the major neoconservatives: Decter, Podhoretz, Abrams, Kirkpatrick, Max Kampelman, Ben Wattenberg, Austin Ranney, and Penn Kemble. Given their three years of harsh attacks, it is hard to imagine how Carter expected to win over the neoconservatives; in the event, he failed miserably. He "indicated that, in fact, he had learned nothing from Afghanistan," recalled Abrams.

> Ranney's efforts to get him to sort of encourage us
> by discussing a change in his view were met with
> complete rejection by Carter . . . far from meeting

this group halfway or indicating that he cared
whether this group stayed Democrats, he basically
indicated that he didn't give a goddamn. That he
had always been right in all of his views on everything. And the universal reaction after the meeting was that this guy was hopeless.

Mondale tried to soothe the coalition group and, according to
Abrams, "made a very good pitch after Carter left the room. . . . But
we had just met Carter and he had been hopeless." After the meetings
ended, Decter remembers, "Jeane [Kirkpatrick] walked right out . . .
right in front of the cameras, and said she was going for Ronald Reagan." Kirkpatrick was not alone. "I would venture to say that everybody at that meeting voted for Reagan," said Abrams.[76]

The neoconservatives had searched, but no Truman was to be found
in the Democratic party in 1980. Instead, the party seemed to
embody all of their nightmares. In the neoconservatives' view, its foreign policies were firmly in the hands of the left and the party no
longer opposed anti-Semitism or totalitarian thinking—indeed, they
believed that these tendencies were now in the party's mainstream.
Believing that the Democrats no longer had room for them, the neoconservatives began leaving the party during the winter of 1980. By
that point, they were probably only slightly missed. Given their
attacks on Carter and their dislike for Kennedy, it was also clear that
whoever won the nomination would have little sympathy for the neoconservatives' concerns. At the same time, however, they were not
thrown out, but walked away.

Supporting the Republicans brought the neoconservatives a new
set of problems. Their opposition to the Democratic left had built up
a lot of expectations in the neoconservative camp, as if to say that
once we are in power, all will be set straight. Now they were trans-
ferring their hopes to Ronald Reagan and the Republicans, expecting
that a conservative victory would bring them all the opportunities
and rewards they had been denied by the Democrats. Unfortunately,
several neoconservatives were to be sorely disappointed.

5

Coping with
Success,

1980 –1985

Following his victory in the 1980 presidential election, Ronald Reagan's new administration faced a broad range of foreign policy issues. Central America, where anti-government rebels were beginning to attack the new regime in Nicaragua and leftist rebels in El Salvador sought to overthrow the government, was at the top of the list. The administration also faced the questions of how to respond to the continuing Soviet occupation of Afghanistan, unrest in Poland, a growing peace movement in the West which demanded freezes on nuclear weapons and disarmament, as well as how to carry out its planned modernization of American conventional and nuclear forces.[1]

Reagan's victory fulfilled several neoconservative hopes and raised still more. In Reagan, the neoconservatives believed that they had a president who shared their view of the world and, especially, of the overriding importance of resisting Soviet expansionism and Third World leftism. Similarly, they viewed Reagan's victory as proving that the American people had come to share their views of the present danger. The neoconservatives, especially Norman Podhoretz, hoped to consolidate this success and build popular support for a foreign policy that would go beyond mere containment. Echoing the conservatives of the early 1950s, they called for actively working for the rollback and eventual defeat of Communism.

Even when they were flush with success, however, the neoconservative intellectuals felt a nagging sense of vulnerability. Early in the first Reagan administration they focused on communicating their goals to the public, hoping that the call for an anti-Communist crusade would generate deeper and longer-lasting support than a call for containment. Podhoretz was one of the leaders of this effort, which also included Irving Kristol, Robert W. Tucker, and Walter Laqueur. To Podhoretz's dismay, however, it turned out that the weak link was not just inadequate public support but also Reagan himself. Podhoretz became progressively more disillusioned as he realized that Reagan was not consumed with defeating Communism but instead was carefully weighing his foreign policy options and acting cautiously. But in Podhoretz's view, anything less than total victory was tantamount to defeat and he turned on Reagan, bitterly denouncing him for his compromises.

Not all neoconservatives shared Podhoretz's disappointment, however. Those who went to work for the Reagan administration, most notably Jeane Kirkpatrick and Elliott Abrams, were politicians as much as, or more than, they were intellectuals. They did not go to Washington solely to crush Communism but, instead, to establish new policies and to restore the country's strength for the continuing struggle. Another of their major goals was to defend the concept of liberal democracy and, if possible, to expand its influence in the world. They knew that success would not come overnight and, in the tradition of Niebuhr but unlike Podhoretz, they would be satisfied with incremental progress. By 1985 they could point to achievements at the United Nations, in Central America, and in human rights policy which enabled them to assess Reagan's term as a great success..

Daniel Patrick Moynihan created another fissure in the ranks of the neoconservatives. He entered the Reagan era a staunch neoconservative Democrat, criticizing what he saw as disastrous liberal foreign policies for contributing to Jimmy Carter's defeat. But, facing reelection in liberal New York in 1982, Moynihan began softening his rhetoric. He spoke and wrote less about foreign policy and concentrated instead on criticizing Reagan's domestic and social policies. At the same time, Moynihan began to believe that the world was undergoing a shift, and that the Communist and leftist threats were receding. As a result, Moynihan changed his views of what foreign policies were appropriate and, after a confusing transition, broke with the neoconservatives over aid to the government of El Salvador and Nicaraguan rebels fighting the Sandinista government.

Beginning in February 1980, individual neoconservatives gradually drifted into Reagan's camp. As relative latecomers, they could not hope for the highest positions in the campaign, but they still served in significant roles. Jeane Kirkpatrick, for example, worked in the campaign as a foreign policy adviser. In August, Elliott Abrams, motivated by what he recalls as a "combination of a strong desire that Reagan beat Carter and a rolling, fast-growing sense of boredom" with his law practice, joined the campaign and was sent to Florida, where he "worked on Jews." Some neoconservatives remained neutral, however. Richard Perle, Senator Henry Jackson's former aide, was working as a consultant in 1980 and took no part in the campaign.[2]

With Reagan's victory, the neoconservatives shifted their attention to influencing the new administration. In late 1980 Midge Decter began setting up the Committee For the Free World, which officially announced its formation in February 1981. In its founding statement, the committee declared that its aim was to "alter the climate of confusion and complacency, apathy and self-denigration, that has done much to weaken the Western democracies." To do this, the committee—a self-described "group of writers, artists, editors, scientists, trade unionists, teachers, [and] publishers"—would work "to defend and preserve [the free world] against the rising menace of totalitarian barbarism" in "books, newspapers, broadcasts, classrooms and in all public institutions." The committee's statement was signed by

about 400 intellectuals and activists from the United States and
Europe, including Raymond Aron, William J. Bennett, Arthur
Koestler, Robert W. Tucker, Gertrude Himmelfarb, Elie Wiesel, Sid-
ney Hook, Elliott Abrams, and Ernest Lefever.[3]

In building the committee's influence, Decter was determined to
avoid the mistakes she had made with the Coalition For a Democratic Majority. The committee's name was chosen with care; Decter
rejected the name Committee For A Free World because, as she
wrote in October 1980, it was "the kind of generalizing piety that
everyone on earth, including Brezhnev, would give assent to. . . . *The
Free World*, on the other hand . . . means the West and its depen-
dencies and allies." Moreover, there would be no room in the committee for the weak-hearted, one of the flaws Decter saw as crippling
to the Coalition for a Democratic Majority. "If you wanted to join the
Committee, you had to sign [its manifesto]. And if you didn't want to
sign it, you were not one of us," she recalled. Thus, as Decter wrote to
Daniel Bell in December 1980, there would be "no margin for disagreement on the essentials" within the committee's ranks. Furthermore, she steered the committee toward intellectual activism and
away from party politics, which she knew to be her weak point. "We
kept ourselves restricted to . . . publishing, writing, doing what it was
people like us know how to do."[4]

Decter quickly went to work to make the committee a success.
The committee was launched with $125,000 raised from the conser-
vative Scaife, John M. Olin, and Smith Richardson foundations, as
well as from individuals. In the months that followed, Decter solicited
funds from wealthy donors as well as such corporations as Sears,
Roebuck and Mobil Oil; well-connected former cabinet members
William Simon and Donald Rumsfeld helped raise funds. Their efforts
were successful. The committee's financial statement for the year
ended December 31, 1981, showed revenues of about $449,000 and
expenses of $405,000, leaving an almost $44,000 surplus.[5]

With its finances in order, the committee undertook a variety of
activities. It placed newspaper advertisements to spread its views
and began a monthly newsletter, *Contentions*, which declared itself

"devoted to questions and arguments currently being agitated within the political and cultural community." The committee also held conferences, including one in February 1983 on "Our Country and Our Culture." Although the title was borrowed from the *Partisan Review* symposium of 1952 in which liberal intellectuals embraced American culture, the 1983 conference focused on the intellectuals' subsequent betrayals. According to the *New York Times*, it "was dominated by the clear and often gloomily expressed concern that the failure of intellectuals to defend traditional values posed a grave danger to American freedom." Prominent neoconservative intellectuals, including Irving Kristol, art critic Hilton Kramer, and historian Michael Ledeen lamented the sad state of American culture, anti-Americanism among intellectuals, and the lingering influence of the New Left.[6]

Furthermore, the committee served as a clearinghouse for neoconservative activists, putting them in touch with one another and helping them find support. It was especially eager to help campus groups, providing help to conservative student groups, especially those trying to establish conservative campus newspapers. According to Decter, the committee also helped set up the National Association of Scholars.[7]

The committee enjoyed access to the highest levels of the Reagan administration, which more than made up for its gloom over the state of American culture. Decter herself was a guest at the White House on a number of occasions, including lunches with President Reagan and his assistants, and she corresponded with White House aides. Kenneth Adelman, Jeane Kirkpatrick's deputy at the United Nations, sent Decter a handwritten note asking her to "please let me know how and where I can help." Jed Snyder, special assistant to the director of the State Department's Bureau of Politico-Military Affairs, wrote Decter that the committee was "intellectually very attractive," and that "he would like to become involved" in its programs. Elliott Abrams, who had married Decter's daughter Rachel in March 1980, was another State Department correspondent of the committee. In light of these contacts, Norman Podhoretz was able to remark at the

February 1983 conference that "the work many of us have been doing has not been in vain."

> There is no question that there are more of us
> around today than there were ten years ago. . . .
> Some of [the neoconservatives'] ideas, which were
> dismissed out of hand, ridiculed, derided as little
> as five or ten years ago, have in some instances
> compelled a respectful hearing, and in other
> instances, *mirabile dictu*, actually become the con-
> ventional wisdom.[8]

Neoconservative foreign policy theorists had made their case for strong containment so forcefully during the Carter years that they had little need to state it again after the 1980 election. In fact, they interpreted Reagan's victory over Carter as indicating that the American people had come to support their point of view. Robert W. Tucker, for example, wrote shortly after the election that "a majority among elites and public alike now accepts the imminent prospect— if not the present reality—of an overall arms balance that favors the Soviet Union. The need to redress this actual or prospective imbalance is also broadly accepted." Similarly, Podhoretz wrote that the election demonstrated that there was a "new American majority" which supported the Republican effort to try "to reverse the decline of American power."[9]

The neoconservatives used Reagan's victory to reiterate their views of the major issues facing the new administration. For Tucker, "the essential dimensions of the American security problem" were "a military balance increasingly favorable to the Soviet Union and the steady erosion of Western power and position in the Persian Gulf." For Podhoretz, it was time to "make our defenses invulnerable . . . to contain Soviet expansionism and to protect our vital interests in the Persian Gulf." Kirkpatrick, foreshadowing one of the major policy concerns of the Reagan administration, wrote that the revolutions in Grenada and Nicaragua and the leftist insurgency in El Salvador "confront this country with the unprecedented need to defend itself against a ring of Soviet bases on and around our southern and eastern borders."[10]

The opportunity to take action carried with it the danger that, in the eyes of the neoconservatives, the new consensus would prove too fragile for the job that lay ahead. The neoconservatives had good reason to be worried; one study found that, although most Americans supported increased defense spending in 1981, there was little support for increased commitments or intervention abroad. If the public continued to view the threat from Moscow solely in conventional, balance-of-power terms, then the strength of America's response would soon be dissipated. Podhoretz had warned of this in early 1980 when he wrote that the "new nationalism" lacked a sense that "we *are* fighting for freedom and against Communism, for democracy and against totalitarianism." Tucker echoed Podhoretz's fear that without an "awareness of the deeper meaning of the conflict" to provide political support of the "effort and sacrifice required to sustain the exercise of power," policy would fall prey to "drift and uncertainty."[11]

Podhoretz stepped forward to provide the rationale, but instead of simply calling again for containment he began preaching an anti-Communist crusade. This was the logical extension of his writings from the late 1970s, which had warned of the need to prevent further Communist gains; if a call for containment had only begun to rally America, then a call to something even stronger was needed to sustain unity and provide a cause worth sacrificing for. In this his thinking was similar to the Republicans' of the early 1950s and, like them, he turned to the rhetoric of liberation. There could be, in Podhoretz's view, no middle ground in the struggle with Moscow, which he called "a clash between civilization and barbarism." Just as John Foster Dulles and James Burnham had called mere containment inadequate in 1952, so Podhoretz wrote that a strategy "which defines the problem as Soviet expansionism alone will be unable to sustain the requisite political support."[12]

Podhoretz argued that the goal of the "refurbished strategy of containment" should be the destruction of the Soviet Union. The strategy called for a vigorous assault on Communism, although one that stopped short of direct military confrontation. If, he argued, the United States would send arms to Afghan and Angolan rebels and refuse assistance to Poland's troubled economy, "the internal pressures already boiling behind [the USSR's] present imperial borders will mount of their own accord," which, in turn, "holds out the hope of a breakup of the Soviet empire." This would be, noted Podhoretz, "nothing more than doing unto them what they have been doing to us for a very long time."[13]

Podhoretz's quest to rally support for the new containment led him, once again, to refight old battles. Just as he had earlier fought against what he viewed as new generations of appeasers and Wallaceites, in 1982 Podhoretz turned to defending America's involvement in Vietnam. That year he published *Why We Were in Vietnam* in which, reversing his 1971 support for a "complete and immediate American withdrawal" from Vietnam, he declared that the war had been—as he approvingly quoted Ronald Reagan—"a noble cause." Defeat had come, however, from the same sources that threatened the new containment. "The war had to have a convincing moral justification, and the failure to provide one doomed the entire enterprise," wrote Podhoretz. He singled out President Johnson's decision to justify the war as a way of containing China, a case "much shakier than the moral case" of anti-Communism, and one which was "much easier for critics of the war . . . to beat down."[14]

Podhoretz also used the book to point out the danger liberal intellectuals posed to the anti-Communist cause. He singled out several antiwar intellectual activists—Frances FitzGerald, Susan Sontag, and Noam Chomsky, to name a few—for what he saw as their responsibility for undermining support for the war and not seeing Communist ideology "as the source of the crimes committed" in Southeast Asia after the war ended in 1975. In addition, in Podhoretz's view, the same intellectuals could be expected to oppose Reagan's policies of renewed American strength and containment. His choice of opponents was strange, however, because critics like FitzGerald or Chomsky had little political influence by 1981. His selection of them showed that Podhoretz believed that not only did Communism have to be fought and destroyed on moral grounds, but that the slightest opposition to, or even inadequate support for, the cause was a danger in itself and could not be tolerated.[15]

Despite their efforts to solidify what they viewed as the ideological foundations of the Reagan administration, however, several of the neoconservative intellectuals were soon dismayed by its actual policies. At the end of April 1981, only three months after Reagan's inauguration and barely four weeks after he was wounded in an assassination attempt, Irving Kristol complained of a "muddle" in foreign policy. He praised Reagan for ending the grain embargo imposed on the USSR after the invasion of Afghanistan, but complained that no new, stronger measures had taken its place; he worried that the administration's declared commitment to preventing a leftist revolution in El Salvador was not being matched by its actions; and that arms sales to Pakistan and Saudi Arabia, respectively, were not helping the Afghans and were a threat to Israel, thus undercutting American interests in the Middle East.[16]

Kristol and other neoconservative critics laid the blame for policy confusion on what they viewed as the administration's flawed intellectual framework. But the neoconservatives put forward their arguments with an impatience bordering on arrogance; they spoke with the confidence of intellectuals who had never held public office or faced the realities of governing. They criticized Reagan's failure to solve all of the country's foreign problems immediately, even though just a few months before they had been emphasizing the desperate nature of the situation. "Though this administration came to office with a clear-cut set of attitudes in foreign affairs," Kristol wrote, "It had never thought through the implications of those attitudes for a coherent foreign policy." The muddle would continue, argued Kristol, until the Reagan administration "realizes the inadequacy of the intellectual tools with which it is operating." Kristol also worried that career State Department diplomats would work to tone down policy statements and keep the administration from pursuing activist policies. Similarly, at the end of 1981, Robert W. Tucker deplored new arms sales to the Saudis—"a policy of economic and political appeasement"—as reinforcing the Carter administration's illusion "that there is some way by which we may secure our interests in the Persian Gulf while avoiding the visible and substantial assertion of American power in the region." Such an approach, Tucker warned, would lead only to concessions to Riyadh regarding Israel and the Palestinians without any compensating increase in the security of America's access to oil.[17]

Despite their attention to the Third World, the neoconservatives' greatest concern remained the Soviet Union. While policies toward other regions could be labeled as muddled or misguided, Soviet policy was the litmus test of ideological purity, strength, and consistency, one which Walter Laqueur believed the Reagan administration was failing. In January 1982 he wrote that the previous year had not been an "annus mirabilis," and instead charged that the United States had failed to put Moscow on the ideological defensive over the rise of the Solidarity movement in Poland, had not rallied European support for its defense policies, and was not using foreign broadcasting to take the cultural offensive. Moscow, Laqueur noted, was "aware of the importance of the 'ideological struggle,'" but not so Washington: "A single-minded concentration on the military aspects of containment leads nowhere. Containment is the political struggle for the minds of men at home and abroad; it has reference to friends as well as to neutrals and enemies. The failure of the Reagan administration in this respect has been almost inexplicable." Thus, concluded Laqueur, Reagan's policies did not match the Soviets' with an overall strategy, "only occasional comments, gestures, and reactions."[18]

The harshest, angriest denunciations of Reagan came from Norman Podhoretz, who accused the president of backsliding. Podhoretz wrote with the anger of one whose highest hopes had been betrayed. In January 1981, he had written of Reagan's "truly historic opportunity" to reverse America's decline. Sixteen months later, Podhoretz wrote bitterly that while Reagan had kept his promise to rebuild the military, he had not established sufficiently strong policies toward the Soviet bloc. When Poland repressed the Solidarity movement in

December 1981, for example, Podhoretz noted that Reagan had not cut economic ties and trade with Warsaw or Moscow. "All we had to do was to *stop helping* the Soviets and their Polish quislings," he complained, "to make it harder for them to stabilize the situation." Apparently, not even the Committee for the Free World's influence could change matters, for, as Podhoretz lamented, Reagan's "ruling passion is concern for the domestic economy and [he] conducts foreign policy with that concern chiefly in mind." Thus, Reagan "has in practice been following a strategy of helping the Soviet Union stabilize its empire, rather than a strategy aimed at encouraging the breakup of that empire from within." The continuation of trade and the tolerance of Soviet actions within its empire, in Podhoretz's view, was nothing more than a return to the Nixon-Kissinger strategy for détente: "Indeed, it would be hard to think of a more consistent and more forceful critic of détente than Mr. Reagan. Yet it is equally hard to think of a term that more accurately describes his own foreign policy." Podhoretz saw the problem in apocalyptic terms. In Reagan, he noted, "we thought we had found a political force capable of turning things around. If President Reagan fails . . . there is no one else in sight."[19]

Podhoretz did not let up on his charge that Reagan had given in to the temptations of détente. In the summer of 1983 he argued that political pressure from appeasers, pacifists, and isolationists was forcing Reagan to engage in arms talks and to avoid sending troops to El Salvador, regardless of the consequences—"a world fashioned in the image of the Soviet Union." In his review of the memoirs of Reagan's first secretary of state, Alexander Haig, Podhoretz noted in 1984 that there had "been a case of mistaken identity."

> By taking some of his statements at face value,
> both the President's warmest friends and his most
> virulent enemies imagined that they had found in
> him a champion of the old conservative dream of
> going beyond the containment of Communism to
> the "rollback" of Communist influence and power
> and the "liberation" of the Soviet empire. The

> truth, however, is that Mr. Reagan as President
> has never shown the slightest inclination to
> pursue such an ambitious strategy.[20]

At the end of Reagan's first term, Podhoretz finally admitted the obvious. Reagan, he wrote in *Foreign Affairs*, "was more politician than ideologue."

> As such he would go only so far, and no farther,
> against the pressures of public opinion, and the
> resistance of the media and the permanent govern-
> ment; he would wherever possible cut his political
> losses after doing anything risky or unpopular; and
> in the face of serious opposition, he would usually
> back down even from a policy to which he was
> personally devoted.

Even Reagan's victories were not enough for Podhoretz. The October 1983 invasion of Grenada, in which American forces deposed a Cuban-supported Marxist regime, may have been a blow against Soviet expansionism in the western hemisphere, but it was a poor substitute for direct action against the Soviet Union or its major allies. But Podhoretz also realized that he still had no alternative to Reagan: "In 1984 Mr. Reagan, for all the deficiencies that showed up in his first term, was preferable to [Democratic presidential nominee] Walter Mondale or any of Mr. Mondale's rivals."[21]

By 1985 Podhoretz had become a victim of his own goals and growing ideological rigidity. He had set an absolute standard for measuring Reagan's foreign policy—victory over Communism—against which anything less was automatically defined as failure. It was also an impossible and contradictory standard. If the situation in 1980 had been as bad as Podhoretz had described it, and the Soviet Union as strong, how could he expect victory to be achieved so quickly? Similarly, his anguished discovery that Reagan was first and foremost a politician spoke eloquently about Podhoretz's continuing naiveté about politics. Not even Reagan's defense buildup, which dramatically strengthened American military capabilities, meant much to Podhoretz. He was unable to accept these realities and was left instead to make the strange charge that Ronald Reagan was soft on Communism. Podhoretz's experience, however, was not representative of all the neoconservatives'. Jeane Kirkpatrick and Elliott Abrams, for example, found Reagan's first term to be a golden opportunity to translate their convictions into actions, and they both flourished on the ideological struggles in which they engaged.

The neoconservatives who came to Washington to work for Ronald Reagan, unlike those who stayed in New York, were experienced politicians. Kirkpatrick, who was appointed ambassador to the United Nations, had been active in Montgomery County, Maryland, Democratic politics, and her husband, Evron, had worked closely with Hubert Humphrey. Elliott Abrams, Daniel Patrick Moynihan's former assistant, was made assistant secretary of state for international organizations. Richard Perle became assistant secretary of defense for international security policy. Max Kampelman, a member of the Committee on the Present Danger and another Humphrey associate, remained head of the American delegation to the Madrid meeting of the Conference on Security and Cooperation in Europe, an appointment he had received from Carter in 1980. None had been Republicans and, except for Kirkpatrick, a professor of political science at Georgetown University, none were intellectuals. They understood the realities of governing, however, and knew that ideological purity would sometimes have to be compromised. But, as the cases of Kirkpatrick and Abrams show, they also had strong convictions and the political ability to put their ideas into action.

Kirkpatrick went to the United Nations determined to speak up for the United States. As a member of the Reagan cabinet, she told the Senate Foreign Relations Committee at her confirmation hearing, "I expect to make a regular and meaningful contribution to the development of the foreign policy of the Reagan administration, which, at the UN, it will then be my job to articulate, explain, and defend." Moreover, she told the senators, she would "speak clearly" and let those "engag[ed] in mischievous ideological struggle against the fundamental principles of the United States . . . know that the patience of the American people is running very thin." Her strong stand invited comparisons with Moynihan, but the less flamboyant Kirkpatrick emphasized only their substantive similarities and distinguished between their styles. "I never seek confrontation with anybody," she told the *New York Times* in January 1981. "But if I must, I do. It is useful from time to time to affirm that we are not a racist, genocidal, imperialist power."[22]

Kirkpatrick made it clear as well that she would be the Reagan administration's leading voice for the values of democracy. The United Nations, she noted at her confirmation hearing, had been founded on the principles of "rule of law, individual dignity, human liberty, and the four freedoms," and that "it should become a first priority for the United States . . . to restore the United Nations to these initial commitments and values." Kirkpatrick viewed the assertion of democratic values as the core of Reagan's foreign policy. She and Reagan, Kirkpatrick told the senators, shared "some common purposes and some common understandings about the nature of our world and our problems, and I think that those common understandings relate both to our reading of the American tradition and what the United States stands for, which is, I think above all, individual freedom." Four months later, Kirkpatrick told an audience in Rome that "liberal beliefs and practices lie at the core of the Reagan administration's orientation toward politics, economics, and policy." With these statements Kirkpatrick claimed not only that she and Reagan held the same views but also that she spoke for both of them. As the administration's leading political theorist, moreover, she was in a position to define what was meant by "liberal democracy," taking for herself a prominent role in setting the ideological agenda.[23]

Once confirmed, Kirkpatrick recruited a staff of like-minded individuals, none of whom were professional diplomats. She was suspicious of the State Department officers who worked at the U.S. Mission to the United Nations, many of whom, she told Allan Gerson, "don't really approach issues from the viewpoint of U.S. interests and American policies, values, and concerns." Kirkpatrick hired Gerson, an international lawyer, to be her counsel. Carl Gershman became Kirkpatrick's chief counselor and José Sorzano, a Cuban exile, was made representative to the Economic and Social Council. Kenneth Adelman served as Kirkpatrick's deputy, Charles Lichenstein, an old friend of Kirkpatrick's and a Yale classmate of William F. Buckley, Jr., was responsible for the Security Council, and Joe Shattan wrote speeches. As political scientist Seymour Finger wrote at the end of 1983, "only those of the *Commentary*-Georgetown-neoconservative team are in the inner circle."[24]

Kirkpatrick soon became involved in a running feud with Secretary of State Alexander Haig over the issue of who would control policy at the United Nations. This problem had plagued several administrations, largely because the ambassador to the United Nations is statutorily independent but still must cooperate with overall foreign policy strategies. The ambassador also depends on the State Department for personnel and support. Haig and Kirkpatrick fought for months, with Haig maneuvering behind the scenes to embarrass Kirkpatrick and make her look amateurish. Reagan consistently supported Kirkpatrick, however, and Haig's politicking eventually became an embarrassment to the administration. Haig's resignation in late June 1982 freed Kirkpatrick from significant State Department interference until she left the administration in early 1985.[25]

Even as she fought with Haig, Kirkpatrick made clear what her approach to the United Nations would be. She portrayed herself as the true successor to Moynihan, taking the United Nations and its rhetoric seriously and making it clear that she would stand up for the United States. In 1982, she told the Foreign Policy Association: "*I begin from the proposition that the United Nations is important.* It is not, as some would like to pretend, a world unto itself, insulated, without consequences for events . . . the alliances and the rhetoric that develop there—have consequences cumulatively important beyond Turtle Bay." She freely and approvingly quoted Moynihan in her speeches in 1981 and 1982 and sometimes implicitly compared her performance to his, and she happily noted the attention paid to her speeches, as when an "amiable European colleague accused me of 'Libyan rhetoric.'" Like Moynihan, Kirkpatrick wanted to make it clear that attacking the United States carried a price. Her goal, she told a correspondent from *National Review*, was "to treat multilateral diplomacy not as diplomacy, but as politics," and, as Carl Gershman noted, "to introduce more accountability into voting."[26]

Kirkpatrick began her Moynihan-style counteroffensive in October 1981, when she responded to an anti-American communiqué issued by the Nonaligned Movement. The report, adopted in late September by the 93 Third World states in the movement, blamed many of the world's ills—including the nuclear arms race, the problems of the Palestinians, and the destabilizations of Nicaragua, Cuba, and Grenada—squarely on the United States. A week later, Kirkpatrick wrote to the UN ambassadors of 40 of the signatories, telling each that "I think you no more believe these vicious lies than I do," and asking for explanations of their countries' stands. With some grumbling, about half the recipients replied. According to Allan Gerson, "most said, in apologetic tones, that it was not their intention to malign the United States; indeed, they didn't even think that their communiqué would be taken seriously by U.S. officials." Kirkpatrick had, in effect, served notice that those countries which criticized the United States, however ritualistic or hollow their rhetoric, would be held accountable for their words.[27]

Kirkpatrick and her staff orchestrated the defense of American and Western interests on other fronts as well. She consistently supported Israel in the Security Council and the General Assembly against "an ongoing process whose goals are to delegitimize . . . [Israel and] to deny it the right to self-defense, to secure borders, to survival." In September 1983, after the Soviets shot down a Korean airliner that had strayed into Soviet airspace, killing 269 passengers and crew, Kirkpatrick called the incident a "calculated attack on a civilian airliner." She bluntly told the Security Council that "violence and lies are regular instruments of Soviet policy," and that the USSR was "a state based on the dual principles of callousness and mendacity." In another case, Gershman defended Wilsonian principles before the Third Committee and contrasted them with Soviet behavior:

> The consequences of the Wilsonian idea of self-determination may be observed in . . . the disman-tling of the European colonial possessions and the corresponding emergence of scores of independent nation states.
>
> The Leninist approach has resulted in the consolidation and expansion of the last remaining empire on earth. The fact that this latter development has been justified in terms of the fulfillment of the right of self-determination . . . is a powerful example of the perversion of language.

Gershman had clearly struck a nerve, for an entire session of the Third Committee then had to be devoted to the infuriated responses of the Soviet Union and its allies. Gershman dismissed these as merely rationalizing "the projection and pursuit of power."[28]

Kirkpatrick did not measure her success in these efforts by the outcome of United Nations votes. The United States continued to be outvoted and Kirkpatrick herself continued to be criticized for a confrontational style that served "the interests neither of the United States nor the United Nations," in Seymour Finger's words. But Kirkpatrick and her staff saw it differently. They took words very seriously, believing that they had real consequences. For them, conducting ideological warfare was important for its own sake and merely speaking up represented progress from what they saw as the disastrous passivity of the Carter era. Gerson caught this mood when he recalled that "the United States would not be a willing victim . . . the 'kick me' sign . . . [was] off the door."[29]

In addition to her defense of the United States, Kirkpatrick spoke frequently on the nature and problems of democracy and provided important ideological support for the Reagan administration's policies. "There is only one kind of government I approve of and should like all people to live under—democratic government," she told George Urban in late 1984. In addition, she told Urban, "There has developed, among representatives of Western nations, a strange timidity . . . that has left us deficient in our affirmation of the superiority of freedom. . . . The President has given a lead by quashing this timidity." Kirkpatrick continued to see democracy in evolutionary terms. Following the reasoning she had outlined in 1979 in "Dictatorships and Double Standards," she argued that such a system could not be imposed from without or perfected overnight. Instead, she noted, the political and social bases which support majority rule and protect minority rights did not exist in most countries and, until they were firmly established, democratic governments would be "difficult to establish and maintain."[30]

Kirkpatrick used this framework most effectively to support the administration's policies in the Caribbean and Central America. Democracies, she argued, have a right to defend themselves and each other against totalitarian challenges. Following the invasion of Grenada Kirkpatrick told the Security Council that "the [UN] charter does not require that people submit supinely to terror, nor that their neighbors be indifferent to their terrorization." Kirkpatrick applied this argument in other situations. "We do not think it is moral to leave small countries and helpless people defenseless against conquest by violent minorities," she said of El Salvador in 1984.[31]

The Reagan policy of supporting El Salvador's gradual democratization while helping it fight Marxist insurgents was another application of Kirkpatrick's theories of democratic development. She readily admitted that El Salvador's problems were complex, telling European audiences in the spring of 1984, "The government headed by Ronald Reagan has not the slightest tendency to imagine that the political turmoil in Central America has no roots in social and economic problems . . . neglect, unmet needs, unfulfilled hopes." She further acknowledged that democracy had not yet taken firm root in the region, but insisted that progress was being made. "The government of El Salvador is made up of democrats who respect the right of the El Salvadorean people to choose their rulers," she told the Third

Committee in late 1981. Such a fledgling democracy, she concluded, had to be helped: "Actions that weaken the government of El Salvador today strengthen those who all over the world undermine peace, democracy, national independence, and the self-determination of peoples." Thus, by looking at the situation in El Salvador in 1984—"a process of democratic development in El Salvador . . . warmly supported by the Salvadorean people"—through the perspective she had established in 1979 and 1980, Kirkpatrick was satisfied with results of the administration's policies.[32]

In contrast to Jeane Kirkpatrick, Elliott Abrams had not come to the State Department with a clear sense of mission. Although an intelligent and hard-driving man, he was not as original a thinker as Kirkpatrick and he tended to follow the ideological paths set out by other neoconservatives. Abrams saw a job in the new administration as a reward for his campaign work and, given his interests, decided to seek a position at State. "I looked at the bureaus at State," he recalled in 1990. "The one that it seemed to me was the best . . . was IO [International Organizations] because it did a little bit of ideological warfare, which I knew about, and it had the UN." Abrams recalls planning to ask for the job of deputy assistant secretary, but that Daniel Patrick Moynihan told him to aim one step higher, for the job of assistant secretary. Abrams made his bid, was nominated, and was quickly confirmed.[33]

Abrams was assistant secretary of state for international organization affairs for less than a year, during which time he learned a great deal about the State Department, but otherwise did little. In one sense, the bureau was a backwater: "What was controversial in 1981? Infant formula, UNESCO, a little bit. . . . The UN budget, which is of no interest to anybody. . . . I testified a couple of times. I think I did actually make very few statements at IO." But other aspects of the job compensated for its obscurity. Abrams had turned 33 soon after Reagan's inauguration and had a tremendous sense of personal achievement. "I was on an almost vertical learning curve about the Department of State and the U.S. government's foreign affairs," he remembered.[34]

Abrams's exhilaration over his job did not last. Although he was nominally in charge of American policy at the United Nations, he found that Kirkpatrick was determined to run her own show in New York. Abrams was as strong-willed as Kirkpatrick, but because she was a cabinet member as well as a friend of Reagan's, she outranked him and could easily outmaneuver him. Abrams and Kirkpatrick first clashed in June 1981, when Kirkpatrick supported, and Abrams opposed, a Security Council resolution condemning Israel's air attack on an Iraqi nuclear reactor. Kirkpatrick won and Abrams probably began to see that his power at IO—and perhaps his tenure—would be limited. "It was an unfortunate situation, since Jeane and I were friends . . . there was a surfeit of neoconservatives there," he recalled later. Fortunately for Abrams, the situation was soon resolved. The nomination of Ernest Lefever to be assistant secretary of state for human rights affairs had become stalled in the Senate and was withdrawn in June 1981. That fall, with the position still vacant, Abrams volunteered to take Lefever's place, thereby getting out of Kirkpatrick's way and taking a job that had a higher public profile and, as Abrams told the *New York Times*, was "more interesting, more intellectual." He was confirmed by the Senate in November 1981.[35]

Abrams came to his human rights assignment with a much clearer plan of action than he had had for IO. His experience with Kirkpatrick had shown him that he would have to have well-defined goals and authority if he was to secure his bureaucratic power. In late October 1981, a memo from Deputy Secretary of State William Clark to Haig—drafted by Abrams, according to the *New Republic*—claimed that human rights would have to be "at the core" of foreign policy, largely because it represented what was "ultimately at issue in our contest with the Soviet bloc." Furthermore, the memo claimed that a strong human rights stand was vital to maintaining domestic support for the administration's policies. Clark urged a two-track policy, attacking rights violations and speaking out in support of moral standards, while restraining criticisms and retaliations when they went against broader American interests. The overall argument drew heavily on points made by Kirkpatrick and Moynihan during the 1970s. "Our struggle is for political liberty," noted the memo, although it cautioned that "human rights is not advanced by replacing a bad regime with a worse one, or a corrupt dictator with a zealous Communist politburo." The memo specifically warned that a strong human rights policy would not be without costs, a point that the neoconservatives believed the Carter administration, at least initially, had not fully grasped: "A human rights policy means trouble, for it means hard choices which may adversely affect certain bilateral relations. At the very least, we will have to speak honestly about our friends' human rights violations." Finally, the memo recommended broad authority for Abrams to make new appointments in the Human Rights Bureau and to make policy on his own. The memo and its recommendations were approved, reportedly by Reagan himself, and Abrams set out to remake human rights policy.[36]

Following Kirkpatrick's ideological lead, Abrams portrayed Communism as the greatest threat to human rights. "To prevent virtually any country from being taken over by a Communist regime tied to the Soviet Union is in our view a very real victory for the cause of human rights," he said in March 1982. This thinking was also quickly integrated into policy statements. "It is a significant service to the cause of human rights to limit the influence the USSR . . . can exert," he wrote in the introduction to *Country Reports on Human Rights Practices for 1981*. In addition, Abrams followed Kirkpatrick in seeing a strong United States as an integral part of promoting human rights: "The strength and prestige of the most powerful democratic nation is inevitably important for human rights."[37]

Despite their similar outlooks, there were important stylistic differences between Abrams and Kirkpatrick. Kirkpatrick spoke in cool professorial tones, often supporting her arguments with scholarly references. In contrast, Abrams frequently used blunt language in merciless attacks against his opponents, whether they were Cuban Communists or American leftists. In preparing for a speech, he later recalled, "Sometimes . . . I would say [to speechwriter Joe Shattan] . . . let's talk about all the morons who have been pro-Cuba over the years. See if you can dig out the disgraceful record of these people."

The result would be a speech which was as frank as the office discussion: "The facts about Cuban repression have been available for many years now. Yet for just as many years, not a few intellectuals and journalists have been systematically denying these facts. I will not attempt, at this time, to describe this rather disgraceful episode in detail." Abrams relished the responses to his attacks as indicators of his effectiveness. In March 1982, shortly after the Cuban Communist Party's newspaper *Granma* called him "an animal," Abrams sent a copy of the editorial to Norman Podhoretz with a note claiming, "I have achieved greatness."[38]

Abrams used his combative style not only to bash leftists, but also to pursue vigorously the approach to human rights outlined in the October 1981 memo. "Our foreign policy must be shaped by the moral ideals and values of the American people," he wrote in June 1983. Much of his effort was devoted to fighting the double standard which he and many other neoconservatives believed governed most liberals' human rights thinking. In the 1981 edition of *Country Reports on Human Rights Practices*, for example, he wrote of the administration's efforts to fight "the hypocrisy of current double standards, discrimination against Latin American countries and indifference to violations by the Soviet Union and its Communist allies." Clarifying standards and facing difficult issues honestly, Abrams believed, would strengthen the human rights effort, and in his speeches and articles he often combined these efforts with support for American policy in Central America. In a September 1982 speech, for example, he argued that "the debate [over human rights in Central America] has been flawed by an unwillingness to come to grips with certain key issues." The focus, according to Abrams, had been skewed as "Those who insist on examining El Salvador with a microscope, while seeing no evil in Nicaragua, are undermining the claim of the human rights movement to be interested in people, rather than in politics."[39]

Abrams also followed Kirkpatrick's intellectual lead in not just defending, but encouraging the spread of democracy. Democratic systems, Abrams believed, were the best protection for human rights. The administration, he wrote in early 1983, saw a "connection between human rights and democracy. . . . The administration is indeed ideologically committed to democracy. We believe, moreover, that there is a clear connection between respect for human rights and a democratic form of government." Abrams gradually became more specific in his definition of democracy. His model was unabashedly American, in which democracy was "a form of government which is based on the freely given consent of the governed," with guaranteed rights of free expression and dissent as well as protection of minority rights. Like Kirkpatrick, Abrams saw the building and spreading of democracy as a gradual process. Unlike Norman Podhoretz, Kirkpatrick and Abrams did not require the rollback of the Soviet empire before they could claim any successes. "The task of believers in democracy is not to impose democracy on a world bitterly opposed to it, but rather to help fulfill the expectations that every people acknowledges for itself," Abrams argued. He further noted, in terms reminiscent of Niebuhr, that "any efforts we make on behalf of democracy, small as they may be, are sustained by democracy's gradual expansion since the days of the American Revolution."[40]

Abrams did not see these ideas as mere abstractions; rather, they had an immediacy that reflected reality. In El Salvador, he noted in July 1982, conditions for establishing democracy and improving human rights "could hardly be worse," and "progress has been measured in inches, not miles." Nonetheless, he argued, the government had to be supported against the insurgents. "Democracy is the central issue in El Salvador. Its strengthening will lead to a further reduction of human rights violations. The current government must be given the opportunity to complete what it has begun." The following year Abrams strongly defended the invasion of Grenada by saying "we are interested in attaining results and not in issuing pious pronouncements," and that "we generally commit ourselves to effective action on behalf of our principles."[41]

Along with his public rhetoric, Abrams used traditional diplomatic methods to advance the causes of human rights and democracy. He sought to tailor the means to the situation, preferring a quiet approach even though it left him open to criticism for appearing to be inactive:

> While public pressure from the United States Gov-
> ernment is occasionally the only possible hope of
> curtailing specific abuses in specific countries,
> quiet diplomacy has often been found more likely
> to obtain concrete results. Let me emphasize here
> that such "quiet" diplomacy requires frank and
> thorough exchanges with the countries involved.

Abrams remained sensitive to the charge of inactivity. In his introduction to the 1983 edition of *Country Reports* he argued that "the phrase 'quiet diplomacy' does not fully convey either the intensity of American efforts, or the depth of our concern . . . in many cases, this kind of intercession has proven an effective response to human rights violations."[42]

One of Abrams's most tenacious efforts at quiet diplomacy involved Chile, where General Augusto Pinochet had ruled since overthrowing President Salvador Allende in 1973. The Reagan administration was initially sympathetic to Pinochet, seeing him as the man who stood between Chile and a Communist takeover. Abrams, however, stood out for his opposition to this view. According to Thomas Carothers, who served in the State Department's Office of the Legal Adviser during the second Reagan administration, Abrams "argued forcefully within the administration for a vigorous policy of pressure against Pinochet on human rights and democracy issues." Abrams based much of his argument on the need to oppose right wing dictators if the administration were to retain its credibility as an opponent of leftist rulers, according to Carothers. Abrams later recalled that this position earned him some hostility from conservatives. "I figure prominently as a villain for trying to get rid of Pinochet. That view is widespread on the right." Abrams stuck to his position through intense policy arguments in 1983 and 1984, managing to moderate policy. According to Carothers, "the administration maintained a basically friendly policy toward Pinochet but began leavening it with more pointed private discussions . . . regarding U.S. human rights concerns and a somewhat less uniformly positive public line." In 1985, after Abrams became assistant secretary of state for inter-American affairs, policy shifted to full support for democratization in Chile.[43]

Kirkpatrick and Abrams viewed the Reagan administration's foreign policies as greatly successful. Unlike Podhoretz, their goals and expectations had been limited. Instead of seeing their partial victories as failures, they viewed them as progress and took pride in them, remembering Niebuhr's point about the "fragmentary and broken character of all historic achievements." Kirkpatrick told the *New York Times* that "four years ago the United States could be and was isolated and humiliated, and that is not easy anymore," but that now, "a great deal less time is spent in the UN on festivals of hate, invective, and abuse." For Abrams, these were the years in which Reagan "stopped their [the Soviets'] free, or at least easy, victories in the Third World . . . [and] made the Soviets realize that these were now going to be expensive."[44]

Reagan's term had also brought personal rewards. Kirkpatrick's keynote speech to the 1984 Republican convention—a proud recitation of Reagan's achievements and a gleeful assault on "the San Francisco Democrats" who "always blame America first" for the world's ills—made headlines the next day and led to speculation about a presidential candidacy in 1988. Abrams's promotion to inter-American affairs, the job he held until Reagan left office, made him the administration's point man for Central American policy.[45]

Abrams's and Kirkpatrick's taste and talent for ideological combat and influence also demonstrated how the neoconservative's Wilsonian strain had come to the fore. This impulse, which sought to spread democracy actively rather than wait for it to spread gradually, was not original with the neoconservatives. In fact, its post-1945 incarnation can be traced to Arthur M. Schlesinger's call to make democracy a fighting faith—a Wilsonian point which remained a part of the neoconservative worldview. For example, in May 1974 (almost a year before he went to the United Nations), Daniel Patrick Moynihan wrote of "the duty to defend and, where feasible, to advance democratic principles in the world at large." In the shaken atmosphere of the mid-1970s, however, while battling Henry Kissinger almost as much as Third World extremism, Moynihan had been unable to have his Wilsonian vision adopted by the Ford administration.[46]

In the 1980s, however, the neoconservatives were able to pursue the institutionalization of Wilsonian and democratic goals within the government's foreign policy establishment. With a friendly president who was predisposed toward such a view, and figures such as Abrams, Kirkpatrick, and Kampelman sprinkled around the administration, the situation was radically different from the Ford-Kissinger years. Reagan's June 1982 address to the British Parliament demonstrated how influential neoconservative Wilsonian thinking had become. "We must take actions to assist the campaign for democracy," Reagan said. "The objective I propose is quite simple to state: to foster the infrastructure of democracy, the system of a free press, unions, political parties, universities, which allows a people to choose their own way to develop their own culture, to reconcile their own differences through peaceful means."[47]

The administration moved to institutionalize these views during the year that followed Reagan's London speech. It established Project Democracy, involving the chairmen of the Democratic and Republican parties, the president of the AFL-CIO, and congressional representatives and business executives to study "how the United States— particularly its nongovernmental organizations—can work to strengthen democracy abroad," Secretary of State George P. Shultz told the House Foreign Affairs Committee in February 1983. Furthermore, said Shultz, the project would emphasize leadership training, education, conveying ideas, and aiding foreign democratic institutions. The guiding philosophy of Project Democracy showed Kirkpatrick's influence. According to Shultz, "We are interested in assisting constructive change which can lead to greater political stability, social justice, and economic progress. We do not seek destabilization. Change must come from within, not be imposed from outside. It must follow a path dictated by national and local traditions." In the fall of 1983, Congress established the National Endowment for Democracy to funnel money to foreign groups and to assist democratic institution building efforts. Carl Gershman was appointed president. By the end of the decade, Gershman and the endowment were active throughout the developing world and Eastern Europe, providing training, money, and technical assistance, such as helping to administer orderly elections, to individuals, groups, and governments in newly democratizing countries.[48]

The establishment of the endowment was a significant triumph for the neoconservative politicians. Not only was there a quasi-governmental agency in place to help democrats overseas, but its underlying concept and goals were in accordance with neoconservative ideas. Moreover, the endowment formed a visible link to the neoconservatives' roots in the vital center—especially with its bipartisan support and connections to organized labor—with the added advantage that its establishment strengthened their claim to being the legitimate heirs of liberal internationalism. It also provided a base for promoting the neoconservative vision of internationalism once the neoconservatives themselves left the government. Ironically, however, Daniel Patrick Moynihan, to whom the endowment owed as great an intellectual debt as anyone, did not share in the triumph. By 1984 he had been expelled from the neoconservative ranks.

Moynihan remained firmly in the neoconservative camp after the election of 1980. The Democrats, he claimed in mid-November, had lost because they had no new ideas to offer, only old ones that were far to the left of most Americans' beliefs. Liberal Democrats, in Moynihan's view, believed that "government should be powerful and America should be weak," and he pledged to fight a takeover of the party "by some of the most vigorous supporters of Senator Kennedy," who had weakened the Democrats through their insistence on "doctrinal purity." In addition, he was among those who, according to the *Washington Post*, "spoke glowingly" of Kirkpatrick at a February

1981 Washington luncheon held by the Coalition for a Democratic Majority to celebrate her confirmation as ambassador.[49]

Also in February 1981, Moynihan took a retrospective look at the Carter administration's foreign policy failings and tried to draw some conclusions about what they meant for liberals. His analysis, which appeared in *Commentary*, focused on American behavior at the United Nations, where the Carter administration, Moynihan asserted, had adopted the liberal view that the United States was "a principal source of instability and injustice in the world . . . [that] the status quo we were trying to preserve was abominable." In order to maintain good relations with Third World nations in general, Moynihan argued, and to gain their support at the United Nations in particular, the administration had specifically rejected his confrontational style and started with the "proposition that if the United States put itself on the 'right' side of history, we would find the nations of the world, most of which of course were 'new,' coming over to our side in turn."[50]

Specifically, Moynihan charged, the United States had given up its defense of Israel. Not only had Washington acquiesced in the March 1980 Security Council resolution on Jerusalem—the vote "was no mistake at all," Moynihan concluded, for it reflected the administration's "conception of the world"—it had vetoed only one of nine anti-Israel Security Council resolutions in 1979 and 1980, and accepted the gradual redefinition of Israel as an outlaw state. Thus, according to Moynihan, the administration blinded itself to the "genuine hostility toward the United States in the world and true conflicts of interest between this nation and others."[51]

Moynihan linked the Carter administration's performance at the United Nations with the Democrats' troubles. He repeated the core of his argument from the mid-1970s, that the Soviet-Arab campaign against Israel was also one against Western democracy and peaceful nations. The administration, he noted, had avoided conflict at the United Nations by remaining silent in the face of the onslaught. But, Moynihan explained, the failure to fight back had led to a surrender—"thus in our flight from 'confrontation' did we end not by

understanding the perspectives of others but by adopting them"—
with disastrous results both at home and abroad:

> American failure was total. And it was squalid.
> These men [Secretary Vance, and UN Ambas-
> sadors Young and McHenry], in New York and
> Washington, helped to destroy the President who
> appointed them, deeply injured the President's
> party, hurt the United States, and hurt nations
> that have stood with the United States in seeking
> something like peace in the Middle East. They
> came to office full of themselves and empty of any
> steady understanding of the world. The world was
> a more dangerous place when at last they went
> away.

Thus, Moynihan concluded, "so long as the ideas underlying the
Carter administration's UN policy are dominant within the Democratic party, we Democrats will be out of power."[52]

Moynihan remained a supporter of a hardline foreign policy
through the remainder of 1981. At times, in fact, he was critical of
the Reagan administration for being too soft. He viewed the resump-
tion of grain sales to the Soviet Union as "feeding the army that's
bent on raping Poland," and called it "an act of contempt" when,
immediately after the United States agreed to sell arms to China, Bei-
jing announced that it was resuming border talks with Moscow. "The
administration has proclaimed a foreign policy of heroes and is car-
rying out a foreign policy of Babbitts," he declared. All was not bleak,
however. In October, Moynihan supported Kirkpatrick's attack on the
nonaligned nations' communique by introducing, and seeing passed,
an amendment to the Foreign Assistance Bill requiring the president
to consider a country's stand on the declaration when making aid
decisions.[53]

Moynihan remained largely silent on foreign issues in 1982, focusing instead on domestic issues of greater relevance to his reelection
campaign. Mindful of the dangers he faced running in a liberal state,

Moynihan distanced himself from the Reagan administration. Many of his writings, for example, were critical of the administration's budgetary, fiscal, and economic policies. He also emphasized his traditional theme of the family, wondering, in one case, how to "provide ways to support dependent children without introducing incentives to child abandonment." The strategy was effective; Moynihan defeated a weak Republican challenger by more than a million votes.[54]

When Moynihan resumed speaking on foreign affairs in 1983, it soon became clear that his views on the danger from Third World radicalism had changed significantly. For the first time, his statements sounded confused and contradictory, particularly when he spoke on Latin American issues; this stood in stark contrast to his clear, strident rhetoric of the previous ten years. Sometimes, for example, he supported aid to El Salvador: "We have a right to help El Salvador, and we have a responsibility to do so," he remarked in the spring of 1983. But Moynihan made other statements which indicated that his commitment to helping El Salvador was limited. In April 1983, for example, he cast doubt on the effectiveness of aid, commenting that some argued that "if we could just train the Salvadorans, why all would be well," but "we've been training the Salvadorans for a quarter of a century."[55]

Moynihan gradually became less convinced that a leftist victory in El Salvador would be disastrous or was even likely. At the same time, however, his public statements became only more confusing. In June 1983, for example, when asked if a guerrilla victory would affect American security, he replied: "These things are still fundamentally internal and won't go external unless the Soviet Union decides that's what they should do." In January 1984, however, Moynihan told an interviewer that he was not convinced that Soviet and Cuban policies in Central America represented a threat to the United States. Furthermore, according to Moynihan, the insurgents in El Salvador had come to see that Washington would defend its interests in the region and, therefore, saw the "necessity of an accommodation with the United States."[56]

Moynihan's confusing statements on El Salvador in 1983 and 1984 reflected his increasing tendency to question some of the basic premises of the Reagan administration's view of the world. Moynihan concluded that the looming totalitarian danger which had justified the administration's actions was passing rapidly. In May 1984, he told the graduating class of New York University:

> The Soviet idea is spent. It commands some influence in the world; and fear. But it summons no loyalty. History is moving away from it with astounding speed.
>
> We must be less obsessed with the Soviets. If we must learn to live with military parity, let us keep all the more in mind that we have consolidated an overwhelming economic advantage.

Instead of concentrating on military and ideological rivalries, Moynihan suggested that the United States should begin paying attention to a new set of global problems, including the world monetary system, terrorism, and what he called "tribalism . . . challenging the traditions of modernity."[57]

In accordance with his changing priorities, Moynihan opposed the Reagan administration more strongly and consistently on the other major Latin American issue of 1983 and 1984, aid to the contra rebels fighting the Marxist Sandinista government of Nicaragua. This was often connected to aid for the government of El Salvador, because the Sandinistas were supplying arms to the Salvadoran rebels, and aid to the contras was viewed as one way of pressuring the Sandinistas to end their assistance. Moynihan, however, was not convinced this could be done or, apparently, that it should be attempted: "One hates to say it, but the capacity to control events in a consolidating Marxist-Leninist country like Nicaragua is very limited and we have to face that."[58]

Moynihan was especially disturbed by the way aid to the contras was administered. In 1982, Congress made it illegal for the United States to aid rebel groups in their efforts to overthrow the Sandinistas; instead, aid was to be given to groups only for limited, tangential purposes, such as helping them interdict Nicaraguan arms shipments to El Salvador. In practice, these distinctions were virtually impossible to enforce. Moreover, the Central Intelligence Agency served as the conduit for assistance to the contras, and the agency's secrecy inevitably led to suspicions that the administration was ignoring the law. "A growing number of my colleagues question whether the CIA is complying with the law," Moynihan said in April 1983. "We may have to rewrite the law to make more explicit what our intentions are. I don't think intelligence officials have taken the measure of our concern."[59]

Moynihan's misgivings about the administration's policies came to a head in the spring of 1984, just as he was concluding that the Soviet threat was fading. In January the contras laid small mines in Nicaraguan harbors. In early April, the *Wall Street Journal* disclosed that the CIA had helped the contras with the mining. A dispute developed over whether the CIA had told the Senate Intelligence Committee about its role in the operation, as required by law. Moynihan and committee chairman Barry Goldwater claimed it had not, but Director of Central Intelligence William Casey disagreed, arguing that the agency had fulfilled its obligations by telling the committee of the mining, in passing, during a long briefing in March 1984. Moynihan was more upset by Casey's cavalier attitude toward the committee than by the mining. If Casey had simply said, "I'm sorry, we goofed, we won't do it again," noted Moynihan, "that would be acceptable."[60]

Moynihan sought a way to make his anger with the CIA public, prominent, and effective. On April 15, he announced that he was resigning as vice-chairman of the Intelligence Committee. The action, he declared, was "the most emphatic way I can express my view that the Senate committee was *not* properly briefed on the mining." Moynihan's maneuver had its desired impact. On April 26, following an agreement in which the committee said that it had not been adequately briefed and Casey concurred and apologized, Moynihan retracted his resignation. The episode must have been satisfying to Moynihan. He had made headlines by standing up to the administration and the CIA, although he had not opposed the contras them-

selves, and he had been able to resign publicly over a matter of principle and still keep his post. If nothing else, it was another demonstration of the political skills Moynihan had developed during his two
decades in Washington.[61]

The mining affair also highlighted Moynihan's increasing interest
in international law. Legal issues had long been implicit in his thinking, as shown by his concern over the effects of the attacks on the
legitimacy of Israel. Starting in 1983, however, he had begun to wonder if the United States was itself becoming a violator of law and
international norms. Discussing the October 1983 invasion of
Grenada, he remarked, "We have a set of propositions the countries
of the world have committed themselves to. We should hold the countries of the world to those commitments, ourselves included." Not
even the defense of democracy justified the invasion, in Moynihan's
view. "I don't think they should have gone in the way they did," he
told the *New York Times*, noting that "in the long run, the principle of
nonintervention is so important."[62]

The Nicaraguan mining controversy came six months after
Grenada and, to Moynihan, was another blatant violation of international law. "A commitment to law," he wrote, "ought to be understood
not as a commitment never to use force, but rather to use force only
as an instrument of law." The mining, however, had gone "considerably beyond the law—both American law as the Senate meant it to
be understood, and international law as the world understands it."[63]

The hardline neoconservatives were perplexed by Moynihan's
seeming defection. At first they rationalized his change as a temporary political ploy, a case of a politician saying things in order to be
reelected, and therefore as only a temporary deviation. Conservative
writer Dinesh D'Souza quoted one unnamed neoconservative as saying, "I expected Pat to give up his political posturing around November 10, 1982," a week after the election. But by mid-1983, the
realization was growing that Moynihan meant what he was saying.
"We all believe Pat is making an error," said Elliott Abrams in June.[64]

Just as important as Moynihan's apparent ideological defection
was the personal dimension of the split. The angriest reaction came,

not surprisingly, from Norman Podhoretz. His July 1983 attack on "the new isolationists [who] would like to see a Marxist regime take over in El Salvador," and those who believed it "would . . . not . . . be a blow to the interests of the United States" was, according to the *New York Times*, "an implicit criticism" of Moynihan. Others were upset as well, if not as harsh in their words. Recalling that Podhoretz had "played a major role in the political emergence of Mr. Moynihan," *National Review* commented, it was "clearly the metamorphosis of Moynihan . . . that really hurts." Or, as Midge Decter put it in early 1991, "he broke our hearts."[65]

Worst of all, without Moynihan the neoconservatives no longer had a voice in the Democratic Party, let alone any chance for influence. Henry Jackson died in September 1983, by which time Moynihan's apostasy was acknowledged. Michael Novak asked, "Who remains within the Democratic Party to lead the Jackson Democrats, and where, now, will they find a home?" Abrams commented, "Senator Jackson is no longer with us and Senator Moynihan is no longer with us." In March 1984, Fred Barnes came to the obvious conclusion—without Moynihan, "the Jackson wing died."[66]

The neoconservatives became increasingly bitter over Moynihan's apparent betrayal, largely because of its effects on their own illusions. When Novak and Barnes wrote that the Jackson wing had died with the senator, they were writing almost four years too late. In truth, it had died in January 1980, when many of its most prominent members turned to Ronald Reagan, forfeiting whatever claim they had to influence within the Democratic party. It was Moynihan who had remained loyal to the party and it seems strange, in retrospect, that the neoconservatives believed that he still owed them complete loyalty or that they were entitled to a role in the party. That the neoconservatives felt that they were still somehow due such a role was yet another example of their innocence as politicians.[67]

Moynihan's shifts starkly revealed the tensions between neoconservative intellectuals and politicians. Moynihan still opposed radical leftism in the world but, in the early 1980s, preferred to see it as less of a threat than before. Not only did this make sense for him as a politician facing reelection but, by returning to his old and familiar themes of family and social issues, Moynihan could focus his energies on his areas of intellectual strength. Moreover, it enabled him to bolster his credentials as an opponent of the Republican administration and, therefore, as a Democrat in good standing with his party.

Podhoretz, on the other hand, had become so wedded to his views that he refused to accept that the situation could be changing, let alone improving. For over a decade, Podhoretz had been one of the towering figures of neoconservatism, a movement which he had done much to create and which relied on fighting radicalism for much of its cohesion. With a waning threat neoconservatism could begin to splinter and Podhoretz's influence, even with *Commentary* as a platform, might decrease. Consequently, Podhoretz had a good reason for following as hard a line as possible and attacking as heretics any who doubted that radicalism was as great a threat as ever. Whatever his remaining personal sympathies for Podhoretz, Moynihan the politician could not allow himself to follow such a trail, one which would soon lead to oblivion in liberal New York. Once again, ideology and politics had parted ways.

By early 1985 the neoconservatives' period of greatest success was drawing to a close. The departure of Kirkpatrick from the United Nations deprived them of their highest level and most influential voice in the administration. Although Abrams continued to fight for the hardline in Central America and support for the contras, Congressional opposition and a lack of popular support steadily undermined the policy. The Iran-contra scandal, which broke in November 1986, doomed any remaining prospects for all-out support to the contras. In the meantime, the momentum for an arms control agreement with the Soviets—which *Commentary* continued to oppose—grew steadily.

The greatest challenge to neoconservative ideology during the second Reagan administration, however, came not from Washington but from Moscow. Mikhail Gorbachev became the leader of the Soviet Union in March 1985 and soon began to implement a series of domestic reforms and a more conciliatory policy toward the West. Although these changes would contribute to the collapse of the Soviet empire between 1989 and 1991, their long-range implications were by no means clear during the early years of Gorbachev's tenure. Instead, a vigorous debate began in the United States over what, if anything, his reforms signified and how the West should react. This controversy led to further splits among the neoconservatives and, eventually, the marginalization of Norman Podhoretz and *Commentary* as voices in American foreign policy discussions.

6

After the
Cold War,

1985–1992

After their successes during Ronald Reagan's first term, the neoconservatives entered a period of increasing confusion. In large part, this was caused by an intellectual failure. The neoconservatives' view of the world assumed a stable, malevolent Soviet Union that was immune from drastic change; consequently, many contributors to *Commentary* first underestimated, and then tried to dismiss, the magnitude of the reforms and changes begun by the new Soviet leader, Mikhail Gorbachev. Some neoconservatives, however, realized that vast changes were afoot and that the cold war world would soon change. Led by Irving Kristol, they began debating the changing role of America in the world. By 1990 this group, clustered around Kristol's new magazine, the *National Interest*, was consistently producing more interesting and relevant articles than *Commentary*.

Simultaneously, the neoconservatives merged with the larger conservative movement. Their service in the Reagan administration, continuing estrangement from the Democrats, and their intellectual leadership of the right made the conservative movement their natural home. Nonetheless, the neoconservatives continued to be distinct from traditional midwestern and southern conservatives for their northeastern roots, combative style, and secularism. Their cohabitation on the right has been uneasy; many traditional conservatives, such as Russell Kirk and Patrick J. Buchanan, have viewed them as interlopers and the two factions have assaulted each other over allegations of anti-Semitism and in debates over who is a true conservative.

The neoconservative movement also began a generational transition. Younger neoconservatives and analysts influenced by neoconservatism—Elliott Abrams, William Kristol, Charles Krauthammer —began to assume the leadership positions long held by Irving Kristol, Norman Podhoretz, and Jeane Kirkpatrick. The first generation has many intellectual and political achievements to its credit. Although it is unlikely that the younger neoconservatives will go through the same series of intellectual and ideological shifts, they too appear poised for long and influential careers.

The quality of *Commentary*'s foreign policy writings declined sharply after 1984. From the early 1970s, one of *Commentary*'s virtues had been Norman Podhoretz's presentation of an unyielding anti-Communist, pro-American point of view. For traditional conservatives and neoconservatives alike, this had provided a steady ideological point of reference during a time of Soviet gains and uncertain American responses. Although Washington's policies shifted dramatically after Ronald Reagan became president in 1981, *Commentary* still provided its readers with a coherent analysis of the Soviet threat, even if its perception of Reagan's responses had become confused. This analytical framework worked well as long as Leonid Brezhnev and his immediate successors ruled the Soviet Union and kept their policies largely unchanged. Beginning in 1985, however, Mikhail Gorbachev's ascension to power in Moscow led to vast changes in the USSR and its international behavior, changes which *Commentary* was ill equipped to understand and which left its analyses increasingly divorced from reality.

In the view of *Commentary* and its contributors, the Soviet Union remained an expansionist power in the late 1980s. In fall of 1985, Walter Laqueur argued that the Soviet system was unchanged and would remain so: "No dissent will be tolerated which will endanger the perpetuation of the regime and the hold of the leadership. Basic political reform . . . is not possible under the Soviet system." Eugene Rostow echoed this view in 1987, when he claimed that Moscow's external behavior was fixed. "The Soviet program of indefinite expansion achieved by the aggressive use of force," he wrote, was still "the central problem . . . of world politics and American national security." When viewed in this context, any improvements in Western-Soviet, and particularly in American-Soviet, relations during Reagan's second term were illusory. "The case for the proposition that 'peace is breaking out all over' rests, at best, on American hopes attached to Soviet actions," wrote Angelo Codevilla in November 1988.[1]

Also in this period, some of *Commentary*'s writers began to view the Soviet Union as virtually invincible. Their pessimism, based on the belief that Reagan had helped the Soviets stabilize their empire in the early 1980s, was so deep that they interpreted Gorbachev's domestic reforms as evidence of the strength of the Communist system. "If there has been a certain relaxation of domestic pressure in the Eastern bloc," lamented Laqueur, "this is a consequence of the triumph rather than the failure of totalitarianism; the opposition has been crushed, large parts of the populations successfully indoctrinated, and in these circumstances there is no need for more drastic measures such as mass purges and executions." Similarly, the French intellectual Jean-François Revel told *Commentary*'s readers that Gorbachev's policy of glasnost was not to be believed. "It is an instrument through which the General Secretary can consolidate his own power by using the press to indict and, little by little, eliminate his predecessors' men." Consequently, no great changes could be expected in the USSR—"the glasnost era reached its climax in 1987 and . . . no substantial advances should be expected for years to come," wrote Laqueur in mid-1988—and the dictatorship in Moscow was as secure as ever.[2]

Commentary also believed that the United States remained vulnerable to Soviet military pressure, and contributors did not doubt that the pressure would be forthcoming. Somehow, in this view, the Reagan defense buildup had accomplished little or had not even kept the United States from falling further behind. According to Rostow, "The Soviet Union is a stronger military power than the United States, and . . . its military strength is growing more rapidly than ours, despite our rearmament efforts . . . [Gorbachev] knows that it is now on the verge of achieving overwhelming strength." In such an environment, arms control talks were viewed as simply foolish. According to Patrick Glynn, writing about the 1987 Intermediate Nuclear Force (INF) Treaty, under which intermediate range nuclear missiles would be eliminated, the Reagan administration had broken its promise to end America's strategic vulnerability. Instead, Glynn charged, it was "prepared at the end of seven years to sign an agreement which . . . will not only deepen our vulnerability but seal it for all time."[3]

By 1990 *Commentary*'s ideology had the same problem that had crippled the Progressives' beliefs 40 years earlier: its views were no longer an adequate guide for interpreting a changing reality. Since 1970, Podhoretz had increasingly defined *Commentary*'s stands by a rigid opposition to any compromise or flexibility in foreign policy. Indeed, since the Carter years Podhoretz's view of the world had been defined by what it opposed more than by what it favored, and dissenting views gradually disappeared from *Commentary*'s pages. As a result, *Commentary* had little to say about what kind of world it sought or what plans it proposed for creating it. As the Soviet Union and Communism deteriorated in the late 1980s, at first slowly but then with a rush after mid-1989, Podhoretz was robbed of his familiar world, left without direction, and saw his relevance decrease. Although Podhoretz was not the only foreign policy commentator overtaken by events and quickly confused, his long record of strident statements marked by a tone of absolute certainty left him with little cover for his misinterpretations.

Another sign of Podhoretz's growing disarray was the tone of

Commentary's attacks on opponents at home. These assaults had never been gentle, but now they took on an added note of hysteria. In January 1987, for example, Peter Collier and David Horowitz, former editors of the radical magazine *Ramparts*, warned that the remnants of the New Left were trying to turn the 1980s into another "low, dishonest decade"—W. H. Auden's label for the 1930s. Because the "post-Vietnam Left" still supported totalitarian movements, concluded Collier and Horowitz, "the time has come in the life of this nation to name these attitudes for what they are and to eliminate the taboos that prevent discussion of the dangers they pose." In addition to watching for signs of a New Left resurgence during Reagan's presidency, *Commentary* kept up its vigilance on mainstream liberalism, which could not be trusted, even after the Soviet threat was undeniably dead. In the fall of 1991, following the collapse of the USSR, Owen Harries (a Welsh-born political scientist and former Australian ambassador to UNESCO living in the United States) denounced those who had preferred "an anti-anti-Communist posture to a simple anti-Communist one," and who had given "higher priority to ending the cold war than to winning it."[4]

Podhoretz's rigidity cost *Commentary* dearly. After 1980, the journal lost many of the contributors who could have provided new insights or goals for its foreign policy writings. Daniel Patrick Moynihan was no longer welcome in its pages, Jeane Kirkpatrick contributed only one unimportant article after she left the United Nations, Robert W. Tucker, Nathan Glazer, Daniel Bell, and Seymour Martin Lipset no longer wrote for it, leaving the magazine without moderating influences to counter its outbursts of hysteria. Furthermore, Podhoretz had not cultivated a new generation of contributors with anywhere near the stature of Glazer, Bell, or Moynihan. The glory days of the 1970s—when a *Commentary* article could lead to an ambassadorship, establish policy for an administration, or become the focus of intellectuals' discussions across the country—were gone.

In the fall of 1985, Irving Kristol stepped forward to fill the vacuum created by *Commentary*'s decline, launching a foreign affairs

journal, the *National Interest*. Kristol wanted the new journal to
serve as a conservative platform "for thinking coherently about foreign policy," as he recalled in 1993, much as the *Public Interest* had
for domestic affairs. Editors Robert W. Tucker and Owen Harries
made this clear in the first issue: the *National Interest* would discuss
"the ideas that inform" American foreign policy and work "to make
that policy more effective and coherent." They frankly proclaimed
that in a world driven by power politics, "the primary and overriding
purpose of American foreign policy must be to defend and advance
the national interest of the United States," to which "the Soviet Union
constitutes the greatest threat." Kristol served as publisher, and
Midge Decter, Jeane Kirkpatrick, and Edward Luttwak were among
the largely neoconservative advisory board. The conservative Olin
and Smith Richardson foundations provided financial support.[5]

The *National Interest*'s neoconservatives quickly developed a
point of view that differed significantly with *Commentary*'s. Although
at first glance their assumptions did not seem far apart, the *National
Interest*'s contributors quickly sensed that the Soviets were weakening and that important changes might be coming. Henry Rowen, a
scholar at the Hoover Institution and a former government official,
wrote in early 1986 that Soviet "domestic problems are so basic and
intractable that we should expect important initiatives towards the
West in the next several years. . . . a significant foreign policy shift is
likely." Economic and technological problems, Rowen argued, were
likely to lead to a decline in Soviet military spending and renewed
efforts to obtain Western aid, although Moscow would still maintain
its "long term goal of trying to do the West in." Similarly, Tucker
wrote in late 1986 that the political, military, and economic issues
"that were found so threatening by the Reagan administration on
entering office have clearly, and in some instances dramatically,
turned for the better . . . the Soviet position has visibly declined."
Even as *Commentary* continued to warn against the Soviet threat,
other contributors to the *National Interest*, including a somewhat
inconsistent Luttwak, pointed to the USSR's growing troubles and
shrinking power.[6]

The most provocative piece to appear in the *National Interest*, however, focused on political theory rather than policy issues. In the summer of 1989, a few months before the East European Communist regimes collapsed, Harries published Francis Fukuyama's article "The End of History?" Fukuyama, a former RAND Corporation analyst and then deputy director of the State Department's Policy Planning Staff, used a Hegelian approach to interpret the meaning of the decline of Communism and concluded that the "triumph of the West, of the Western *idea* is evident . . . in the total exhaustion of viable systematic alternatives to Western liberalism." Consequently, "in the realm of ideas," argued Fukuyama, there would be the "universalization of Western liberal democracy as the final form of human government." Fukuyama's theory ignited a lively controversy among intellectuals and was soon the subject of numerous articles—both favorable and unfavorable—in op-ed pages, Sunday supplements, and magazines around the world. It was the "hottest topic around," according to James Atlas, an editor of the *New York Times Magazine*, even though it was not always clear that the discussants had read or understood what they were talking about.[7]

"The End of History?" made clear the *National Interest*'s ascendancy over *Commentary*. Like "The United States in Opposition," and "Dictatorships and Double Standards," more than a decade earlier, Fukuyama's article had created a new reference point for debate and a new buzzword for intellectuals. If Fukuyama was correct, for example, the question of how to respond to Gorbachev was irrelevant, for liberal, Western political values were simply extending themselves. The question of how to ensure national security would also be superseded, for Fukuyama had postulated the continuing "diminution of the likelihood of large-scale conflict between states." Suddenly, *Commentary* appeared not only to be providing old answers to old questions, but it no longer seemed even to be making the right inquiries. The fact that "The End of History?" had not appeared in *Commentary*, or in any New York-based publication, further underscored how the *National Interest* and Washington-based writers had seized the intellectual leadership in foreign affairs from their New York counterparts.[8]

The end of the cold war forced neoconservative foreign policy writers to face a question they had not seen in 40 years: what should be the focus of American efforts abroad? The issue, posed as a challenge to define America's purpose, became the subject of a lengthy debate in the *National Interest*. That it dealt with the future and took place largely within the *National Interest*'s pages was further evidence of the journal's importance. Just as significant, however, was what the debate revealed about neoconservatism's continuing reliance on Reinhold Niebuhr and its relationship with the American conservative movement.

The debate revolved around the issue of whether the United States should pursue a Wilsonian foreign policy, dedicated to spreading democracy throughout the world, or if policy should be based on the narrower foundation of national self-interest. The discussion began in 1986 with Robert W. Tucker's reassertion of a point he had made in the 1960s, that Americans believe that their purposes transcend mere survival and include a mission to spread liberty:

> From the outset of our existence as a nation we
> have believed that our security and survival are
> synonymous with the security and survival of free-
> dom in the world. This is why our reason of state
> has not only had a dimension above and beyond a
> conventional reason of state, but has been regu-
> larly seen as somehow qualitatively different from
> it. This is also why we have always believed that
> what we do for ourselves we do for others as well.

As a result, according to Tucker, Reagan's policies of seeking to extend freedom, as well as neoconservatism's Wilsonian impulse, were consistent with American customs. Put into practice in the 1980s, they benefitted further from the decline of the Soviet Union and the spread of democracy in the Third World, both of which appeared to bolster American interests at little cost. As he had done 20 years earlier, however, Tucker warned against the temptation to embark on a crusade for freedom, and instead advocated building "a framework of stability and moderation within which democratic institutions may take root and grow," with the United States acting as "a force for self-government simply by virtue of our example."[9]

Tucker's argument caught the mood of most of the neoconservatives. In articles of their own over the following six years most neoconservatives tended to side with Tucker's caution, noting that the spread of democracy abroad was of immense benefit to the United States but that Americans should avoid open-ended crusades. The end of the ideological threat posed by Communism—the threat that had been of the greatest concern to the neoconservatives—led some to believe that the United States could take a less active role in the world. Jeane Kirkpatrick, for example, wrote, "It is enormously desirable for the U.S. and others to encourage democratic institutions wherever possible." She also pointed out, however, that "there is no mystical American 'mission' or purposes" that should compel the United States to try to spread its democracy around the world and asserted, instead, the primacy of American domestic concerns. Similarly, Irving Kristol advocated basing policy solely on American interests—which, with the demise of the Soviet Union, had become more limited—thereby escaping the "incubus of liberal internationalism, with its utopian expectations."[10]

For the most part, other neoconservatives failed to produce compelling counterarguments to the neo-realism of Tucker, Kristol, and Kirkpatrick. The strongest case for continued activism on issues many neoconservatives ignored was, in fact, articulated by Charles Krauthammer, whose writings were heavily influenced by neoconservatism. Krauthammer, born in 1950, is a Harvard-trained psychiatrist who turned to journalism and foreign affairs commentary in the early 1980s. His writings during the decade frequently allied him with the neoconservatives. He opposed calls for a nuclear weapons freeze, defended deterrence theory, and strongly criticized the isolationist tendencies of both liberals and conservatives.

Krauthammer consistently advocated that the United States be prepared to defend its interests, even if its allies were not prepared to
support it. "Unilateral American action is often necessary," he wrote
in 1985. "The allies are often simply not free agents. If the United
States does not act—in Grenada, in Nicaragua, in the Middle East, as
it once did in Greece and Berlin—no one will." But Krauthammer
was not an unquestioning cheerleader for Reagan-era policy. He took
issue with the morality of the administration's seemingly indiscrimi-
nate willingness to support anti-Communist guerrilla groups and, in
the wake of the Iran-contra scandal, insisted that Americans look
closely at the effects of an activist foreign policy on constitutional
norms at home.[11]

Krauthammer's response to the end of the cold war, after some
early confusion, was largely consistent with what he had written
before. At first he rejected both Wilsonian aims and realpolitik in
favor of creating a confederation of advanced Western and Asian
states that could dominate world politics. Their example, Krauthammer argued at the end of 1989, would lead to gradual political and
economic liberalization by less advanced states, which could then
join their circle. Krauthammer abandoned this idea, which sounded
eerily like Brzezinski's technetronic analysis of the late 1960s, within
a year. The Iraqi invasion of Kuwait in August 1990 and subsequent
American-led military response reminded Krauthammer that Western security still depended on Washington's willingness to lead.
"Where the United States does not tread, the alliance does not follow," he wrote.[12]

Krauthammer drew on the lessons of the Gulf war as well as his
willingness to support unilateralism to provide a blueprint for American policy in the 1990s. He warned conservatives against slipping
into isolationism simply because the "anti-Communist emergency is
over." A new and major problem, he wrote in July 1991, would be
that ballistic missile and other advanced weapons technologies
would enable "relatively small, peripheral, and backward states . . .
to emerge rapidly as threats not only to regional but to world security." The United States would have to be prepared "to act alone,

backed by as many of its allies as will join," to face down or disarm countries threatening to use their weapons to upset international stability. The United States would also have to be prepared to change many of the rules of national sovereignty to accommodate the rise of "aggressive nationalisms," which had been kept in check by the Americans and Soviets during the cold war. Krauthammer's analysis found at least one supporter among the neoconservatives. In 1992, Elliott Abrams advocated an American role centered on using its preponderance of power to enforce international norms of conduct, much as the British had during the nineteenth century, but with the overarching goal of keeping violence among nations from spinning out of control.[13]

Except for Abrams, Krauthammer's approach did not catch on among neoconservatives. Krauthammer presented a middle way for policy, avoiding Wilsonian crusades while trying to identify potential interests rather than simply those that already exist. Instead, the dominant post-cold war neoconservative position has been the narrower, anti-utopian view, which takes a more restricted view of the national interest. In his 1992 book *The Imperial Temptation*, Robert W. Tucker (writing with his frequent collaborator David C. Hendrickson) presented it as a return to traditional American diplomatic principles, in which the United States "refrained from intervention in the internal affairs of other states," and sought instead to spread democracy by example rather than by force. Indeed, argued Tucker, interventionism would have changed "the fundamental maxims of American policy 'from *liberty* to *force*.'"[14]

Unfortunately for many other neoconservatives, identifying national interests and deciding when to apply American power has proven as difficult in practice as in theory. Some decisions have been easy: the neoconservatives unanimously supported the war against Iraq and condemned opposition to Operation Desert Storm in January and February 1991. The civil war which broke out in Bosnia-Herzegovina in 1992, on the other hand, confused them and led to some unexpected alliances. The combination of Serbian aggression against a fledgling democracy, European inaction, and Bosnian suffering added a moral dimension to the question of whether the United States had Balkan interests worth an intervention. Realist Jeane Kirkpatrick and Wilsonian Joshua Muravchik were on the same side, urging the use of American force to stop the war. Other neoconservatives, such as Irving Kristol, remained strikingly silent on the issue, apparently not seeing a pressing American concern in the Balkans and willing to leave the Bosnians to their fate.[15]

Despite their strong defense of liberal democracy during the 1970s and 1980s, it is not surprising that the neoconservatives have backed away from a democratic crusade. Irving Kristol maintains that much of the neoconservative ideological battle against the Soviet Union was defensive, made necessary by Moscow's offensive against the West, and neoconservatism's history bears out Kristol's point. Even as he defended Woodrow Wilson in 1975, Daniel Patrick Moynihan spoke only of assisting democratic states and forces, not creating them. Similarly, the Reagan administration had restrained the Wilsonian impulse; Jeane Kirkpatrick had offered a strong defense of liberal democracy, but only a defense, and the National Endowment for Democracy did not try to start movements or revolutions. The rhetoric of rollback was a relatively small part of neoconservative writings, with a marginal influence on policy. When neoconservatism is viewed in this light, Carl Gershman and Joshua Muravchik stand out for their continued advocacy of spreading democracy, but mostly because their views make them exceptions within the neoconservative community.[16]

The neoconservatives' general reluctance to crusade also provides a glimpse of Reinhold Niebuhr's continuing influence. Even in the 1990s, they looked to him as their most reliable guide. In 1992, on Niebuhr's hundredth birthday, Michael Novak celebrated his teachings in *National Review*, particularly those which emphasized man's limitations and the need to balance power with power. The idea that the United States is destined to spread its democracy and remake the world would undoubtedly have struck Niebuhr as naive and utopian, a point which is not lost on realists like Kristol. The neoconservative dependence on Niebuhr appears in more subtle ways as well, whether it is in Kristol's dismissal of utopian expectations at home, or Krauthammer's warnings that the end of the cold war will not bring an end to international dangers and suffering.[17]

Niebuhr's influence and the policy confusion within the neoconservative camp would be of little consequence were they not related to broader controversies among the neoconservatives and other American conservatives. The end of the cold war coincided with the completion of the neoconservatives' slow transition from liberalism to mainstream conservatism. Several factors had led to this. For one, their years in the Reagan camp had made them de facto conservatives. Elliott Abrams and Jeane Kirkpatrick, for example, had formulated, defended, and carried out conservative policies, often with the enthusiastic approval of the right. In addition, their battles with Congressional critics and the Democrats widened the existing rifts between them and even moderate liberals. Consequently, they had no conceivable political home other than within the conservative movement—a stark contrast with their hesitation to join the Republicans in 1980 that became clear after they left office. Abrams, for example, became a contributing editor for *National Review*. He was enthusiastically applauded when he spoke at the *National Review*-sponsored January 1993 conservative convention in Washington, D.C., which also featured Norman Podhoretz and Jeane Kirkpatrick.[18]

Even as they entered the conservative mainstream, however, the neoconservatives were careful to maintain an identity apart from that of traditional southern and midwestern American conservatism. Writing in 1986 of the differences between "our conservatism and theirs," Brigitte and Peter Berger explained:

> We have defined ourselves politically in the American situation in response to the sudden descent of the elite culture and political liberalism into an orgy of utopian lunacies. We have been kept in this political self-definition by the fact that . . . the lunacies have become organized into a cultural and political establishment. . . . We are, if you will, conservatives not by faith but by skepticism.

Two years later, another *Commentary* contributor explained that "neoconservatives belong to the tradition of liberal-democratic modernity, the tradition of Montesquieu, Madison and Tocqueville; paleoconservatives [as the traditional conservatives are often labeled] are the heirs to the Christian and aristocratic Middle Ages, to Augustine, Aquinas, and Hooker." He might have added as well that, as heirs to Robert Taft and the tradition of midwestern isolationism, the traditional conservatives are suspicious of internationalism, let alone any hint of a Wilsonian crusade.[19]

For their part, the traditional conservatives have been happy to accept these differences and add still others to the list. Not all of the distinctions have been explained in friendly tones, however. Their most inflammatory charge has been that the neoconservatives do not place American interests first. In a celebrated remark, Russell Kirk—one of the founders of the post-World War II conservative intellectual movement—claimed that "not seldom it has seemed as if some eminent neoconservatives mistook Tel Aviv for the capital of the United States." Similarly, Patrick Buchanan, who had been skeptical of the need for war with Iraq and challenged George Bush for the 1992 Republican presidential nomination, commented that neoconservative "tactics—including the smearing of opponents as racists, nativists, fascists, and anti-Semites—left many conservatives wondering if we hadn't made a terrible mistake when we brought these ideological vagrants in off the street and gave them a warm place by the fire." Although no one seriously suspected Kirk of being an anti-Semite, a lively debate ensued over whether or not Buchanan was one. Other disputes centered around foundation grants and allegations that the neoconservatives had come to dominate conservative publications. Underlying much of the traditional conservatives' anger, undoubtedly, was a feeling that the conservative movement was now dominated—had been hijacked—by a small group of latecomers from the northeast.[20]

The traditional conservatives' distrust of the neoconservatives is justified to a limited extent. During the 1992 campaign, Democratic presidential candidate Bill Clinton made a concerted effort to woo the neoconservatives back to the party. Clinton, running as a moderate Democrat, based his appeal on the claim that he was taking the party back toward the center and was forcing it to give up many of the policies which had angered the neoconservatives. Most neoconservatives ignored Clinton's appeal and remained firmly in the Republican camp, but several returned to the Democratic fold. Clearly, whatever their service to Ronald Reagan, in the eyes of the paleoconservatives the neoconservatives could not be trusted not to make another ideological shift.[21]

The battle between neoconservatives and traditional conservatives is likely to continue, and it holds particular dangers for the neoconservatives. A view based on Niebuhr will always be outward looking. Even if the neoconservatives remain suspicious of Wilsonian crusades, the Gulf war, Bosnia, and the influence of Krauthammer and Abrams virtually guarantee that they will advocate continued American activism abroad. It is hard to see how this outlook can be reconciled with Russell Kirk's inward-looking tendencies. Trading charges and name calling—something neoconservatives are prone to do—at a time when they are trying to build a new view of the future will only distract them from their task. Too bitter a fight against the traditional right, which could easily happen should its power among conservatives continue to grow, could also lead the neoconservatives to become an isolated faction on the right. Although they would still have their platforms of *Commentary* and the *National Interest* as outlets for their writing, they would risk losing their place in any rebuilt conservative coalition as well as their voice in Republican party policymaking.

The journey from *The Vital Center* to "The End of History?" was a short one. Despite the shift from left to right and various diversions in between, the neoconservatives finished close to where they had started. Both Arthur M. Schlesinger, Jr., and Francis Fukuyama expressed a remarkable, perhaps naive, faith in the eventual triumph of liberal democracy. The other foundations of neoconservative thinking—Niebuhr, Schumpeter, and Arendt—also date from the time of *The Vital Center*. They gave the neoconservatives a way to view the world, and it served them well. For 40 years they used the concepts of Schumpeter and Arendt to tell friend from foe; of Niebuhr to understand that progress would be gradual and victories incomplete; and of Schlesinger to remember that liberalism has to fight for survival.

Schlesinger was right when he called liberal democracy a faith. Democracy, as he described it in a 1948 speech, had "two articles of faith": "One characteristic is the belief in the inalienable rights of the individual. The other is the belief in the necessity for democratic control of political and economic life." The struggle with the Soviet Union was simply one between those who believed in this concept of freedom and those who would have abolished it. Both Schlesinger and Niebuhr warned that the struggle for democracy would be a long one and urged liberals not to give up when the world failed to live up to their expectations. Even though the United States was not a utopia, Schlesinger said in 1948, there was no reason "to decide that it is therefore a mass of hypocrisy" and give up. Containment promised an eventual triumph and, in the meantime, the democratic faith enabled its adherents to avoid losing their way, forgetting what their purpose was, or simply compromising out of despair when the cold war seemed endless and American fortunes were at their lowest.[22]

One of the neoconservatives' major accomplishments, therefore, was to maintain their anti-Communist faith when many liberals were ready to give it up. They never forgot Schlesinger's teaching that Communism posed the greatest threat to true liberalism as well as liberal democracy. By the late 1960s, the number of liberals who still believed this was dwindling rapidly under the twin assaults of Vietnam and cold war revisionism. Many liberals focused instead on America's failures and shortcomings to the exclusion of any appreciation of its successes and virtues. Unfortunately, however, they had little to offer in place of the democratic faith. Despite the efforts of academics like Stanley Hoffmann, new theories and proposals were overwhelmed by the realities of totalitarianism, the continuing cold war, and had little to say about ideological competition or the virtues of democracy.

By sticking to their anti-Communism the neoconservatives avoided falling into this vacuum. Instead, the simplicity of containment doctrine and their anti-Communism gave them several advantages over their liberal opponents. The neoconservatives had a comprehensive world view and policy approach at hand; they did not have to explain or defend a new theory; and, having worked out their views long before, they were free to attack the follies of world order theory, Jimmy Carter's failures, or any other weaknesses they spotted. The contrast with the post-1968 Democrats, whose positions shifted, became muddled, and contributed to their electoral troubles, is striking. The neoconservatives had another advantage as well. Because they did not forget a fundamental truth—that the Soviet Union posed terrible threats to American security—and were not distracted by dissenting theories, the neoconservatives were able to focus public attention on their points.

Norman Podhoretz notwithstanding, this outlook led most neoconservatives to see Ronald Reagan's record in foreign affairs as a triumph. Their summations of Reagan's two terms usually centered on the contrast between the Soviet Union's seeming omnipotence in 1981 and its clear decrepitude in 1989. "Is it too fanciful to suggest," asked Aaron Wildavsky as Reagan left office, "that an outspoken moral rejection of the Soviet system and a confident affirmation of democratic capitalism by an American president may have helped the Soviets face up to their inability to justify dictatorial Communism?" While the neoconservatives acknowledged that much of the Soviet Union's plight had come about for internal reasons unrelated to American policy and that Reagan had sometimes been lucky, an emphasis on moral and intangible factors allowed them to believe that their writings and crusade for strict containment had paid off. What Elliott Abrams remembered in 1987 as a "little outpost of voices in opposition" had come to power and seen its policies and ideas succeed in practice.[23]

Another neoconservative contribution has been to help kick the props out from under revisionist thinking and related policies. The collapse of the Communist regimes in eastern Europe and Moscow vindicated much of what the neoconservatives had written in the 1970s and 1980s—they had been repressive, corrupt, brutal, totalitarian states which used every opportunity to attack Western interests. It is now difficult to find an influential thinker who defends, or even advocates a hands-off approach toward, hostile Third World dictatorships or revolutionaries. Arguments against the war with Iraq, for example, had none of the intellectual underpinnings— America only makes things worse, we should be on the right side of history—of those opposing intervention in Third World conflicts after the Vietnam war. This was by no means solely a neoconservative achievement, for Jimmy Carter's troubles had discredited many of these theories. When the time came, however, to use force to face down a dictator, 20 years of neoconservative arguments helped prepare the case for defending American interests.

If there has been a neoconservative failure, it has been one of overzealousness. Neoconservatives have not infrequently viewed their enemies as embodiments of evil who must be destroyed, rather than as opponents to be debated or persuaded. Consequently, *Commentary* has had a tendency to carry on its fights against the New Left and anti-anti-Communism long after these forces ceased to matter. Similarly, Daniel Patrick Moynihan was cast out of the neoconservative ranks because of his seeming apostasy over Latin America. Moynihan had come to believe that the waning of the Soviet ideological threat meant the revolutions in Central America presented little long-term threat. For Podhoretz, however, it was inconceivable that Moynihan had made an objective analysis of the situation, one that could be legitimately considered. Instead, he made it clear that Moynihan was no longer welcome in the pages of *Commentary*, leaving the journal that much poorer.

Another neoconservative failing has been an inability to understand politicians and politics. Few politicians can meet the expectations of intellectuals. As people committed to the purity and abstractions of their ideas, intellectuals are uncomfortable with (and repelled by) the compromising that is instinctive to successful politicians. At the same time, however, Podhoretz's relationship with Moynihan was an example of the dependence of political intellectuals on actual politicians if their ideas are to be translated into policy. Intellectuals who openly scorn politicians quickly see their influence wane, which only adds to their distrust. Nor do intellectuals always appraise their own roles realistically. Conversely, it is those intellectuals, like Jeane Kirkpatrick, who understand and can work in politics that have the most realistic expectations and can claim the most success.

In fact, it is the small group of neoconservative politicians that has coped the best with the end of the cold war and the resulting uncertainties. The breadth and resilience of their politics meant that they had never been dependent on the ideological conflict of the cold war for their sustenance. Moynihan, who stands out for his ability to shift from one set of problems to another, is probably the most successful of all. Since leaving the neoconservative ranks he has returned to many of the domestic social welfare issues which concerned him in the 1960s and has also become a powerful senator. In 1993, following the selection of Texas Senator Lloyd Bentsen to be secretary of the treasury, Moynihan became chairman of the Senate Finance Committee and has played a major role in supporting the Clinton administration's budget and fiscal proposals. In addition, Moynihan's writings continue to attract attention. One 1993 article, "Defining Deviancy Down," noted that "the amount of deviant behavior in American society has increased" to the point where deviancy has been redefined to make previously unacceptable behavior seem normal. It quickly became a reference point for discussions of many social problems.[24]

As for the future, the neoconservatives are on the verge of both intellectual and generational transitions. Their anti-Communist struggle lasted more than 40 years and required a continually activist posture, both in domestic politics as well as in their preferences for American foreign policy. The end of the external Communist threat will encourage them to favor a more relaxed set of policies; no longer will small countries and minor events be magnified by superpower competition, and the neoconservatives will feel free to ignore large parts of the world. This attitude—consistent with the inclinations of many other American conservatives—is already evident. Although once they would have rushed to speak out, the neoconservatives have had little to say about the growing chaos in Africa, continuing Sandinista machinations in Nicaragua, or the democratic transitions in Eastern Europe.

The first generation of neoconservatives will soon give way to the second. Irving Kristol, Jeane Kirkpatrick, Midge Decter, and Norman Podhoretz are either approaching or are already over 70. Although they are still active and may remain so for years to come, they and the other veterans of the vital center will gradually fade away. Their heirs are prepared to take their places. William Kristol, Irving's son, served as chief of staff to Vice-President Dan Quayle and appears to have a bright future in conservative politics and intellectual affairs. Daniel Pipes, son of historian Richard Pipes, edits the foreign affairs journal *Orbis*, and is a respected Middle East specialist. Elliott Abrams will remain an important voice as well, although his conviction on charges related to the Iran-contra scandal will probably keep him from ever holding another appointive office.[25]

The second generation neoconservatives will be an important part of the conservative movement. Some of the major traditional conservatives, like Patrick Buchanan or the leaders of the religious right, have a good chance of marginalizing themselves as national leaders, either by alienating potential supporters or by leading their movements to electoral disasters reminiscent of George McGovern's. The younger neoconservatives, whose Reagan and Bush era credentials give them good standing in conservative circles, will not be as ideologically suspect as their predecessors and are already skilled at building and working within coalitions. Predominantly northeastern and Jewish, they will bring their intellectual tradition as well as an ethnic and scholarly balance to American conservatism. Consequently, they may be expected to play major roles in any future conservative administration.

Epilogue:

The Early
Clinton
Administration,
1993–1994

Although Bill Clinton attracted the support of several neoconservatives during his 1992 presidential campaign, by the end of 1993 they were united in opposition to him. Clinton's neoconservative supporters, most notably Joshua Muravchik, had turned to him because they were disappointed with many of President Bush's policies and unsure of their position within the Republican party. Clinton ran as a moderate Democrat and asserted his willingness to use force, if necessary, to defend American interests abroad. To the unhappy neoconservatives, he appeared to be the type of Democrat that they had long hoped would arise.

In office, however, Clinton disappointed his neoconservative supporters. Paying the price for their earlier support of Reagan and Bush, and also because of Clinton's need to satisfy the Democrats' many factions, the neoconservatives did not receive any significant appointments in the new administration. In fact, many of Clinton's appointees—especially Secretary of State Warren Christopher and National Security Adviser Anthony Lake—were suspect in neoconservative eyes because of their positions in the Carter administration and their continued adherence to world order theories. When the administration's foreign policy performance came under fire in the fall of 1993, the neoconservatives enthusiastically joined in the denunciations. Their criticisms revealed both a strengthening commitment to realism in foreign policy as well as the ascendancy of several new neoconservative policy intellectuals.

Bill Clinton came to the presidency better prepared to handle foreign affairs than the last Democrat to hold the office, Jimmy Carter. Clinton had studied international affairs as an undergraduate at Georgetown University in the 1960s, had lived in England as a Rhodes scholar, and had worked for Arkansas Senator J. William Fulbright. As governor of Arkansas, Clinton made several trips to Asia and Europe to try to stimulate foreign investment and business interest in the state. Like Carter, however, he had virtually no pre-presidential experience dealing with significant foreign issues, crises, or leaders. Moreover, Arkansas politics had never required him to deal with deeply hostile political opponents like Saddam Hussein or Kim Il-Sung, the dictators of Iraq and North Korea.

During the 1992 campaign, Clinton portrayed himself as a strong defender of American foreign and economic interests abroad, as well as favoring a strongly pro-democratic policy. The result was that Clinton frequently criticized President Bush for being too soft, turning the tables on the Republicans' 1980s strategy of depicting Democratic candidates as dangerously weak. For example, in a June 1992 interview with the *New York Times*, Clinton criticized Bush for not providing military assistance to Bosnia, not being tough enough with Iraq before the invasion of Kuwait, and having only a "very tepid response to Tiananmen Square," where Chinese authorities brutally repressed student demonstrators in 1989. After the war with Iraq, Clinton noted that Bush had "left the Kurds and the Shiites twisting" while Saddam Hussein crushed their rebellions.[1]

When explaining what he would do differently, Clinton made proposals designed to appeal to moderate and conservative Democrats.

As a so-called New Democrat, he proclaimed a strong commitment to democracy, telling the Los Angeles World Affairs Council that "we will offer international assistance to emerging fragile democracies in the former Soviet Union, and Eastern Europe, and create a democracy core to help them develop free institutions." Clinton also made clear his determination to maintain a strong defense and his willingness to use force if necessary: "This world is still a dangerous place. Military power still matters. And I am committed to maintaining a strong and ready defense. I will use that strength where necessary to defend our vital interests." Clinton also pledged himself to defending American interests against new threats, especially the proliferation of weapons of mass destruction, and to enhancing the economic security of the United States.[2]

Despite Clinton's condemnations of President Bush, some analysts noted that in many cases their positions were not very different. Clinton largely agreed with several of Bush's major policies: a continued hard line against Iraq, assisting United Nations efforts to deliver humanitarian supplies to Bosnia, and continuing the Middle East peace process, for example. Zbigniew Brzezinski said that both men were within the internationalist mainstream, and the *Washington Post* noted that Clinton offered mainly "midcourse corrections" to existing policies. These statements support journalist Leon Sigal's post-election observation that Clinton had used a "hugging tactic" to stay close to Bush's policies, and "fudged differences instead of sharpening them."[3]

Foreign issues played only a secondary role in the 1992 campaign, which contributed to the success of Clinton's strategy. The 1992 election was fought mostly on such domestic issues as the economy, budget deficits, and health care. In addition, the collapse of the Soviet Union removed the foreign issue on which a Democratic candidate was most vulnerable. Not only did it free Clinton from having to make any claims about being resolutely dedicated to containment, but it also made it virtually impossible for the Republicans to use the memory of Jimmy Carter's failures and allegations of Democratic softness to discredit Clinton. Moreover, the demise of the major threat to American security made Clinton's lack of experience seem much less risky to the electorate.[4]

Clinton was also a talented politician who could tailor his message to his audience. The *Wall Street Journal* noted that Clinton wanted "so much to be liked by people that he will . . . pick just those parts [of issues that] appeal to his audience, and jettison the less appealing parts." The *New York Times* commented that his statements combined "idealism and pragmatism, internationalism and protectionism, use of force and reliance on multinational institutions." Consequently, his listeners had ample opportunities to hear what they wanted to hear, helping those looking for an alternative to Bush view him favorably. In endorsing Clinton, for example, the *New Republic* found "Clinton's internationalism a refreshing change from the narrow confines" of Bush's policies, and that his "addresses . . . reflected a deep understanding of this country's need to remain engaged in Europe and Asia, to refocus our defenses rather than run them down."[5]

Clinton's combination of moderate internationalism and pro-democracy attacks on Bush came at a time when many neoconservatives had become uneasy in their alliance with the Republicans. In addition to the discomfort caused by Patrick Buchanan's presidential campaign and what many perceived as the growing strength of the Christian right within the party, the neoconservatives tended to be disappointed by Bush's policies, frequently viewing them as half-hearted and ineffective. Bush's failure to destroy Saddam Hussein's regime made the war with Iraq a lightning rod for their criticisms. According to Angelo Codevilla, Bush had wanted influence in the Middle East but was unwilling to involve the United States decisively; another article in *Commentary* argued that this put America's role as an honest and reliable broker in the region in doubt.[6]

Concern over policy toward Israel added to the tensions between the neoconservatives and Bush. Shortly after the war with Iraq, Arab-Israeli bilateral peace talks began, with Washington and, to a lesser extent, Moscow acting as facilitators. The talks soon bogged down, and the administration began pressuring Israel to be more flexible. At the same time, a nasty domestic political fight erupted in early 1992 over a proposal to provide $10 billion in loan guarantees to Israel, much of which would be used to house Russian Jewish immigrants. Before providing the guarantees, the administration wanted assurances that the money would not be used to establish additional Israeli settlements in the occupied territories. Frustrated by the Israelis as well as their political allies in the United States, Secretary of State James A. Baker lost his temper. "Fuck the Jews. They didn't vote for us," he said in a private remark which, unfortunately for the Bush administration, was leaked to the press.[7]

In this atmosphere, some neoconservatives found Clinton an attractive alternative. Many still called themselves Democrats, and they took Clinton's moderate policies and commitment to maintaining American strength as evidence that the party had returned to true liberalism. His pro-democracy speeches, furthermore, told them what they had been waiting to hear. "In . . . the emphasis he has given in his speeches to democracy and human rights, he has demonstrated a much better feel [than Bush] for the idealism that must inform U.S. policy," wrote Joshua Muravchik in his endorsement of Clinton. Several other neoconservatives also supported or worked for Clinton, including Richard Schifter (Elliott Abrams's successor as assistant secretary of state for human rights), Ben Wattenberg, and Penn Kemble. In addition, after the Republican convention in August, neoconservatives who were tempted to support Clinton may also have seen him as the likely victor in November and, therefore, as their best chance for continued influence in Washington.[8]

Not all neoconservatives abandoned Bush, however, for suspicions of the Democrats and Clinton's advisers ran deep. Indeed, several prominent neoconservatives—especially those who, like Abrams, Norman Podhoretz, and Jeane Kirkpatrick, had long before switched to Reagan and the Republicans—remained loyal to Bush. Podhoretz worried that Clinton would have "an administration not all that different from Jimmy Carter's," and Abrams argued that Clinton's future appointees would be "more or less the same people [1988 Democratic nominee] Mike Dukakis would have appointed. They're just four years older." William Kristol sniffed, "Any neocon who drifts back to the Democratic Party is a pseudo-neocon."[9]

Because of his ambitious domestic plans and lack of experience, Clinton left it to his top level appointees to turn his campaign statements into a foreign policy. For secretary of state, Clinton chose Warren Christopher, a well-to-do Los Angeles lawyer who had been deputy attorney general from 1967 to 1969 and, as deputy secretary of state from 1977 to 1981, had been the number-two man in Cyrus Vance's State Department. Christopher was a loyal Democrat and had played a prominent role in the Clinton campaign, both as a foreign policy adviser and, most notably, in overseeing the process of choosing the Democrats' vice-presidential candidate, Tennessee Senator Al Gore.

Despite his background, there was little in the public record to reveal Christopher's views on foreign affairs. He had been an able deputy to Vance—in 1980 and 1981 he had been in charge of the negotiations to free the Americans held hostage in Iran—but, other than a privately published book, an introduction to a book on the hostage crisis, one article in *Foreign Affairs*, and some speeches, he had done little to defend the Carter administration's record or to define his own views. In the *Foreign Affairs* article, for example, he limited himself to a review of the constitutional tensions between Congress and the president in the conduct of foreign relations, noting that the "Constitution is, in fact, ambiguous . . . the framers left a great deal of room for their successors to adopt methods and apply values of their own." Christopher's suggested approach was for the two branches to exempt foreign policy from politics and to work together—"to complement each other, each bringing unique qualities to bear on the decisions they were expected to share,"—and to act with "a renewed spirit of bipartisanship." Most other evaluations of Christopher noted that he abhorred the use of force and believed deeply in relying on diplomacy and negotiations to settle differences among states. Christopher's lawyerly approach led the *New Republic* to editorialize, in comments dripping with sarcasm, that it could not be sure if his appointment was a bad sign "because we cannot say with any certainty what he represents."[10]

Clinton appointed Anthony Lake to be his national security adviser. Lake had become an academic after serving as director of policy planning at the State Department from 1977 to 1980, most recently as a professor at Mount Holyoke. Not surprisingly, Lake had explained his views in a number of articles and books and had clearly thought through the problems of the Carter administration's efforts abroad. He acknowledged, for example, that one reason Carter's policies had been discredited "was his failure ever to fashion a coherent policy toward the Soviet Union," and that in both Iran and Nicaragua Carter's efforts to push the regimes toward reform only further undermined them.[11]

When it came to relating these lessons to the realities of policy making in Washington—an inherently political process fraught with difficulties for any administration—Lake had trouble offering suggestions any more concrete than Christopher's. In fact, his approach was technocratic and even narrower than Christopher's. He noted, for example, that "influencing . . . events is as much a test of American foresight as it is of American power," and stressed the importance of an administration being "sufficiently led, organized and disposed to the sustained attention and kinds of compromises necessary to the conduct of . . . traditional diplomacy." He further argued that the president and secretary of state, while promoting their agendas, must still pay close attention to the government's foreign policy professionals and experts. This idealized approach to policy making was pervasive in Lake's writings. On southern Africa, for example, Lake urged the United States to avoid "excessive optimism in either thinking or rhetoric," and, when vital American interests were not threatened, to rely on "brains more than muscle."[12]

Put into practice in 1993, these proposals resulted in policies that combined an update of the Carter administration's world order approach with Wilsonianism. At his confirmation hearings in January 1993, Christopher told the Senate Foreign Relations Committee that policy would have to be adjusted to the new strategic environment and emphasize such issues as rising ethnic conflicts, global economic changes, and the challenges of environmental problems, AIDS, overpopulation, and drug trafficking. Unlike Carter, however, Christopher and Lake also emphasized encouraging the further spread of democracy. In September 1993, for example, Lake told an audience in Washington that containment had been replaced by a "strategy of enlargement—enlargement of the world's free community of market democracies," which Christopher had earlier noted would be a "strategic investment in our nation's security."[13]

This approach provided the administration with a clear guide for action for dealing with world order and democratization issues. In November 1993, the administration secured congressional approval of the North American Free Trade Agreement (NAFTA) after a hard political battle. A month later, the United States made significant progress toward liberalizing international trade at the General Agreement on Tariffs and Trade (GATT) talks in Geneva. Elsewhere, Clinton firmly backed Russian President Boris Yeltsin in his confrontations with former Communists and other opponents of his reforms, continued to assist the Middle East peace talks, and committed the United States to aiding the implementation of the Israeli-Palestinian agreement. Although the ultimate fate of many of Clinton's policies, especially in the Middle East and Russia, remains unpredictable, the administration's theories enabled it to make quick and coherent decisions in these situations.[14]

The Clinton administration did not perform as well in situations involving the use of force. The administration's theories provided little guidance for dealing with states or leaders who pursued their own goals without regard for international norms. Despite acknowledging the necessity of, and proclaiming their willingness to use force against such opponents, neither Lake nor Christopher nor Clinton appear to have given careful thought to how, when, or where they would employ military means. The problems surfaced within a few weeks of Clinton's inauguration, as the administration came under pressure to live up to its campaign rhetoric about aiding the embattled Bosnian government. Beginning in February 1993, Christopher, Lake, Secretary of Defense Les Aspin, and their aides considered numerous proposals, including airstrikes against Serb forces. On several occasions, most notably in early August 1993, after consulting with NATO, the United States threatened to attack if the Serbs did not alter their behavior; the United States only followed through once, in April 1994, with a minor air attack. The Serbs never made more than symbolic concessions and the United States backed down.

A second, and equally serious, example of confusion over the use of force took place in Somalia. President Bush had sent troops there in December 1992 to safeguard humanitarian deliveries to famine victims, and Clinton inherited the commitment. Although most American troops were withdrawn during the first half of 1993, the remaining U.S. forces became increasingly involved in United Nations efforts to build a functioning government in the war-torn country. The main obstacle appeared to be a local warlord named Mohammed Farra Aideed, who wanted to rule Somalia himself, and he became the object of an extensive manhunt by American forces. In early October, a raid aimed at capturing some of Aideed's lieutenants went wrong as Somali gunmen shot down an American helicopter, killed thirteen GIs, captured one, and wounded nearly eighty more. A few days later, Clinton tacitly agreed to a cease-fire with Aideed and promised to withdraw all American forces by March 31, 1994.

The uproar that followed the raid showed the administration at its weakest. In a meeting with congressional representatives two days after the raid, Aspin was unable to give a coherent explanation of American goals or strategy in Somalia and then asked them what they believed should be done. "Never have I heard a more confused, disjointed, vague defense of American foreign policy," fumed one Republican lawmaker, while one Democrat left the room because he found Aspin's performance "painful to watch." The next day, it was revealed that in September, Aspin had turned down a request from the American commander in Mogadishu for tanks and reinforcements.[15]

The administration's disarray revealed important weaknesses in its attempt to combine world order theory and Wilsonianism. The situations in Bosnia and Somalia were confusing, American interests were not always clear, and the administration had failed to provide compelling explanations for American involvement. In both places, Clinton, Lake, and Christopher made threats but then shied away from using force once they saw that vital American interests were not directly threatened and that casualties were unlikely to be justified by immediate results. Finally, television coverage, especially in Somalia, added to the confusion and sense of panic in Washington. Not surprisingly, foreign affairs commentators of all persuasions pounced on the administration, questioning its foreign policy competence. Clinton's problems were soon reflected in public opinion polls; a *Time*/CNN poll after the Somali raid showed 52 percent of respondents disapproving of Clinton's conduct of foreign policy.[16]

Adding to Clinton's troubles was the abandonment by the neoconservatives who had supported him in 1992. The new administration gave no jobs to the neoconservatives or their allies. Muravchik, for example, lobbied hard for the human rights position at the State Department, and Richard Schifter reportedly wanted to head the Agency for International Development. The neoconservatives also hoped that former representative Steven Solarz (D-New York)—a strong supporter of Israel and the war with Iraq—would be appointed deputy secretary of state, Christopher's position under Vance. Not only were none of these hopes realized (although Schifter was appointed to the National Security Council staff in June), but some disappointments were perceived as particularly galling. Clifton Wharton, Jr., appointed deputy secretary of state, was a respected black educator and administrator for a college pension fund, but had little experience in foreign policy; his appointment was widely viewed as a form of affirmative action. Peter Tarnoff, appointed under secretary for political affairs (the State Department's third highest position) had been Vance's chief of staff and ambivalent about the use of force against Iraq. The neoconservatives were also shut out of major domestic policy appointments.[17]

Although the neoconservatives would disagree, Clinton had good reasons for not appointing them to major posts. In choosing his appointees, Clinton was executing a difficult balancing act in which he had to satisfy several factions within the Democratic Party as well as to try to expand his popular base (he had won the three-way election with only 43 percent of the popular vote). Consequently, Clinton made his personnel selections according to a complex calculus. Moderate Democrats—Christopher and Secretary of the Treasury Bentsen—received some of the most visible and important cabinet positions. Liberal Democrats were represented by Secretary of Health and Human Services Donna Shalala, blacks and Hispanics by Secretary of Commerce Ron Brown and Secretary of Housing and Urban Development Henry Cisneros, and women by Attorney General Janet Reno. At the secondary level, nominees included Roberta Achtenberg, a lesbian, and Lani Guinier, a controversial civil rights lawyer whose nomination was withdrawn under fire. In itself, satisfying all these groups would have left few jobs for the neoconservatives, even if Clinton had been inclined to hire them. Given that Muravchik, Schifter, Kemble, and their allies had been criticizing the Democrats bitterly for two decades and had cooperated enthusiastically with the Reagan and Bush administrations, it is not at all surprising that they were frozen out. Indeed, as Muravchik realized too late, neoconservatives remained "particularly abhorrent to many Democratic liberals."[18]

The neoconservatives began attacking Clinton in the spring of 1993. Without a role in policy making, the neoconservatives had no stake in Clinton's success and no reason to defend him. The thrust of their charges was that Clinton had never truly been a moderate Democrat but, rather, a member of the party's left wing disguising himself to win the election. During the summer, Muravchik, lamenting his previous support for Clinton, wrote a comprehensive critique of the president's first six months in office, concluding that Clinton's "inner compass . . . was forged in the McGovern campaign, and perhaps in his marriage to Hillary, [and] pulls him to the Left."[19]

The neoconservatives also focused on Clinton's failure to rescue the Bosnians. The issue had grown in importance to them since 1992, as the Bosnian's military situation deteriorated and the administration's indecision led the neoconservatives to worry that foreign governments might perceive the United States as turning isolationist and weakening militarily. Muravchik saw the failure to intervene as evidence both of Clinton's perfidy and Christopher's incompetence. In October 1993, Edward Luttwak wrote acidly that, had the Bosnians been bottle-nosed dolphins, the administration would have stopped their slaughter; Luttwak accused the administration of misunderstanding the nature of the post-cold war world, the continuing importance of force in international affairs, and turning over America's leadership role to the weak and corrupt United Nations.[20]

Clinton's troubles in October and November spurred a new round of neoconservative criticism. Their attacks soon became as savage as those they had leveled against Jimmy Carter and Andrew Young 15 years earlier. This time, Charles Krauthammer led the charge. Clinton, he argued in late October, excelled at campaigning, when "talk is cheap, and promises have no consequences." In foreign policy, however, Krauthammer pointed out that talk quickly turns into commitments and that Clinton had "made various commitments in Bosnia, Somalia, and Haiti, but upon waking to the cost, backed down," thereby showing himself to be "easily cowed and dangerously weak."[21]

Krauthammer also attacked the conceptual foundations of administration policy. Rather than face their problems and opponents squarely, Krauthammer wrote, Clinton and Christopher preferred to negotiate in search of unobtainable agreements with untrustworthy dictators, regardless of the damage to American interests. Talks with North Korea aimed at getting Pyongyang to honor its Nuclear Nonproliferation Treaty obligations were, according to Krauthammer, an "absurd example of the administration's parchment fetish," and involved compromises amounting to capitulation. When Clinton explained his difficulties by noting that world problems were much more complex than they had been during the cold war, Krauthammer contemptuously dismissed this "alibi." Krauthammer pointed out that for years liberals had used "cold warrior" as an insult, but suddenly,

after 20 years of deriding anti-Communists for
being blinded by the Soviet threat, they wistfully
recall how the Soviet threat brilliantly illuminated
the foreign policy landscape—and lament how
obscure it all is with the lodestar gone. Ah, the
Golden Age when everything was easy and we all
joined hands in the cold war battles of Vietnam
and Nicaragua and the Euromissiles.

Despite the end of the cold war, the neoconservatives remained
unforgiving of those who had not been firmly anti-Communist as well
as critical of attempts to deal with Communist regimes.[22]

Clinton's difficulties confirmed the neoconservatives' continuing
bias against what they viewed as utopianism and drove them further
in the direction of realist thinking. Accepting Krauthammer and
Tucker's arguments, they increasingly emphasized that, in a post-
containment world, the United States should no longer undertake
universal, ideologically based, commitments. In addition, the neoconservatives made their points in harsher tones than they did during the euphoria that followed the collapse of the Soviet empire
between 1989 and 1991. Fareed Zakaria, managing editor of *Foreign Affairs*, wrote approvingly in the *National Interest* of the realist
proposition that the few great powers should "undertake to provide
'public goods' for [their] neighbors, chiefly security," while Muravchik
wrote after the Mogadishu debacle that "we ought . . . to be skeptical
of UN-led multilateralism."[23]

Instead, the neoconservatives advocated applying American
power only in carefully selected instances. Even within the great
power concert, according to Zakaria, "there will not be a universal
commitment to respond to *every* act of aggression," and only conflicts threatening to spill out of control will merit attention. In his
view, securing American interests should be Washington's primary
task, with far less attention given to peripheral problems. Both
Krauthammer and Jeane Kirkpatrick made similar statements in the
fall of 1993. Krauthammer called the tendency "to engage our blood
and treasure in places of little interest" a "prescription for mindless

interventionism," and Kirkpatrick noted a need for the United States to distinguish among what could be achieved multilaterally, unilaterally, and "what cannot be done at all."[24]

As a consequence of accepting the realist position, the neoconservatives' willingness to campaign for democracy has continued to decline. In part, this is because the task has proven more difficult than they anticipated during what Tucker has called their "time of triumphalism and unbounded optimism." Indeed, instead of democracies, small wars have blossomed in the former Soviet republics, and Vladimir Zhirinovsky, an opportunistic demagogue, emerged as a major figure after the December 1993 Russian parliamentary election. In light of these events, even Muravchik wrote less enthusiastically of spreading democracy, realizing that the process is more complex and potentially more painful than he had anticipated. Accepting what Zakaria called a "'second-best' arrangement that works most of the time," the neoconservatives appear content instead to consolidate the gains of the 1980s while isolating the troublemakers of the 1990s, such as North Korea.[25]

Despite being out of power, the first year of the Clinton presidency was good for the neoconservatives. Freed from their ambivalent ties to George Bush, they were able to focus their polemics on Clinton, his appointees, and his policies. Their opposition role forced them to develop and articulate fresh positions and sharpen their writing. In addition, Charles Krauthammer's continued intellectual leadership and the appearance of new writers, such as Zakaria, in *Commentary* and the *National Interest* signaled the ascendancy of a new generation of thinkers who could take over from Tucker, Kirkpatrick, and the other neoconservative leaders of the 1970s and 1980s. Their strengthening commitment to realism and a narrowed view of American vital interests also coincided with a growing tendency among the American people toward restraint overseas. Given these conditions, it appears that there will be a renewal of neoconservative foreign policy thinking in the mid-1990s.

Notes

Preface

1. Reinhold Niebuhr, *Moral Man and Immoral Society* (1932; reprint, New York: Charles Scribner's Sons, 1960), p. xi; Reinhold Niebuhr, *The Children of Light and the Children of Darkness* (New York: Charles Scribner's Sons, 1945), p. 178.
2. Fred Barnes, "They're Back!" *New Republic*, August 3, 1992, p. 12.

Chapter One   The Liberal Foreign Policy Consensus and After, 1948–1976

1. "Getting Along With Russia," *New Republic*, August 27, 1945, p. 247; Arthur M. Schlesinger, Jr., *The Vital Center*, Sentry edition (Boston: Houghton Mifflin, 1962), pp. 10, 235; John Kenneth Galbraith, "An Agenda for American Liberals," *Commentary*, June 1966, p. 31.
2. Sidney Hook, *Out of Step* (New York: Harper & Row, 1987), p. 136. For additional information on Communist influence in intellectual life during the 1930s, see John P. Diggins, *The Rise and Fall of the American Left* (New York: W. W. Norton, 1992), chapter 5.
3. Edward A. Purcell, Jr., *The Crisis of Democratic Theory* (Lexington: University Press of Kentucky, 1973), p. 117. For a thorough discussion of the effects of scientific naturalism, relativism, and legal realism on democratic theory, see Purcell, chapters 1–6.
4. Alexander Bloom, *Prodigal Sons* (New York: Oxford University Press, 1986), p. 45. For a discussion of American liberals' and intellectuals' sympathy for the Soviet Union and Stalinism, see Paul Hollander, *Political Pilgrims* (New York:

Oxford University Press, 1981), and Sidney Hook, *Marxism and Beyond* (Totowa, N.J.: Rowman and Littlefield, 1983).

5. William L. O'Neill, *A Better World* (New York: Simon and Schuster, 1982), p. 13 (italics in the original); Hook, *Out of Step*, p. 220.

6. Purcell, *The Crisis of Democratic Theory*, pp. 135, 138, 156; "New Group Fights Any Freedom Curb," *New York Times*, May 15, 1939, p. 13; Reinhold Niebuhr, "Fighting Chance for a Sick Society," *Nation*, March 22, 1941, p. 360; "Ex-Pacifists Favor War If Necessary," *New York Times*, April 29, 1941, p. 9.

7. Reinhold Niebuhr, "Russia and the West," *Nation*, January 16, 1943, p. 83; Jerome Davis, "Religion in the USSR," *New Republic*, March 5, 1945, p. 331. For a brief summary of the Soviet Union's ideological rehabilitation in 1941, see John Lewis Gaddis, *The United States and the Origins of the Cold War* (New York: Columbia University Press, 1972), chapter 2.

8. "War Aims and Peace Aims," *New Republic*, February 26, 1940, p. 263; "Ex-Pacifists Favor War If Necessary," *New York Times*, April 29, 1941; Alonzo L. Hamby, "Henry A. Wallace, the Liberals, and Soviet-American Relations," *Review of Politics* 30 (April 1968): 154. For a summary of Wallace's ideas for the postwar world, see Henry A. Wallace, *Democracy Reborn*, ed. Russell Lord (New York: Reynal & Hitchcock), 1944. Wallace's leadership of the liberals is covered in Edward L. Schapsmeier and Frederick H. Schapsmeier, *Prophet in Politics: Henry A. Wallace and the War Years, 1940–1965* (Ames: Iowa State University Press, 1970), chapter 3, and Alonzo L. Hamby, *Beyond the New Deal* (New York: Columbia University Press, 1973, chapters 1 and 2.

9. Joseph E. Davies, "Russia Today," *Vital Speeches*, August 1, 1943, p. 640; Richard W. Fox, "Reinhold Niebuhr and the Emergence of the Liberal Realist Faith, 1930-1945," *The Review of Politics* 38 (April 1976): 260; Niebuhr, "Russia and The West," p. 83; "The Great Pravda Mystery," *New Republic*, January 31, 1944, p. 136. For a portrait of Stalin emphasizing his acceptance of democratic values, see "Four Strong Men, East and West, Who Lead the United Nations," *New York Times Magazine*, July 4, 1943, p. 15.

10. "Drive Is On To Oust All 'Isolationists,'" *New York Times*, May 10, 1942, p. 34; "The Great Pravda Mystery," p. 135; "A Purge Needed in State," *New Republic*, July 9, 1945, p. 38.

11. Reinhold Niebuhr, *The Children of Light and the Children of Darkness* (New York: Charles Scribner's Sons, 1945), p. x. Niebuhr's biographer, Richard W. Fox, rightly points out that Niebuhr's attitude toward the USSR during the war was ambivalent and shifted with events. See Fox, "Reinhold Niebuhr and the Emergence of the Liberal Realist Faith, 1930-1945," p. 261.

12. Niebuhr, *Children*, pp. 187, 183.

13. Reinhold Niebuhr, "The Basis of World Order," *Nation*, October 21, 1944, p. 489; Niebuhr, *Children*, pp. 186, 189.

14. Hamby, "Henry A. Wallace, the Liberals, Soviet-American Relations," p. 157.

15. "A New Three-Power Conference," *Nation*, October 27, 1945, p. 420; "Relations with Russia," *New Republic*, November 5, 1945, p. 588; "The World Must Choose!" *New Republic*, November 19, 1945, p. 660; "Sixty Days to War or Peace!" *New Republic*, November 26, 1945, p. 692.

16. William Mandel, "Russia and the Peace," *New Republic*, November 19, 1945, p.

664; "Living with the USSR," *New Republic*, April 8, 1946, p. 462; Irving Brant, "Eyewitness in Poland," *New Republic*, January 7, 1946, pp. 15, 17; "One Year After," *New Republic*, May 20, 1946, p. 715.

17. O'Neill, *A Better World*, p. 131. For a description of Truman's lack of preparation in foreign affairs and an analysis of who were his important early advisers, see Daniel Yergin, *Shattered Peace*, revised edition (New York: Penguin Books, 1990), chapter 3.

18. Arthur Hays Sulzberger, "With Faith in Our Democratic System," *New York Times Magazine*, January 20, 1946, pp. 51, 52.

19. Joseph Alsop and Stewart Alsop, "Tragedy of Liberalism," *Life*, May 20, 1946 pp. 68, 69, 70, 72, 74.

20. Arthur M. Schlesinger, Jr., "The U.S. Communist Party," *Life*, July 29, 1946, pp. 85, 94, 96; "The 'Liberal' Fifth Column," *Partisan Review*, Summer 1946, pp. 283, 292.

21. Reinhold Niebuhr, "Europe, Russia, and America," *Nation*, September 14, 1946, pp. 288, 289.

22. Richard W. Fox, *Reinhold Niebuhr* (New York: Pantheon Books, 1985), p. 228; Reinhold Niebuhr, "The Fight for Germany," *Life*, October 21, 1946, pp. 65, 67, 72.

23. Fox, *Reinhold Niebuhr*, p. 229; Niebuhr, "The Fight for Germany," p. 72; Irving Kristol, interview by author, July 21, 1993, Washington, D.C.

24. Steven M. Gillon, *Politics and Vision* (New York: Oxford University Press, 1987), pp. 10, 12–21; *New York Times*, January 5, 1947. For further information on the founding of the ADA and the liberal split, see Hamby, *Beyond the New Deal*, chapter 6, and Mary McAuliffe, *Crisis on the Left* (Amherst: University of Massachusetts Press, 1976).

25. Gillon, *Politics and Vision*, pp. 26, 27, 30; Hamby, *Beyond the New Deal*, p. 165; McAuliffe, *Crisis on the Left*, p. 31.

26. "Faith to Combat Communism Urged," *New York Times*, October 22, 1947, p. 24; Arthur M. Schlesinger, Jr., "Not Left, Not Right, But a Vital Center," *New York Times Magazine*, April 4, 1948, p. 45; Arthur M. Schlesinger, Jr., "Democracy; What Does it Mean?" *Vital Speeches*, April 15, 1948, p. 401; Arthur M. Schlesinger, Jr., "What is Loyalty? A Difficult Question," *New York Times Magazine*, November 2, 1947, p. 7.

27. Reinhold Niebuhr, "For Peace, We Must Risk War," *Life*, September 20, 1948, pp. 38, 39; Arthur M. Schlesinger, Jr., "Adding Guns to ECA Butter," *New Republic*, November 22, 1948, pp. 19, 21.

28. George F. Kennan, *Memoirs, 1925-1950* (Boston: Little, Brown, 1967), p. 354; X [George F. Kennan], "The Sources of Soviet Conduct," *Foreign Affairs*, July 1947, reprinted in Kennan, *American Diplomacy 1900-1950* (Chicago: University of Chicago Press, 1951), p. 128; Brooks Atkinson, "America's Global Planner," *New York Times Magazine*, July 13, 1947, p. 33. For Kennan's comments in 1944, in which he expressed doubts about the prospects for good postwar relations with the Soviets, see "Russia—Seven Years Later," Memorandum by the Counselor of Embassy in the Soviet Union, September 1944, reprinted in *Memoirs*.

29. Schlesinger, *The Vital Center*, pp. 1, 170, 130, 219, 224, 234–235, 256.

30. The reviewers' comments cited are from Irwin Ross, "Liberalism's Enemies," *Commentary*, October 1949, p. 400; *New York Times*, September 8, 1949; Robert

Bendiner, "Schlesinger's 'Vital Center'," *Nation*, September 17, 1949, p. 267; Jonathan Daniels, "Ready to Be Radical," *Saturday Review*, September 10, 1949, p. 12.

31. For the events leading to the founding of the Congress for Cultural Freedom, see Peter Coleman, *The Liberal Conspiracy* (New York: The Free Press, 1989).

32. Paul Nitze, *From Hiroshima to Glasnost* (New York: Grove Weidenfeld, 1989), p. 93; John Lewis Gaddis and Thomas H. Etzold, *Containment: Documents on American Policy and Strategy, 1945-1950* (New York: Columbia University Press, 1978), p. 385. One of the best analyses of NSC-68 and its implications may be found in John Lewis Gaddis, *Strategies of Containment* (New York: Oxford University Press, 1982), chapter 4. Other discussions about the drafting and impact of the report are in Daniel Yergin, *Shattered Peace*, pp. 401-404, and Steven E. Ambrose, *Rise to Globalism*, 6th ed. (New York: Penguin Books, 1991).

33. Gaddis, *Strategies of Containment*, p. 107; Nitze, *From Hiroshima to Glasnost*, p. 95. NSC 20/4, November 23, 1948, is reprinted in Gaddis and Etzold, *Containment*, p. 203.

34. NSC-68, April 14, 1950, reprinted in Gaddis and Etzold, *Containment*, pp. 385, 386, 389.

35. Alonzo L. Hamby, *Liberalism and its Challengers* (New York: Oxford University Press, 1985), p. 344.

36. William A. Williams, "The Frontier Thesis and American Foreign Policy," *Pacific Historical Review* 24 (November 1955): 380; John Lewis Gaddis, *The Long Peace* (New York: Oxford University Press, 1987), p. 227. Further examples of Williams's early thinking on open door imperialism may be found in *American Russian Relations, 1781-1947* (New York: Rinehart, 1952), pp. 32-34, 39-42. Biographical details on Williams and his conversion to radicalism may be found in an interview published in *Visions of History*, ed. Henry Abelove, et al. (Manchester: Manchester University Press, 1983).

37. William A. Williams, "Irony of Containment," *Nation*, May 5, 1956, pp. 379, 376; William A. Williams, "Babbitt's New Fables," *Nation*, January 7, 1956, pp. 6, 3.

38. William A. Williams, *The Tragedy of American Diplomacy* (Cleveland: World, 1959), pp. 47, 150, 163.

39. Williams, *Tragedy*, pp. 196, 201, 202, 212.

40. William A. Williams, "Needed: Production for Peace," *Nation*, February 21, 1959, p. 153; William A. Williams, "Foreign Policy and the American Mind," *Commentary*, February 1962, p. 158; William A. Williams, *The Tragedy of American Diplomacy*, revised edition (New York: W. W. Norton, 1972), p. 312. This passage in the concluding chapter was unchanged from the 1962 edition.

41. Bradford Perkins, "The *Tragedy of American Diplomacy*: Twenty-five Years After," *Reviews in American History* 12 (March 1984), reprinted in William A. Williams, *The Tragedy of American Diplomacy*, revised edition (New York: W. W. Norton, 1988), p. 313; Abelove, et al., *Visions of History*, p. 133.

42. Robert W. Tucker, *Nation or Empire?* (Baltimore: Johns Hopkins University Press, 1968), p. 9; Christopher Lasch, "The Cold War, Revisited and Re-Visioned," *New York Times Magazine*, January 14, 1968, p. 51.

43. "Johnson's World," *New Republic*, May 2, 1964, p. 4; Townsend Hoopes, *The Limits of Intervention*, revised edition (New York: David McKay, 1973), pp. 1-2.

44. Maurice J. Goldbloom, "Foreign Policy," *Commentary*, June 1965, pp. 47, 54, 55.

45. J. William Fulbright, "Old Myths and New Realities," *Vital Speeches*, April 15, 1964, p. 388; J. William Fulbright, "The Fatal Arrogance of Power," *New York Times Magazine*, May 18, 1966, p. 29. For contemporary discussions of Fulbright's challenge to Johnson, see Hans J. Morgenthau, "Senator Fulbright's New Foreign Policy," *Commentary*, May 1964, and Maurice J. Goldbloom, "The Fulbright Revolt," *Commentary*, September 1966.

46. Tucker, *Nation or Empire?*, pp. 2, 20; John Kenneth Galbraith, "An Agenda for American Liberals," *Commentary*, June 1966, p. 31; McGeorge Bundy, "The End of Either/Or," *Foreign Affairs*, January 1967, pp. 189, 191, 200.

47. Henry Steele Commager, "How Not to Be a World Power," *New York Times Magazine*, March 12, 1967, p. 135; Theodore Draper, "The American Crisis: Vietnam, Cuba & the Dominican Republic," *Commentary*, January 1967, p. 27; Norman Podhoretz, "Liberal Anti-Communism Revisited," *Commentary*, September 1967, p. 31.

48. Hubert H. Humphrey, "Constructive Initiatives for Freedom and Peace," *Department of State Bulletin*, May 13, 1968, p. 603; Herbert S. Parmet, *The Democrats* (New York: Macmillan, 1976), p. 286; Gillon, *Politics and Vision*, pp. 228–229.

49. "Why Foreign Policy?" *Foreign Policy*, Winter 1970–1971, p. 4.

50. Richard J. Barnet and Marcus Raskin, *After 20 Years* (New York: Random House, 1965), pp. 32, 69, 72, 178.

51. Barnet and Raskin, *After 20 Years*, p. 193.

52. Richard J. Barnet, *Intervention and Revolution* (New York: New American Library, 1968), pp. 16, 15, 261.

53. Barnet, *Intervention and Revolution*, pp. 273, 276.

54. Richard J. Barnet, "The Illusion of Security," *Foreign Policy*, Summer 1971, pp. 84, 72, 83; Richard J. Barnet, "The Game of Nations," *Harper's*, November 1971, p. 53; Richard J. Barnet, "The Great Foreign Policy Debate We Ought to Be Having," *New Republic*, January 17, 1976, pp. 20, 21; Richard J. Barnet and Ronald E. Müller, *Global Reach* (New York: Simon and Schuster, 1974), p. 151.

55. The reviews cited are Henry Kissinger, "Answers Aren't Easy," *New York Times Book Review*, June 27, 1965, p. 3; Anthony Sampson, "Global Reach," *New York Times Book Review*, January 26, 1975, p. 2; and David Fromkin, "Who's Managing the World?" *New Republic*, April 19, 1975, p. 23. John Kenneth Galbraith, "The Decline of American Power," *Esquire*, March 1972, pp. 82, 84.

56. Stanley Hoffmann, *Gulliver's Troubles* (New York: McGraw-Hill, 1968), p. 80; Stanley Hoffmann, "A Great Power Cannot Treat Every Tremor as a Major Threat," *Commonweal*, March 21, 1969, p. 14; Stanley Hoffmann, "Policy for the 70s," *Life*, March 21, 1969, p. 70.

57. Stanley Hoffmann, "Notes on the Elusiveness of Modern Power," *International Journal* 30 (Spring 1975): 183, 203; Stanley Hoffmann, "Weighing the Balance of Power," *Foreign Affairs*, July 1975, p. 643. For Hoffmann's approach to the practical problems of developing a world order, see Stanley Hoffmann, "Choices," *Foreign Policy*, Fall 1973. For a summary of issues facing the international community, see Stanley Hoffmann, *Primacy or World Order* (New York: McGraw-Hill, 1978), pp. 190–192.

58. Hoffmann, *Primacy or World Order*, p. 220, 258, 286.

59. Richard J. Gardner, "The Hard Road to World Order," *Foreign Affairs*, April 1974, pp. 576, 563; Richard A. Melanson, "World Order Theorists and the Carter Administration," in Kenneth W. Thompson, ed., *Traditions and Values* (Lanham, Md.: University Press of America, 1984), p. 105; Cyrus Vance, "Overview of Foreign Policy Issues and Positions," reprinted in Cyrus Vance, *Hard Choices* (New York: Simon and Schuster, 1983), p. 441.

60. Zbigniew Brzezinski, *Between Two Ages* (New York: Viking, 1971), pp. xiv, 281, 282, 301, 308. For an early example of Brzezinski's ideas on the technetronic age, see Zbigniew Brzezinski, "The Implications of Change for United States Foreign Policy," *Department of State Bulletin*, July 3, 1967, pp. 19-23.

61. Zbigniew Brzezinski, "A Community of the Developed Nations," *Newsweek*, February 1, 1971, p. 40; Brzezinski, *Between Two Ages*, p. 293; Zbigniew Brzezinski, "America and Europe," *Foreign Affairs*, October 1970, pp. 17, 20.

62. Zbigniew Brzezinski, "U.S. Foreign Policy: The Search for Focus," *Foreign Affairs*, July 1973, pp. 712, 722, 724; Zbigniew Brzezinski, "Unmanifest Destiny: Where Do We Go From Here?" *New York*, March 3, 1975, reprinted in *Current*, April 1975, p. 58; Zbigniew Brzezinski, "America in a Hostile World," *Foreign Policy*, Summer 1976, pp. 76, 95.

63. Brzezinski, "America in a Hostile World," p. 92.

Chapter Two   Liberalism's Split

1. The neoconservatives are notable for having published virtually no memoirs about themselves and their politics. Only Norman Podhoretz has written autobiographical works, *Making It* (New York: Random House, 1967), and *Breaking Ranks* (New York: Harper & Row, 1979). Other neoconservatives have published book-length collections of their essays which give insights into the development of their thinking but no personal reflections. See Midge Decter, *The Liberated Woman and Other Americans* (New York: Coward, McCann & Geoghegan, 1971), and *Liberal Parents, Radical Children* (New York: Coward, McCann & Geoghegan, 1975); Irving Kristol, *On the Democratic Idea in America* (New York: Harper & Row, 1972), and *Reflections of a Neoconservative* (New York: Basic Books, 1976). For an example of the lessons drawn from failed social reforms, see Daniel Patrick Moynihan, *Maximum Feasible Misunderstanding* (New York: The Free Press, 1969).

There are several good secondary sources which describe neoconservatism and its emergence in the late 1960s and early 1970s. George H. Nash, *The Conservative Intellectual Movement in America Since 1945* (New York: Basic Books, 1976), describes the intellectual context of neoconservatism's appearance. Alexander Bloom's *Prodigal Sons* (New York: Oxford University Press, 1986) is an exhaustive treatment of the New York intellectuals, many of whom became identified as neoconservatives, and is a good source of biographical information. Neil Jumonville, *Critical Crossings* (Berkeley and Los Angeles: University of California Press, 1991) tells largely the same story. J. David Hoeveler, Jr., *Watch on the Right* (Madison: University of Wisconsin Press, 1991) has useful biographical sketches and summaries of the thinking of Irving Kristol, Jeane Kirkpatrick, and Michael Novak. Gary Dorrien, *The Neoconservative Mind* (Philadelphia: Temple University Press, 1993) contains thorough intellectual biographies of Kristol,

Podhoretz, Novak, and Peter Berger and places them in the context of the larger American conservative movement. More hostile treatments of neoconservatism may be found in Peter Steinfels, *The Neoconservatives* (New York: Simon and Schuster, 1979), and Sidney Blumenthal, *The Rise of the Counter-Establishment* (New York: Harper & Row, 1986).

2. Mark J. Rozell, "Jeane Kirkpatrick's Public Philosophy and Rhetoric," in Mark J. Rozell and James F. Pontuso, eds., *American Conservative Opinion Leaders* (Boulder: Westview Press, 1990), p. 137; Nathan Glazer, "On Being Deradicalized," *Commentary*, October 1970, p. 80.

3. Norman Podhoretz, *Making It* (New York: Random House, 1967), p. 288; Norman Podhoretz, *Breaking Ranks* (New York: Harper & Row, 1979), pp. 81, 86; Glazer, "On Being Deradicalized," p. 76.

4. Alexander Bloom, *Prodigal Sons* (New York: Oxford University Press, 1986), p. 351; Irving Howe, "The New York Intellectuals: A Chronicle and a Critique," *Commentary*, October 1968, p. 45; Irving Kristol, "The Old Politics, the New Politics, The *New*, New Politics," *New York Times Magazine*, November 24, 1968, p. 174. For a concise history of the New Left, see John P. Diggins, *The Rise and Fall of the American Left* (New York: W. W. Norton, 1992), chapter 6.

5. Moynihan, *Maximum Feasible Misunderstanding*, p. 170; Kristol, "The Old Politics," p. 164.

6. Aaron Wildavsky, "The Empty-Head Blues: Black Rebellion and White Reaction," *Public Interest* 11, Spring 1968, pp. 3; Aristede and Vera Zolberg, "The Americanization of Frantz Fanon," *Public Interest* 9, Fall 1967, p. 62; Kristol, "The New Politics," p. 176.

7. Daniel Patrick Moynihan, "The Politics of Stability," *New Leader*, October 9, 1967, pp. 7, 9; Joseph A. Loftus, "Moynihan Calls on ADA to Seek Ties With Conservatives," *New York Times*, September 24, 1967, p. 1; Tom Wicker, "Which Law and Whose Order?" *New York Times*, October 3, 1967, p. 46.

8. Nathan Glazer, "Negroes & Jews: The New Challenge to Pluralism," *Commentary*, December 1964, pp. 28, 29; M. S. Handler, "4-City Study of Negroes Finds Majority Hold Moderate Views," *New York Times*, May 26, 1967, p. 32.

9. James Baldwin, "Negroes Are Anti-Semitic Because They're Anti-White," *New York Times Magazine*, April 9, 1967, p. 139; Earl Raab, "The Black Revolution & The Jewish Question," *Commentary*, January 1969, p. 29.

10. Gene Roberts, "SNCC Charges Israel Atrocities," *New York Times*, August 15, 1967, p. 1; Douglas Robinson, "New Carmichael Trip," *New York Times*, August 19, 1967, p. 8.

11. Robert Alter, "Israel & The Intellectuals," *Commentary*, October 1967, p. 49. See also Martin Peretz, "The American Left And Israel," *Commentary*, November 1967; Irving Spiegel, "Rising Hostility to Jews is Seen," *New York Times*, December 2, 1967, p. 42.

12. Nathan Glazer, "Remembering the Answers," *Atlantic*, July 1969, reprinted in Nathan Glazer, *Remembering the Answers* (New York: Basic Books, 1969), p. 275.

13. Steven Donadio, "Black Power at Columbia," *Commentary*, September 1968, p. 68.

14. Sylvan Fox, "Faculty's Effort Fails to Resolve Columbia Dispute," *New York Times*, April 27, 1968, p. 18; Steven V. Roberts, "Black and White," *New Leader*, May 20, 1968, p. 15.

15. Dotson Rader and Craig Anderson, "Rebellion at Columbia," *New Republic*, May 11, 1968, p. 10; Diana Trilling, "On the Steps of Low Library: Liberalism & the Revolution of the Young," *Commentary*, November 1968, reprinted in Diana Trilling, *We Must March My Darlings* (New York: Harcourt Brace Jovanovich, 1977), pp. 115, 127.

16. Nathan Glazer, "Blacks, Jews, & Intellectuals," *Commentary*, April 1969, p. 36. For details of the *Commentary-New York Review* quarrel, see Merle Miller, "Why Norman and Jason Aren't Talking," *New York Times Magazine*, March 26, 1972, and Dennis Wrong, "The Case of the *New York Review*," *Commentary*, November 1970.

17. Podhoretz, *Breaking Ranks*, p. 47; *Time*, May 20, 1966, pp. 56-57.
    For further discussions of Podhoretz and the origins of his counterattacks, see Bloom, *Prodigal Sons*, chapter 14; Jumonville, *Critical Crossings*, pp. 193–202; and Dorrien, *The Neoconservative Mind*, chapter 4.

18. Podhoretz, *Breaking Ranks*, p. 305; Robert L. Bartley, "A Most Improbable 'Conservative,'" *Wall Street Journal*, November 10, 1970, p. 18; Israel Shenker, "Ideological Labels Changing Along With the Label-Makers," *New York Times*, November 12, 1970, p. 45.

19. Eugene Goodheart, "The Deradicalized Intellectuals," *Nation*, February 8, 1971, pp. 177, 178; Sol Stern, "My Jewish Problem—And Ours," *Ramparts*, August 1971, pp. 38, 40.

20. Peter Steinfels, "The Cooling of the Intellectuals," *Commonweal*, May 21, 1971, pp. 256, 260.

21. Joseph Epstein, "The New Conservatives: Intellectuals in Retreat," *Dissent*, Spring 1973, pp. 155, 156, 154.

22. "Split in the Family?" *National Review*, December 15, 1970, p. 1335; "Come On In, the Water's Fine," *National Review*, March 9, 1971, pp. 249, 250.

23. Seymour Martin Lipset, "Neoconservatism: Myth and Reality," *Society*, July-August, 1988, p. 29; James Q. Wilson in "Neoconservatism: Pro and Con," *Partisan Review*, 1980, no. 4, p. 509; Irving Kristol, "What is a 'Neo-Conservative'?" *Newsweek*, January 19, 1976, p. 17; Irving Kristol, "Confessions of a True, Self-Confessed—Perhaps the Only—'Neoconservative,'" *Public Opinion*, October/November 1979, reprinted in Kristol, *Reflections of a Neoconservative* (New York: Basic Books, 1983), pp. 74, 75.

24. Daniel Bell, *The Cultural Contradictions of Capitalism* (New York: Basic Books, 1978), p. xi; Midge Decter in "What is a Liberal—Who is a Conservative?" *Commentary*, September 1976, p. 51; Midge Decter, interview by author, February 25, 1991, New York City; Tom Buckley, "For the Senate: The Main Event East," *New York Times Magazine*, October 31, 1976, p. 57; Bloom, *Prodigal Sons*, p. 372.

25. Jeane J. Kirkpatrick, ed., *The Strategy of Deception* (New York: Farrar, Straus, 1963), p. xi.

26. Irving Kristol, "Memoirs of a Trotskyist," *New York Times Magazine*, January 23, 1977, reprinted in Kristol, *Reflections of a Neoconservative*, p. 11; David Sidorsky, discussion with author, February 26, 1991, New York City.

27. Midge Decter, interview by author, February 25, 1991; Hoeveler, *Watch on the Right*, pp. 154-155; Podhoretz, *Breaking Ranks*, p. 27; Lloyd Grove, "The Con-

trary Evolution of Elliott Abrams," *Washington Post*, January 14, 1987; Elliott Abrams, interview by author, July 6, 1990, Alexandria, Va.

28. Kenneth Crawford, "Isolationist Again?" *Newsweek*, November 20, 1967, p. 72; Walter Lippmann, "Relapse into Isolationism?" *Newsweek*, December 16, 1968, p. 27; "The Limits of Commitment: A Time-Louis Harris Poll," *Time*, May 2, 1969, p. 16; James A. Johnson, "The New Generation of Isolationists," *Foreign Affairs*, October 1970, pp. 141, 146.

29. Irving Kristol, "American Intellectuals and Foreign Policy," *Foreign Affairs*, July 1967, pp. 608-609.

30. Kristol, "American Intellectuals and Foreign Policy," p. 609; Irving Kristol, "We Can't Resign As 'Policeman of the World,'" *New York Times Magazine*, May 12, 1968, pp. 26, 27 (italics in the original).
    Kristol was not the only neoconservative to look to Niebuhr during this period. For another, and more conscious example, see Michael Novak, "Needing Niebuhr Again," *Commentary*, September 1972.

31. Kristol, "Why We Can't Resign," p. 106; Irving Kristol, "Why I Am For Humphrey," *New Republic*, June 8, 1968, p. 22; Irving Kristol, "A Foolish American Ism— Utopianism," *New York Times Magazine*, November 14, 1971, p. 103.

32. It is not surprising that Kristol left it to others to write the books. In mid-1993 he remarked that he prefers to write essays and lacks the patience to write a book-length manuscript. In any case, be believes that books are frequently just overly long essays (Irving Kristol, interview by author, July 21, 1993, Washington, D.C.).

33. Robert W. Tucker, *The Radical Left and American Foreign Policy* (Baltimore: Johns Hopkins University Press, 1971), pp. 152, 148.

34. Robert W. Tucker, *Nation or Empire?* (Baltimore: Johns Hopkins University Press, 1968), pp. 85, 155.

35. Tucker, *Nation or Empire*, pp. 52, 37, 160.

36. Robert W. Tucker, *A New Isolationism: Threat or Promise?* (New York: Universe, 1972), pp. 12, 17, 46, 64, 89.

37. Robert W. Tucker, "Oil: The Issue of American Intervention," *Commentary*, January 1975, p. 28.

38. Tucker, "Oil," pp. 22, 31, 29–30 (italics in the original).

39. Robert W. Tucker, "A New International Order?" *Commentary*, February 1975, pp. 41, 42, 45

40. Tucker, "A New International Order?" pp. 45, 47, 48-49; Tucker, "Oil," p. 31.

41. Walter Laqueur, "The Fall of Europe?" *Commentary*, January 1972, p. 37; Walter Laqueur, "The World of the 70s," *Commentary*, August 1972, p. 24; Walter Laqueur, "Rewriting History," *Commentary*, March 1973, p. 63; Walter Laqueur, "Lost Illusions: The End of the Postwar World?" *Social Research* 42 (Spring 1975): 18.

42. Walter Laqueur, "The West in Retreat," *Commentary*, August 1975, p. 50; Laqueur, "The Fall of Europe?" p. 33; Laqueur, "The World of the 70s," p. 24.

43. Laqueur, "The World of the 70s," p. 28; Laqueur, "The West in Retreat," p. 49; Walter Laqueur, "From Globalism to Isolationism," *Commentary*, September 1972, pp. 67, 66.

44. Walter Laqueur, "The Gathering Storm," *Commentary*, August 1974, pp. 24, 28, 29, 32, 33.

45. Decter interview, February 25, 1991.

46. Herbert S. Parmet, *The Democrats* (New York: Macmillan, 1976), pp. 230, 244, 290; Penn Kemble, "The Democrats After 1968," *Commentary*, January 1969, p. 35.

47. William Pfaff, "The Decline of Liberal Politics," *Commentary*, October 1969, p. 50; Penn Kemble, "Who Needs the Liberals?" *Commentary*, October 1970, p. 58, 62; Penn Kemble and Josh Muravchik, "The New Politics & the Democrats," *Commentary*, December 1972, pp. 79, 83, 78, 84.

48. Norman Podhoretz, "What the Voters Sensed," *Commentary*, January 1973, p. 6; Jeane Kirkpatrick, "The Revolt of the Masses," *Commentary*, February 1973, pp. 62, 59-60.

   Kirkpatrick's identification of McGovern as a cultural class enemy drew on Joseph Schumpeter's observations on the sociology of intellectuals. According to Schumpeter, "Capitalism creates a critical frame of mind which, after having destroyed the moral authority of so many other institutions, in the end turns against its own . . . [and] goes on to attack private property and the whole scheme of bourgeois values." The intellectuals "work up and organize resentment, . . . nurse it, . . . voice it and . . . lead it" (Joseph A. Schumpeter, *Capitalism, Socialism, and Democracy*, 3d. ed. [New York: Harper & Brothers, 1950], pp. 143, 145). During the 1970s, the neoconservatives would increasingly rely on Schumpeter's theory for their own analyses of liberal intellectuals.

49. Seymour Martin Lipset and Earl Raab, "The Election and the National Mood," *Commentary*, January 1973, pp. 44, 45.

50. George S. McGovern, "Are Our Military Alliances Meaningful?" *The Annals* 384 (July 1969): 20; Robert Reinhold, "Scholars Starting to Advise McGovern," *New York Times*, June 18, 1972, p. 28; "Text of Statement by Senator McGovern Presenting His Views on Foreign Policy," *New York Times*, October 6, 1972, p. 26; Podhoretz, *Breaking Ranks*, p. 291.

51. Decter interview, February 25, 1991.

52. Christopher Lydon, "5 Governors Fight Democrats' Chief," *New York Times*, November 17, 1972, p. 1; Advertisement in *New York Times*, December 7, 1972, p. 14.

53. Paul R. Wieck, "Chairman Strauss' Hot Seat," *New Republic*, April 20, 1974, p. 18; Paul R. Wieck, "Everything Hunky-dory in Kansas City," *New Republic*, December 21, 1974, p. 12; Richard Perle, telephone interview by author, March 25, 1991.

54. Decter interview, February 25, 1991.

55. Decter interview, February 25, 1991.

Chapter Three   The Intellectual in Politics

1. There is only one book-length biography of Moynihan, Douglas Schoen, *Pat* (New York: Harper & Row, 1979), but Schoen's admiration of his subject leaves the book useful chiefly as a chronology of Moynihan's life until 1979. Moynihan has not written an autobiography, but has produced a large body of writings that detail his intellectual and political development. Chief among these are *Maximum Feasible Misunderstanding* (New York: The Free press, 1969), *The Politics of a Guaranteed Annual Income* (New York: Random House, 1973), and *A Dan-*

gerous Place (Boston: Little Brown, 1978). Moynihan has also published a large number of articles in *Commentary* and *Public Interest*, which demonstrate his approach to social and political problems.

2. Schoen, *Pat*, pp. 7, 11.

3. Schoen, *Pat*, pp. 31-48.

4. Moynihan's first published articles appeared in the *Reporter*, whose editor, Irving Kristol, "encouraged Moynihan to do more writing" (Schoen, *Pat*, p. 62).

5. Schoen, *Pat*, p. 34; Moynihan letter quoted on p. 35.

6. Daniel Patrick Moynihan, "'Bosses' and 'Reformers,'" *Commentary*, June 1961, p. 465; Schoen, *Pat*, pp. 55-56.

7. Lee Rainwater and William L. Yancey, *The Moynihan Report and the Politics of Controversy* (Cambridge: MIT Press, 1967), pp. 18, 19-25, 26-27; Moynihan quoted in Rainwater and Yancey, p. 25.

8. Daniel P. Moynihan, *The Negro Family: The Case for National Action*, Department of Labor, Office of Policy Planning and Research, March 1965, pp. i, 5, 15-21, 27, 30-40, 43, 45, 48, reprinted in Rainwater and Yancey, *Moynihan Report*.

9. Rainwater and Yancey, *Moynihan Report*, pp. 32, 130.

10. "Moynihan Report," *New Republic*, September 11, 1965 p. 8; Moynihan, *Negro Family*, p. 3; Whitney Young, Jr., "The 'Real' Moynihan Report," January 1966, reprinted in Rainwater and Yancey, *Moynihan Report*, p. 416; William Ryan, "Savage Discovery: The Moynihan Report," *Nation*, November 22, 1965, reprinted in Rainwater and Yancey, *Moynihan Report*, pp. 458, 462, 463, 464; Thomas Meehan, "Moynihan of the Moynihan Report," *New York Times Magazine*, July 31, 1966, p. 48.

11. Daniel Patrick Moynihan, "The President & The Negro: The Moment Lost," *Commentary*, February 1967, pp. 31, 33, 34, 37.

12. Moynihan, "The President & The Negro," pp. 41-42, 43.

13. Norman Podhoretz, *Breaking Ranks* (New York: Harper & Row, 1979), p. 354; Daniel Patrick Moynihan, "The Politics of Stability," *New Leader*, October 9, 1967, pp. 10, 9.

14. Fred Powledge, "Idea Broker in the Race Crisis," *Life*, November 3, 1967, p. 75; "Light in the Frightening Corners," *Time*, July 28, 1967, p. 10.

15. Daniel Patrick Moynihan, "The Democrats, Kennedy & "The Murder of Dr. King," *Commentary*, May 1968, pp. 20, 26.

16. Daniel Patrick Moynihan, "Eliteland," *Psychology Today*, September 1970, p. 70; Daniel Patrick Moynihan, "Politics as the Art of the Impossible," *American Scholar*, Autumn 1969, p. 573; Henry Brandon, "A Moynihan Report—After Six Months of 'Benign Neglect,'" *New York Times Magazine*, June 27, 1971, p. 50.

17. Moynihan, "The Democrats, Kennedy & The Murder of Dr. King," p. 29; Schoen, *Pat*, pp. 143-146.

18. For examples of writers attributing a Disraeli strategy for Nixon to Moynihan, see Schoen, *Pat*, p. 147, and Edward D. Berkowitz, *America's Welfare State* (Baltimore: Johns Hopkins University Press, 1991), p. 127.

19. Daniel Patrick Moynihan, *The Politics of a Guaranteed Annual Income* (New York: Random House, 1973), p. 147. The best short summaries of the plan, its demise in Congress, and research about its likely effects may be found in Nathan

Glazer, *The Limits of Social Policy*, (Cambridge: Harvard University Press, 1988), chapter 2, and Berkowitz, *America's Welfare State*, pp. 126–133.

20. Glazer, *Limits of Reform*, pp. 29–32; Moynihan, *Politics of a Guaranteed Annual Income*, p. 353 (italics in the original); Brandon, "A Moynihan Report," p. 55.

21. "Text of the Moynihan Memorandum on the Status of Negroes," *New York Times*, March 1, 1970, p. 69.

22. "Text of the Moynihan Memorandum."

23. "Neglect—but Not 'Benign,'" *New York Times*, March 3, 1970, p. 40; Schoen, *Pat*, p. 166.

24. Bernard Weinraub, "Daniel Moynihan's Passage to India," *New York Times Magazine*, March 31, 1974, p. 68.

25. Daniel Patrick Moynihan, "The Presidency & the Press," *Commentary*, March 1971, pp. 43, 52, 51, 45, 52, 44 (italics in the original). Schumpeter's point about the adversary role of intellectuals remained in Moynihan's mind for some time. For a further example of his thinking on the subject, see Daniel Patrick Moynihan, "An Address to the Entering Class at Harvard College, 1972," *Commentary*, December 1972.

26. Schoen, *Pat*, p. 183.

27. Schoen, *Pat*, p. 188.

28. Weinraub, "Moynihan's Passage to India," pp. 17; Patrick Moynihan, *A Dangerous Place*, p. 18.

29. Moynihan, *A Dangerous Place*, pp. 12; Israel Shenker, "Moynihan Finds U.N. With Head Lost in Cloud of Ideals," *New York Times*, November 10, 1971, p. 16.

30. Moynihan, *A Dangerous Place*, p. 37; Tom Buckley, "Brawler at the U.N.," *New York Times Magazine*, December 7, 1975, p. 111.

Moynihan's account of his diplomatic experiences in India and at the United Nations in *A Dangerous Place* should be approached cautiously. Moynihan is accurate in his recounting of facts and events, but his interpretation of his own role and effectiveness is one-sided and somewhat self-serving. Nevertheless, a careful reading of *A Dangerous Place* provides insights into what Moynihan was thinking and trying to achieve in 1975. For a skeptical review of the book, see Gaddis Smith, "Bugling the Red, White and Blue," *New York Times Book Review*, December 10, 1978, p. 3.

31. Daniel Patrick Moynihan, "Was Woodrow Wilson Right?" *Commentary*, May 1974, pp. 26, 28, 29.

32. Moynihan "Was Woodrow Wilson Right?" pp. 30, 31; Moynihan, *A Dangerous Place*, pp. 28, 31.

33. Moynihan's cable is reprinted in William F. Buckley, Jr., *United Nations Journal* (New York: G. P. Putnam's Sons, 1974), pp. 258, 260.

34. Moynihan, *A Dangerous Place*, pp. 27, 37.

35. Daniel Patrick Moynihan, "The United States in Opposition," *Commentary*, March 1975, pp. 31, 32, 33, 34, 39–40.

36. Moynihan, "United States in Opposition," pp. 35, 36, 37-38, 40.

37. Moynihan, "United States in Opposition," pp. 41, 42, 43, 44 (italics in the original).

38. Moynihan, *A Dangerous Place*, pp. 59, 61; "On the Disaster," *New Republic*, May 3, 1975, p. 3.

39. Daniel Patrick Moynihan, "Presenting the American Case," *American Scholar*, Autumn 1975, pp. 567, 582.

40. Congress, Senate, Committee on Foreign Relations, *The United States and the United Nations*, 94th Cong., 1st sess., June 4, 1975, pp. 384, 385; Moynihan, *A Dangerous Place*, p. 72.

41. Moynihan, *A Dangerous Place*, pp. 111, 129-139.

42. Moynihan, *A Dangerous Place*, pp. 169-170; Moynihan, "United States in Opposition," p. 42; "Statement by Ambassador Moynihan, Plenary, November 10," reprinted in *Department of State Bulletin*, December 1, 1975, pp. 791, 793, 794.

43. "The Moynihan Controversy," *Newsweek*, October 20, 1975, p. 50; Moynihan, *A Dangerous Place*, pp. 153-154, 162-164.

44. Daniel Patrick Moynihan, "A Diplomat's Rhetoric," *Harper's*, January 1976, p. 42; Daniel Patrick Moynihan, "Soviet Ideology," *Vital Speeches*, January 1, 1976, p. 176.

45. "Benign Attention at the U.N.," *Newsweek*, September 22, 1975, p. 34; Buckley, "Brawler at the U.N.," "Mr. Moynihan's Stellar Finale," *Chicago Tribune*, December 21, 1975, section 2, p. 4; "Man of the Year," *National Review*, January 23, 1976, pp. 20-21; "A Fighting Irishman at the U.N.," *Time*, January 26, 1976, pp. 26, 34.

46. "A Fighting Irishman at the U.N.," p. 27; Midge Decter, interview by author, February 25, 1991, New York City.

47. Moynihan, *A Dangerous Place*, pp. 3, 72 (italics in the original).

48. Moynihan, *A Dangerous Place*, pp. 213, 219; Daniel Patrick Moynihan, "I Say it's Spinach and I Say the Hell With It!" interview by Eric Sevareid, May 30, 1976, in *Society*, November-December 1976, p. 77; Schoen, *Pat*, p. 234; "Playboy Interview: Pat Moynihan," *Playboy*, March 1977, reprinted in G. Barry Golson, ed., *The Playboy Interview* (New York: Playboy Press, 1981), p. 513.

49. "Text of Cablegram Sent by Moynihan to Kissinger and All American Embassies," *New York Times*, January 28, 1976, p. 8.

50. Leslie H. Gelb, "Moynihan Says State Department Fails To Back Policy Against U.S. Foes in U.N.," *New York Times*, January 28, 1976, p. 1.

51. "Administration Backs Moynihan," *New York Times*, January 29, 1976, p. 9; James Reston, "What About Moynihan?" *New York Times*, January 30, 1976, p. 29.

52. "What Next for Pat Moynihan?" *Time*, February 9, 1976, p. 21.

53. Moynihan, *A Dangerous Place*, p. 212.

54. Decter interview, February 25, 1991; Schoen, *Pat*, p. 249.

55. Jon Margolis, "N.Y. Race Could Produce a President," *Chicago Tribune*, October 26, 1976, p. 5; Daniel Patrick Moynihan, "The Liberals' Dilemma," *New Republic*, January 22, 1977, pp. 58, 60.

56. Decter interview, February 25, 1991; Charles Horner, interview by author, May 7, 1991, Washington, D.C.

57. Daniel Patrick Moynihan in the *Congressional Record*, Senate, March 4, 1977, p. 6396.

58. Golson, *The Playboy Interview*, p. 510; Daniel Patrick Moynihan, "The Politics of Human Rights," *Commentary*, August 1977, p. 20; Daniel Patrick Moynihan, "Unwords and Policy," *New York Times*, November 21, 1978, p. 21.

59. *Congressional Record*, March 4, 1977, p. 6395; Ben J. Wattenberg, "Is There A Crisis of Spirit in the West?" *Public Opinion*, May/June 1978, pp. 4, 7; Moynihan, "The Politics of Human Rights," p. 25.

60. Daniel Patrick Moynihan in the *Congressional Record*, Senate, April 13, 1978, p. 9981.

61. Moynihan, *A Dangerous Place*, p. 278; Moynihan, "The Politics of Human Rights," pp. 23, 24.

Chapter Four   Searching for Truman, 1976–1980

1. There are a number of good sources for the study of Carter and his attitudes toward foreign affairs. For Carter's own statements, see Jimmy Carter, *Why Not the Best?* (New York: Bantam Books, 1975), chapter 13, and Carter's memoir *Keeping Faith* (New York: Bantam, 1983). For first-hand accounts of Carter's diplomacy, see Zbigniew Brzezinski, *Power and Principle* (New York: Farrar, Straus, Giroux, 1983), and Cyrus Vance, *Hard Choices* (New York: Simon and Schuster, 1983).

   Although no definitive works on Carter and his diplomacy have yet been written, there are several good secondary accounts. Betty Glad, *Jimmy Carter* (New York: W. W. Norton, 1980), provides an excellent introduction to Carter and his views. Gaddis Smith, *Morality, Reason & Power* (New York: Hill and Wang, 1986), presents a comprehensive and balanced account of Carter's policies. Donald S. Spencer, *The Carter Implosion* (New York: Praeger, 1988), is comprehensive and unremittingly hostile. Raymond L. Garthoff, *Detente and Confrontation* (Washington: Brookings Institution, 1985), contains an in-depth description of Carter's relations with the USSR. Finally, John Lewis Gaddis has covered Carter in two of his books, *Strategies of Containment* (New York: Oxford University Press, 1982), chapter 11, and *Russia, the Soviet Union, and the United States*, 2d. ed. (New York: McGraw-Hill, 1990), chapter 10.

2. Carter, *Keeping Faith*, p. 51; Carter's speech to the Foreign Policy Association was printed in the *New York Times*, June 24, 1976, p. 22.

3. Carter, *Why Not the Best?* p. 141; Glad, *Jimmy Carter*, pp. 315, 477, 478-483.

4. Christopher Lydon, "Carter, Outlining Foreign Policy Views, Urges Wider Discussion," *New York Times*, March 16, 1976, p. 24; the quote on Israel is from Carter's June speech to the Foreign Policy Association.

5. Leslie H. Gelb, "Carter's Foreign Views Fit Liberal Democratic Mold," *New York Times*, July 7, 1976, pp. 1, 12; Tad Szulc, "Carter's Foreign Policy," *New Republic*, July 17, 1976, p. 15.

6. Vance, *Hard Choices*, p. 441; Congress, Senate, Committee on Foreign Relations, *Vance Nomination: Hearing Before the Committee on Foreign Relations*. 95th Cong., 1st sess., January 11, 1977, p. 5; Leslie H. Gelb, "The Kissinger Legacy," *New York Times Magazine*, October 31, 1976, p. 72.

7. Marshall Shulman, "On Learning to Live with Authoritarian Regimes," *Foreign Affairs*, January 1977, pp. 334, 338, 327, 331, 337.

8. Paul Warnke, "Apes on a Treadmill," *Foreign Policy*, Spring 1975, pp. 19, 18, 21.

9. Andrew Young, "Why I Support Jimmy Carter," *Nation*, April 3, 1976, p. 397; "Playboy Interview: Andrew Young," *Playboy*, July 1977, pp. 78, 76, 68, 82.

10. Commencement address at the University of Notre Dame, May 22, 1977, in

Public Papers of the Presidents of the United States, Jimmy Carter, 1977, vol. 1 (Washington: U.S. Government Printing Office, 1977), p. 956; Raymond L. Garthoff, *Détente and Confrontation* (Washington: Brookings Institution, 1985), p. 565.

11. Midge Decter in "America Now: A Failure of Nerve?" *Commentary*, July 1975, p. 29; Theodore Draper, "Appeasement & Détente," *Commentary*, February 1976, pp. 35, 36.

12. Norman Podhoretz, "Making the World Safe for Communism," *Commentary*, April 1976, pp. 32, 35.

13. Podhoretz, "Making the World Safe for Communism," p. 33; Walter Laqueur, "The West in Retreat," *Commentary*, August 1975, p. 44.

14. Peter L. Berger, "The Greening of American Foreign Policy," *Commentary*, March 1976, pp. 23, 25, 27; Walter Laqueur, "Third World Fantasies," *Commentary*, February 1977, p. 43.

15. Nathan Glazer, "American Values & American Foreign Policy," *Commentary*, July 1976, pp. 33, 34 (italics in the original); Robert W. Tucker, "Beyond Detente," *Commentary*, March 1977, p. 45.

16. Tucker, "Beyond Detente," p. 46; Edward N. Luttwak, "Defense Reconsidered," *Commentary*, March 1977, pp. 57, 58.

17. Bayard Rustin and Carl Gershman, "Africa, Soviet Imperialism & the Retreat of American Power," *Commentary*, October 1977, pp. 33, 36, 37, 38.

18. Laqueur, "The West in Retreat," p. 48; Podhoretz, "Making the World Safe for Communism," pp. 38, 39; Glazer, "American Values & American Foreign Policy," pp. 35, 36.

19. Norman Podhoretz, "The Culture of Appeasement," *Harper's*, October 1977, pp. 29, 31; Walter Laqueur, "Confronting the Problems," *Commentary*, March 1977, p. 35.

20. Norman Podhoretz, "The Abandonment of Israel," *Commentary*, July 1976, pp. 25, 30, 27.

21. Arthur M. Schlesinger, Jr., *The Vital Center*, Sentry edition (Boston: Houghton Mifflin, 1962), p. 50; Berger, "The Greening of American Foreign Policy," p. 27.

22. Podhoretz, "Making the World Safe for Communism," p. 32.

23. Charles Horner, interview by author, May 7, 1991, Washington, D.C. The joke about Micronesia was reported in Morton Kondracke, "The Neoconservative Dilemma," *New Republic*, August 2 and 9, 1980, p. 10.

24. Walter Laqueur, "Containment for the 80s," *Commentary*, October 1980, p. 36; Bayard Rustin and Carl Gershman, "Africa, Soviet Imperialism & the Retreat of American Power," *Commentary*, October 1977, p. 36; Chalmers Johnson, "Carter in Asia: McGovernism without McGovern," *Commentary*, January 1978, p. 39; Carl Gershman, "The Rise & Fall of the New Foreign Policy Establishment," *Commentary*, July 1980, pp. 13, 20.

25. Carl Gershman, "The World According to Andrew Young," *Commentary*, August 1978, p. 22.

26. Walter Laqueur, "The World & President Carter," *Commentary*, February 1978, pp. 63, 56; Robert W. Tucker, "America in Decline: The Foreign Policy of 'Maturity,'" *Foreign Affairs: America and the World, 1979*, pp. 462, 464, 474.

27. Richard Pipes, "Team B: The Reality Behind the Myth," *Commentary*, October 1986, p. 33.

28. Paul Nitze, *From Hiroshima to Glasnost* (New York: Grove Weidenfeld, 1989), pp. 353, 354; "Common Sense and the Common Danger," in Charles Taylor, II, ed., *Alerting America* (Washington: Pergamon-Brassey's, 1984), pp. 5, 4, 6. For Nitze's doubts about SALT before the Team B episode ("I believe the record shows that neither negotiations nor unilateral restraint have operated to dissuade Soviet leaders from seeking a nuclear-war-winning capability"), see Paul Nitze, "Assuring Strategic Stability in an Era of Detente," *Foreign Affairs*, January 1976, p. 230.

  There are three major sources for the history of the Committee on the Present Danger. *Alerting America*, the major primary source, is a collection of the committee's reports and papers. Jerry W. Sanders, *Peddlers of Crisis* (Boston: South End Press, 1983), provides a comparative history of the committee as well as its predecessor (and namesake) from the 1950s, written from a Marxist perspective. Beth Ann Ingold, "The Committee on the Present Danger: A Study of Elite and Public Influence, 1976-1980," Ph.D. diss., University of Pittsburgh, 1989, provides a history of the committee and its influence, concluding that it was effective in undermining public support for Carter's policies while raising public awareness of the Soviet threat and building support for a hardline response.

29. "What is the Soviet Union Up To?" in *Alerting America*, p. 14; Paul Nitze, "A Plea for Action," *New York Times Magazine*, May 7, 1978, p. 117; "Is America Becoming Number 2?" in *Alerting America*, p. 42 (italics in the original); Paul Nitze, "Is SALT II a Fair Deal for the United States?" in *Alerting America*, p. 162.

30. Eugene V. Rostow, "The Case Against Salt II," *Commentary*, February 1979, p. 30; Edward Luttwak, "Ten Questions about SALT II," *Commentary*, August 1979, pp. 25, 30.

31. Ben Wattenberg, "It's Time to Stop America's Retreat," *New York Times Magazine*, July 22, 1979, pp. 14, 16 (italics in the original); Nitze, "A Plea for Action," p. 117; Richard Pipes, "Soviet Global Strategy," *Commentary*, April 1980, p. 39.

32. Walter Laqueur, "Containment for the 80s," pp. 34, 38, 41.

33. Wattenberg, "It's Time to Stop America's Retreat," p. 16; Laqueur, "Containment for the 80s," p. 40.

34. Glazer, "American Values & American Foreign Policy," pp. 33, 34.

  Arendt's description of the difference between authoritarianism and totalitarianism was this: "Totalitarianism differs essentially from other forms of political oppression known to us such as despotism, tyranny and dictatorship. Wherever it rose to power, it developed entirely new political institutions and destroyed all social, legal and political traditions of the country" (Hannah Arendt, *The Origins of Totalitarianism*, revised edition [New York: Harcourt, Brace & World, 1966], p. 460).

35. Maurice Cranston, "Should We Cease to Speak of Totalitarianism," *Survey* 23 (Summer 1977-1978): 62; Raymond Aron, "Ideology and Totalitarianism," *Survey* 23 (Summer 1977-1978): 81; Laqueur, "The World & President Carter," p. 59.

36. Carl Gershman, "After the Dominoes Fell," *Commentary*, May 1978, p. 53; Gershman, "The World According to Andrew Young," p. 23 (italics in the original);

Peter Berger, "Indochina & the American Conscience," *Commentary*, February 1980, p. 36.

37. Allan Gerson, *The Kirkpatrick Mission* (New York: The Free Press, 1991), p. xiii.

38. Jeane J. Kirkpatrick, ed., *The Strategy of Deception* (New York: Farrar, Straus, 1963), p. xviii; Jeane J. Kirkpatrick, *Leader and Vanguard in Mass Society*, (Cambridge: MIT Press, 1971), pp. 40–41; Jeane J. Kirkpatrick. "The Trivialization of Government," in Ernest W. Lefever, ed., *Values in an American Government Textbook* (Washington: Ethics and Public Policy Center, Georgetown University, 1978), p. 21.

    Kirkpatrick took her criteria for determining the non-totalitarian character of Peronism from Carl Friedrich, another political scientist who believed that "totalitarian dictatorship is historically an innovative and *sui generis*," and that "there has never been anything quite like it before" (Carl J. Friedrich, *Totalitarian Dictatorship and Autocracy*, 2d. ed., [Cambridge: Harvard University Press, 1965], pp. 15, 19).

39. Jeane J. Kirkpatrick, *Political Women* (New York: Basic Books, 1974), p. 251.

40. Jeane J. Kirkpatrick, "Dismantling the Parties," (Washington: American Enterprise Institute, 1978), pp. 2, 12, 31. "Dismantling the Parties" drew on Kirkpatrick's extensive research for her book *The New Presidential Elite* (New York: Russell Sage Foundation and the Twentieth Century Fund, 1976).

41. Jeane J. Kirkpatrick, "Politics and the New Class," *Society*, January-February 1979, pp. 43, 42, 44.

42. Jeane J. Kirkpatrick, "Politics and the New Class," p. 48; Jeane J. Kirkpatrick, "Martin Diamond and the American Idea of Democracy," *Publius* 3 (summer 1978): 29; Jeane J. Kirkpatrick, "Regulation, Liberty, and Equality," *Regulation*, November-December 1977, pp. 13, 15 (italics in the original).

43. Jeane J. Kirkpatrick, "Dictatorships and Double Standards," *Commentary*, November 1979, pp. 37, 38.

44. Kirkpatrick, "Dictatorships and Double Standards," pp. 38, 42, 35, 39, 45, 40.

45. Kirkpatrick, "Dictatorships and Double Standards," p. 44.

46. Schlesinger, *The Vital Center*, pp. 243, 234.

    Historian J. David Hoeveler, Jr., sees Kirkpatrick's thinking in the mid- and late 1970s as part of a process which brought her to a Burkean position during the early years of the Reagan administration. On the question of human rights, for example, Hoeveler writes that "she described her skepticism as a Burkean suspicion of grand ideals and high moral principles and demanded with Burke to know how these would be located in specific institutions and how they would affect the habits of a people" (J. David Hoeveler, Jr., *Watch on the Right* [Madison: University of Wisconsin Press, 1991], p. 170).

    Along with Burke, Kirkpatrick also drew on the British political philosopher Michael Oakeshott for her criticisms of reformism. In the introduction to her 1982 collection of essays, *Dictatorships and Double Standards*, she restated her opposition to rational reformism in terms heavily reminiscent of Oakeshott: "Failure to distinguish between the domains of thought and experience, of rhetoric and politics, is, of course, the very essence of rationalism." Compare this with Oakeshott's observation that "rationalism is the assertion . . . that, properly speaking, there is no knowledge which is not technical knowledge" (Jeane J.

Kirkpatrick, *Dictatorships and Double Standards* [New York: Simon and Schuster, 1982], p. 11; Michael Oakeshott, *Rationalism in Politics and Other Essays*, [Indianapolis: Liberty Fund, 1991], p. 15.)

47. James A. Nuechterlein, "Neo-Conservatism and its Critics," *Virginia Quarterly Review*, Autumn 1977, p. 623; "Capitalism, Socialism, and Democracy," *Commentary*, April 1978, p. 29ff.

48. Elliott Abrams in "Why Are There Neoconservatives?" *American Spectator*, November 1979, p. 11.

49. Milton Himmelfarb, "Carter and the Jews," *Commentary*, August 1976, p. 48; Martin E. Marty, "Jimmy Carter is an Evangelical!" *Moment*, September 1976, p. 60; Melvin Urofsky, "President Carter—A New Era?" *Midstream*, January 1977, p. 43.

50. Himmelfarb, "Carter and the Jews," p. 48; Carter quoted in Urofsky, "A New Era?" p. 45. For Carter's efforts to win Jewish voters in 1976, see "Both Campaigns Courting Jewish Voters," *Washington Post*, October 14, 1976, p. A2.

51. George W. Ball, "How to Save Israel in Spite of Herself," *Foreign Affairs*, April 1977, pp. 470, 459.

52. "Clinton, Mass.," *Public Papers of the Presidents of the United States: Jimmy Carter, 1977*, vol. 1, p. 387; Bernard Reich, *The United States and Israel* (New York: Praeger, 1984), p. 53; Schindler quoted in Reich, *The United States and Israel*, p. 54.

53. Eugene V. Rostow, "The American Stake in Israel," *Commentary*, April 1977, pp. 37, 40; Herbert Kampf, "The American Interest in Israel's Security," *Midstream*, June/July 1977, pp. 28, 32.

54. "Don't Deliver Israel," *New Republic*, August 6 & 13, 1977, p. 5; Leonard Fein, "Carter, Israel, and the Jews," *Moment*, December 1977, p. 10.

55. Morton Kondracke, "The Crunch," *New Republic*, March 11, 1978, p. 12; "Carter and the Jews," *Newsweek*, March 20, 1978, p. 28.

56. "Andy Young Strikes Again," *Time*, July 24, 1978, p. 27.

57. Thomas A. Johnson, "Black Leaders Air Grievances on Jews," *New York Times*, August 23, 1979, p. 12.

58. Samuel Allis, "U.S. Jewish Leaders Lash Back After Criticism by Blacks," *Washington Post*, August 24, 1979, p. A16; Leonard Fein, "The Andrew Young Affair . . . To Be Continued," *Moment*, October 1979, p. 12; Cynthia Ozick, "Carter and the Jews," *New Leader*, June 30, 1980, p. 13.

59. "Newly Vulnerable Carter," *Newsweek*, March 17, 1980, pp. 27, 29; "A Sell-Out, Not a Foul-Up," *New Republic*, March 15, 1980, p. 5. Voting and poll results from New York are from *New York Times*, March 26, 1980, p. B5.

60. Wayne King, "Billy Carter's Problems," *New York Times*, February 17, 1979, p. 6; Martin Tolchin, "President Won't Condemn Brother's Remarks on Jews," *New York Times*, February 28, 1979, p. 16; Ozick, "Carter and the Jews," p. 6.

61. Seymour Martin Lipset and William Schneider, "Carter vs. Israel," *Commentary*, November 1977, pp. 26, 27, 29; Pranay Gupte, "Study Finds Dispute With Israel Would Hurt the Carter Race in 1980," *New York Times*, November 1, 1977, p. 9.

62. Carl Gershman, "The Andrew Young Affair," *Commentary*, November 1979, pp. 25, 32, 33.

63. "Liberalism & the Jews," *Commentary*, January 1980, pp. 15, 32, 37, 16, 66.

64. Robert Loewenberg, "The Theft of Liberalism—A Jewish Problem," *Midstream*, May 1977, p. 19; Rael Jean Isaac, "The Institute for Policy Studies: Empire on the Left," *Midstream*, June-July 1980, p. 7; Earl Raab, "Blacks and Jews Asunder?" *Midstream*, November 1979, pp. 3, 6; Earl Raab, "Jewish Unease and the Democratic Party," *Midstream*, October 1980, p. 15.

65. Maurice Carroll, "Carter's Aide is Booed in New York at a Rally for Soviet Jewry," *New York Times*, May 22, 1978, p. 19; Solomon Arbeiter, "Must Black-Jewish Relations Erode?" *New York Times*, October 21, 1979, sec. xi, p. 34; John Herbers, "Aftermath of Andrew Young Affair: Blacks, Jews and Carter All Could Suffer Greatly," *New York Times*, September 6, 1979, p. A18; Jeffrey Hart, "New Directions: Catholics and Jews," *National Review*, April 28, 1978, p. 517; Peter Steinfels, "The Reasonable Right," Esquire, February 13, 1979, p. 24 (italics in the original); Podhoretz, "The Present Danger," p. 38. For a skeptical contemporary view of neoconservatism, see Irving Howe, "The Right Menace," *New Republic*, November 9, 1978.

66. Alan M. Fisher, "Where is the New Jewish Conservatism," *Society*, June 1979, p. 16; Nick Kotz, "Why Not Mondale?" *New Republic*, November 17, 1979, p. 18.

67. Elliott Abrams in "Liberalism & the Jews," p. 16.

68. "Daniel Patrick Moynihan: A *Moment* Interview," *Moment*, August 1978, pp. 12, 16; Daniel Patrick Moynihan, "Exporting Anti-Semitism," *New Leader*, November 5, 1979, pp. 10, 12.

69. Bernard Lewis, review of *A Dangerous Place* by Daniel Patrick Moynihan, in *Commentary*, March 1979, p. 84; Edward N. Luttwak, "Masochism at the UN," *New Republic*, December 16, 1978, p. 17.

70. "Separate Views of Senator Daniel P. Moynihan," in Congress, Senate, Select Committee on Intelligence, Subcommittee on Collection, Production, and Quality, *The National Intelligence Estimates A-B Team Episode Concerning Soviet Strategic Capability and Objectives*, 95th Cong., 2nd sess., p. 9; Daniel Patrick Moynihan, "Reflections: The SALT process," *New Yorker*, November 19, 1979, reprinted in Daniel Patrick Moynihan, *Counting Our Blessings*, (Boston: Little, Brown, 1980), pp. 307, 318, 326, 321, 333.

71. Morton Kondracke, "The Moynihan Movement," *New Republic*, July 22, 1978, pp. 10, 11; Steven Rattner, "Upstart in the Senate," *New York Times Magazine*, January 7, 1979, p. 48.

72. William F. Buckley, Jr., "Why Not Moynihan?" *National Review*, June 22, 1979; "The Perils of Pat," *Nation*, September 22, 1979, p. 227.

In 1974, Buckley had written that Moynihan "identified himself with American left-liberalism" (William F. Buckley, Jr., *United Nations Journal* [New York: G. P. Putnam's Sons, 1974], p. 257).

73. *New York Times*, May 23, 1979; "Moynihan Opens Way for Favorite Son Draft," *New York Times*, August 2, 1979, p. B9; Frank Lynn, "Carter's Backers Begin Lining Up State Democrats," *New York Times*, October 17, 1979, p. B3; Irvin Molotsky, "'Nuke Twins' in Congress Lobby for Nuclear Power," *New York Times*, January 7, 1980, p. D10.

74. Irvin Molotsky, "Moynihan Criticizes Kennedy on Soviet," *New York Times*, January 11, 1980, p. A12; Daniel Patrick Moynihan, "A New American Foreign Policy," *New Republic*, February 9, 1980, p. 20; Irvin Molotsky, "Moynihan Prefers the

Role of a Neutral," *New York Times*, March 17, 1980, p. B1; Irvin Molotsky, "Moynihan Joins Carey in Deciding Not to Be Convention Delegate," *New York Times*, p. 1; "Moynihan Endorses Carter's Bid," *New York Times*, August 18, 1980, p. A14.

75. Elliott Abrams, interviews by author, July 6, 1990, and April 2, 1991, Alexandria, Va.; Horner interview, May 7, 1991.

76. Midge Decter, interview by author, February 25, 1991, New York City; Abrams interview, July 6, 1990.

Chapter Five Coping with Success, 1980–1985

1. Few complete histories of Reagan's diplomacy have been written. For a good overview, see Coral Bell, *The Reagan Paradox* (New Brunswick, N.J.: Rutgers University Press, 1989). Other useful volumes, some written while Reagan was still president, include Thomas Carothers, *In The Name of Democracy* (Berkeley and Los Angeles: University of California Press, 1991), Robert Pastor, *Condemned to Repetition* (Princeton: Princeton University Press, 1987), and Kenneth A. Oye, Robert J. Lieber, and Donald Rothchild, *Eagle Resurgent?* (Boston: Little, Brown, 1987). Few Reagan administration officials have published useful memoirs, although two anthologies by Jeane Kirkpatrick, *The Reagan Phenomenon* (Washington: American Enterprise Institute for Public Policy Research, 1983), and *Legitimacy and Force* (New Brunswick: Transaction Books, 1988) are good guides to the administration's ideology. Reagan appointees were usually willing to speak more bluntly than most diplomats, and the *Department of State Bulletin* provides a running record of their speeches and comments.

   For general background on the Reagan years, see Laurence I. Barret, *Gambling With History* (Garden City: Doubleday, 1983), Haynes Johnson, *Sleepwalking Through History* (New York: W. W. Norton, 1991), Jane Mayer and Doyle McManus, *Landslide* (Boston: Houghton Mifflin, 1988), and Garry Wills, *Reagan's America* (Garden City: Doubleday, 1987).

2. Elliott Abrams, interview by author, July 6, 1990, Alexandria, Va.; Richard Perle, telephone interview, March 25, 1991.

3. "Founding Statement of The Committee For the Free World," February 1981, in Committee For the Free World papers, box 25, Hoover Institution Archives, Stanford, Calif. (hereafter cited as CFW papers.)

4. Midge Decter to Leopold Labedz, October 20, 1980, CFW Papers, Box 5; Midge Decter, interview by author, February 25, 1991, New York City; Midge Decter to Daniel Bell, December 11, 1980, CFW papers, Box 1.

5. Kathleen Tesltsch, "400 Intellectuals Form 'Struggle for Freedom' Unit," *New York Times*, February 19, 1981, p. A19; Gene L. Harmon, Sears, Roebuck and Co., to Midge Decter, March 20, 1984, CFW papers, box 10, Windon folder; Bernard M. Windon, Searle Corp., to Rawleigh Warner, Jr., Mobil Corp., December 21, 1983, CFW papers, box 10, Windon folder; William E. Simon to Donald Rumsfeld, November 16, 1983, CFW papers, box 10, Windon folder; Committee For the Free World, Inc., *Report*, December 31, 1982, CFW papers, box 25.

6. "A Note From the Editor," *Contentions*, August 1981; Richard Bernstein, "Conservatives Gather in City to Defend Their Principles," *New York Times*, February 14, 1983, p. B4. For an amusing and skeptical view of the 1983 CFW conference, see

Alfred Kazin, "Saving My Soul at the Plaza," *New York Review of Books*, March 31, 1983.

7. Decter interview, February 7, 1991.

8. Kenneth Adelman to Midge Decter, undated, CFW papers, box 1; Jed Snyder to Midge Decter, January 25, 1982, CFW papers, box 8, S folder; Richard Williamson, assistant to the President for intergovernmental affairs, to Midge Decter, September 23, 1982, December 13, 1982, April 19, 1983, CFW papers, box 10, W folder; John Lenczowski, National Security Council, to Midge Decter, October 19, 1984, and Franklin L. Lavin, White House Office of Public Liaison, to Midge Decter, June 28, 1984, CFW papers, box 5, L folder; Norman Podhoretz in *Our Country & Our Culture: A Conference of the Committee for the Free World* (New York: Orwell Press, 1983), pp. 111–112.

9. Robert W. Tucker, "The Purposes of American Power," *Foreign Affairs*, Winter 1980-1981, pp. 251; Norman Podhoretz, "The New American Majority," *Commentary*, January 1981, pp. 19, 28.

10. Tucker, "The Purposes of American Power," p. 247; Podhoretz, "The New American Majority," p. 25; Jeane Kirkpatrick, "U.S. Security & Latin America," *Commentary*, January 1981, p. 29.

11. William Schneider, "Conservatism, Not Interventionism: Trends in Foreign Policy Opinion," in Kenneth A. Oye, Robert J. Lieber, and Donald Rothchild, eds., *Eagle Defiant: United States Foreign Policy in the 1980s* (Boston: Little, Brown, 1983), pp. 34, 45; Norman Podhoretz, "The Present Danger," *Commentary*, March 1980, p. 40 (italics in the original); Tucker, "The Purposes of American Power," pp. 262, 265.

12. Norman Podhoretz, "The Future Danger," *Commentary*, April 1981, p. 47. Gary Dorrien argues—probably erroneously—that arguments such as Podhoretz's indicate that James Burnham was a major influence on the neoconservatives' outlook during the latter part of the cold war. See Gary Dorrien, *The Neoconservative Mind* (Philadelphia: Temple University Press, 1993), chapter 2 and pp. 370-373.

13. Podhoretz, "The Future Danger," pp. 40, 37, 45.

14. Norman Podhoretz, "A Note on Vietnamization," *Commentary*, May 1971, p. 9; Norman Podhoretz, *Why We Were in Vietnam* (New York: Simon and Schuster, 1982), pp. 210, 108.

15. Podhoretz, *Why We Were in Vietnam*, 209.

16. Irving Kristol, "The Muddle in Foreign Policy," *Wall Street Journal*, April 29, 1981, p. 28.

17. Kristol, "The Muddle in Foreign Policy," p. 28; Irving Kristol, interview by author, July 21, 1993, Washington, D.C.; Robert W. Tucker, "Appeasement & the AWACS," *Commentary*, December 1981, pp. 29, 30.

18. Walter Laqueur, "Reagan & the Russians," *Commentary*, January 1982, pp. 22, 24, 25, 26.

19. Podhoretz, "The New American Majority," p 28; Norman Podhoretz, "The Neo-Conservative Anguish Over Reagan's Foreign Policy," *New York Times Magazine*, May 2, 1982, pp. 32, 88, 89, 96, 92, 97 (italics in the original).

20. Norman Podhoretz, "Appeasement By Any Other Name," *Commentary*, July 1983, p. 38; Norman Podhoretz, review of *Caveat* by Alexander Haig, in *Commentary*, July 1984, p. 59.

21. Norman Podhoretz, "The Reagan Road to Détente," *Foreign Affairs: America and the World, 1984*, pp. 458, 461, 462.

22. Congress, Senate, Committee on Foreign Relations, *Nomination of Jeane Kirkpatrick*, 97th Cong., 1st sess., January 15, 1981, pp. 6, 7; Bernard D. Nossiter, "U.N. Nominee Envisions Firm Stance," *New York Times*, January 12, 1981, p. A3.

23. *Nomination of Jeane Kirkpatrick*, pp. 8, 16; Jeane J. Kirkpatrick, "The Reagan Phenomenon and the Liberal Tradition," speech to the Centro Studi per la Conceiliazione Internazionale, Rome, Italy, May 28, 1981, reprinted in Kirkpatrick, *The Reagan Phenomenon*, p. 7.

24. Allan Gerson, *The Kirkpatrick Mission* (New York: The Free Press, 1991), p. 23; Seymour Maxwell Finger, "The Reagan-Kirkpatrick Policies and the United Nations," *Foreign Affairs*, Winter 1983-1984, p. 445.

25. For details of the Haig-Kirkpatrick battle, see Gerson, *The Kirkpatrick Mission*, chapters 8 and 9, and Barrett, *Gambling With History*, chapter 14.

26. Jeane J. Kirkpatrick, "The Problem of the United Nations," speech to the Foreign Policy Association, New York, January 26, 1982, reprinted in Kirkpatrick, *The Reagan Phenomenon*, p. 92 (italics in the original); Jeane J. Kirkpatrick, "Standing Alone," speech given at Arizona State University, Tempe, October 23, 1981, reprinted in *The Reagan Phenomenon*, p. 87; Mary Schwartz, "Jeane Kirkpatrick: Our Macho UN Ambassador," *National Review*, January 21, 1983, p. 49.

27. Bernard D. Nossiter, "Mrs. Kirkpatrick Asks 40 Nations To Explain Their Anti-U.S. Stand," *New York Times*, October 14, 1981, p. 1; Gerson, *The Kirkpatrick Mission*, p. 79.

28. Jeane J. Kirkpatrick. "Delegitimizing Israel," statement in the General Assembly, April 23, 1982, reprinted in *The Reagan Phenomenon*, p. 129; "Ambassador Kirkpatrick's Statement, UN Security Council, September 6, 1983," reprinted in *Department of State Bulletin*, October 1982, pp. 8, 10, 11; Carl Gershman, "The Right of Self-determination," *Freedom At Issue*, March-April 1982, pp. 4, 7.

29. Finger, "The Reagan-Kirkpatrick Policies and the United Nations," p. 457; Gerson, *The Kirkpatrick Mission*, p. 80.

30. Jeane Kirkpatrick and George Urban, "American Foreign Policy in a Cold Climate: A Long Conversation," *Encounter*, November 1983, pp. 25, 31; Jeane Kirkpatrick, "Democratic Elections and Democratic Government," address to the American Enterprise Institute and the Department of State, November 4, 1982, reprinted in *World Affairs*, Fall 1984, p. 64.

31. "Ambassador Kirkpatrick's Statement, UN Security Council, October 27, 1983," *Department of State Bulletin*, December 1983, p. 74; Jeane Kirkpatrick, "The Superpowers: Is There a Moral Difference?" *The World Today*, May 1984, p. 184.

32. Jeane Kirkpatrick, "U.S. Foreign Policy," *Vital Speeches*, May 15, 1984, p. 455; Jeane Kirkpatrick, "Human Rights in El Salvador," statement in the Third Committee, December 1, 1981, reprinted in *The Reagan Phenomenon*, pp. 54, 61; Kirkpatrick, "The Superpowers: Is There a Moral Difference?" p. 184.

33. Abrams interview, July 6, 1990.

34. Abrams interview, July 6, 1990.

35. Abrams interview, July 6, 1990; Francis X. Clines and Bernard Weinraub, "Briefing," *New York Times*, November 24, 1981, p. B2.

36. "Human Rights Revisited," *New Republic*, November 25, 1981, p. 5; Christopher

Madison, "Abrams, State's Human Rights Chief, Tries to Tailor a Policy to Suit
Reagan," *National Journal*, May 1, 1982, p. 765; "Excerpts From State Department Memo on Human Rights," *New York Times*, November 5, 1981, p. A10.

37. Madison, "Abrams, State's Human Rights Chief," p. 763; introduction to *Country
Reports on Human Rights Practices for 1981*, reprinted in *Department of State
Bulletin*, April 1982, p. 75.

38. Abrams interview, July 6, 1990; Elliott Abrams, "The Cuban Revolution and Its
Impact on Human Rights," *Department of State Bulletin*, December 1983, p. 28;
Elliott Abrams to Norman Podhoretz, March 5, 1982, CFW papers, box 1,
Abrams folder.

39. Elliott Abrams, "Human Rights and the Reagan Administration: Another View,"
America, June 4, 1983, p. 433; introduction to *Country Reports on Human Rights
Practices for 1981*, p. 72; Elliott Abrams, "The Situation We Face in Central
America," *Vital Speeches*, December 1, 1982, pp. 102, 103.

40. Elliott Abrams, letter to the editor, *Foreign Policy*, Winter 1983–1984, p. 174;
introduction to *Country Reports on Human Rights Practices for 1983*, reprinted
in *Department of State Bulletin*, April 1984, pp. 54, 56, 57.

41. Elliott Abrams, "Human Rights Conditions in El Salvador," *Department of State
Bulletin*, September 1982, pp. 42, 43; Elliott Abrams, "Human Rights Implications for U.S. Action in Grenada," speech before the Los Angeles World Affairs
Council, November 22, 1983, reprinted in *Department of State Bulletin*, February
1984, p. 26.

42. Abrams, "Human Rights and the Reagan Administration," p. 453; introduction to
Country Reports on Human Rights Practices for 1983, p. 53.

43. Thomas Carothers, *In the Name of Democracy*, (Berkeley and Los Angeles: University of California Press, 1991), p. 153; Abrams interview.

44. Bernard Weinraub, "Kirkpatrick Asserts Some in Washington Distorted Her
Views," *New York Times*, February 1, 1985, p. A9; Abrams interview, July 6, 1990.

45. "Text of Jeane J. Kirkpatrick's Remarks at Republican Convention in Dallas," *New
York Times*, August 21, 1984, p. A22.

46. Daniel Patrick Moynihan, "Was Woodrow Wilson Right?" *Commentary*, May
1974, p. 28.

47. Ronald Reagan, "Address to Members of the British parliament," June 8, 1982,
reprinted in *Public Papers of the Presidents of the United States: Ronald Reagan,
1982*, vol. 1, pp. 745, 746.

48. "Project Democracy," *Department of State Bulletin*, April 1983, pp. 47, 48.

49. Irvin Molotsky, "Moynihan Vows to Resist a 'Cadre' of Kennedy Backers From the
Left," *New York Times*, November 12, 1980, pp. A1, A24; Mary Battiata, "The
U.N. Envoy, the Coalition and Human Rights," *Washington Post*, February 3,
1981, p. B4.

50. Daniel Patrick Moynihan, "'Joining the Jackals': The U.S. at the U.N.
1977–1980," *Commentary*, February 1981, pp. 24, 28.

51. Moynihan, "Joining the Jackals," pp. 29, 30, 25, 29.

52. Moynihan, "Joining the Jackals," pp. 30, 31, 23.

53. Moynihan quoted in Fred Barnes, "Pat Moynihan, Neo-Liberal," *New Republic*,
October 21, 1981, p. 17; Barbara Crossette, "Senate Approves '82 Foreign Assistance Bill, 40-33," *New York Times*, October 23, 1981, p. A9.

54. Daniel Patrick Moynihan, "One-Third of a Nation," *New Republic*, June 9, 1982, p. 21.

55. "Kissinger and Moynihan: Five Years Later," *Public Opinion*, April–May 1983, p. 54; Jane Perlez, "New York Region's Senators Are Divided on Latin Policies," *New York Times*, April 30, 1983, p. 25;

56. Jane Perlez, "After Much in Common, a Split on Central America," *New York Times*, June 30, 1983, p. B6; Jane Perlez, "Latin Panel's Soviet Finding Is Challenged by Moynihan," *New York Times*, January 13, 1984, p. A8.

57. Daniel Patrick Moynihan, commencement address, New York University, May 24, 1984, reprinted in Moynihan, *Came the Revolution*, pp. 190, 191.

   Moynihan has since claimed that he saw the exhaustion of the Soviet threat as early as 1979, usually pointing to his statement in *Newsweek* that "the Soviet empire is coming under tremendous strain. It could blow up." His perception of the threat and prediction were not as accurate as he likes to imply; in the same piece he warned that Moscow would probably try to take the Persian Gulf oil fields "in order to reverse the decline at home and preserve national unity" (Daniel Patrick Moynihan, "Will Russia Blow Up?" *Newsweek*, November 19, 1979, pp. 144, 147). For Moynihan's retrospective explanation of his shift in point of view, see Daniel Patrick Moynihan, *Pandaemonium* (New York: Oxford University Press, 1993), pp. 38–41.

58. "Kissinger and Moynihan: Five Years Later," p. 54.

59. Philip Taubman, "Moynihan Questions C.I.A.'s Latin Role," *New York Times*, April 1, 1983, p. A3.

60. Bernard Gwertzman, "Moynihan To Quit Senate Panel Post in Dispute on C.I.A.," *New York Times*, April 16, 1984, p. A8.

61. "Text of Moynihan Statement," *New York Times*, April 16, 1984, p. A8 (italics in the original); Philip Taubman, "Moynihan To Keep Intelligence Post," *New York Times*, April 27, 1984, p. A1.

62. Dinesh D'Souza and Adam Meyerson, "An Interview with Senator Moynihan," *Policy Review*, Spring 1984, p. 46; Jane Perlez, "Senators Talk About Beirut And Takeover of Grenada," *New York Times*, October 30, 1983, p. 22.

63. Daniel Patrick Moynihan, "U.S. Has Abandoned International Law," *Newsday*, April 13, 1984, reprinted in Moynihan, *Came the Revolution*, pp. 173, 174.

64. Dinesh D'Souza, "Paddy, We Hardly Knew Ye," *Policy Review*, Spring 1984, p. 49; Perlez, "After Much in Common," p. B6.

65. Podhoretz, "Appeasement By Any Other Name," pp. 34, 35; Perlez, "After Much in Common," p. B6; "Et Tu, Moynihan," *National Review*, August 5, 1983, p. 913; Decter interview, February 25, 1991.

66. Michael Novak, "In Memorium: Henry M. Jackson," *Commentary*, January 1984, p. 50; Abrams quoted in Fred Barnes, "The Death of the Jackson Wing," *American Spectator*, March 1984, reprinted in R. Emmett Tyrell, Jr., ed., *Orthodoxies* (New York: Harper & Row, 1987), p. 484; Barnes, "Death of the Jackson Wing," p. 485.

67. The depth of the neoconservatives' continuing bad feelings toward Moynihan is evident, for example, in the first explicitly anti-Moynihan article published in *Commentary*. See Glenn C. Loury, "The Family, the Nation, and Senator Moynihan," *Commentary*, June 1986, in which Moynihan was denounced as a defender

of the "liberal policy edifice against both the promptings of experience and the encroaching judgment of the American electorate." In early 1991, Norman Podhoretz was reluctant even to talk about his experiences with Moynihan, citing the tenuous nature of their once warm personal relationship (Norman Podhoretz, telephone discussion with author, February 15, 1991).

Chapter 6   After the Cold War, 1985–1992

1. Walter Laqueur, "Is There Now, or Has There Ever Been, Such a Thing as Totalitarianism?" *Commentary,* October 1985, p. 34; Eugene V. Rostow, "Why the Soviets Want An Arms-Control Agreement, And Why They Want It Now," *Commentary*, February 1987, p. 20; Angelo M. Codevilla, "Is There Still a Soviet Threat?" *Commentary*, November 1988, p. 23.

2. Laqueur, "Is There Now . . . ?" p. 32; Jean-François Revel, "Is Communism Reversible?" *Commentary*, January 1989, p. 19; Walter Laqueur, "Glasnost & Its Limits," *Commentary* July 1988, p. 18.

3. Rostow, "Why the Soviets Want An Arms-Control Agreement," p. 26; Patrick Glynn, "Reagan's Rush to Disarm," *Commentary*, March 1988, p. 20.

4. Peter Collier and David Horowitz, "Another 'Low Dishonest Decade' on the Left," *Commentary*, January 1987, p. 24; Owen Harries, "The Cold War & the Intellectuals," *Commentary*, October 1991, p. 19.

5. Irving Kristol, interview by author, July 21, 1993, Washington D.C.; "A Note on *The National Interest*," *National Interest*, Fall 1985, p. 3.

6. Henry S. Rowen, "Living with a Sick Bear," *National Interest*, Winter 1986, pp. 14, 15, 18; Robert W. Tucker, "Exemplar or Crusader?" *National Interest*, Fall 1986, p. 66.

7. Francis Fukuyama, "The End of History?" *National Interest*, Summer 1989, pp. 3, 4 (italics in the original); James Atlas, "What is Fukuyama Saying?" *New York Times Magazine*, October 22, 1989, p. 38.

8. Fukuyama, "The End of History?" p. 18.

9. Tucker, "Exemplar or Crusader?" pp. 69, 74, 75.

10. Jeane J. Kirkpatrick, "A Normal Country in a Normal Time," *National Interest*, Fall 1990, pp. 43, 42, 41, 40; Irving Kristol, "Defining Our National Interests," *National Interest*, Fall 1990, p. 25; Kristol interview, July 21, 1993.

11. Charles Krauthammer, "The Multilateral Fallacy," *New Republic*, December 9, 1985, p. 19; Charles Krauthammer, "Morality and the Reagan Doctrine," *New Republic*, September 8, 1986; Charles Krauthammer, "The Price of Power," *New Republic*, February 9, 1987.

12. Charles Krauthammer, "Universal Dominion: Toward a Unipolar World," *National Interest*, Winter 1989-1990, pp. 48, 49; Charles Krauthammer, "The Unipolar Moment," *Foreign Affairs: America and the World, 1990/91*, p. 24.

13. Charles Krauthammer, "The Lonely Superpower," *New Republic*, July 29, 1991, pp. 26, 27; Elliott Abrams, "Why America Must Lead," *National Interest*, Summer 1992, p. 59.

14. Robert W. Tucker and David C. Hendrickson, *The Imperial Temptation* (New York: Council on Foreign Relations Press, 1992), p. 210 (italics in the original).
   Tucker and Hendrickson wrote this book in 1992 as a post-Gulf war critique of President Bush's policies for a new world order. In addition to criticizing

democratic crusades, Tucker and Hendrickson criticized what they viewed as the growing American perception that war has become a cheap and easy solution to foreign problems: "We have fastened upon a formula for going to war—in which American casualties are minimized and protracted engagements are avoided—that requires the massive use of American firepower and a speedy withdrawal from the scenes of destruction. . . . It creates an anarchy and calls it peace" (Tucker and Hendrickson, *Imperial Temptation,* p. 162). Tucker and Hendrickson's suspicion of democratic crusades is also reminiscent of Tucker's arguments in *A New Isolationism.*

15. For Jeane Kirkpatrick on Bosnia, see "To Die in Sarajevo," *Policy Review,* Fall 1992, p. 38. See also Joshua Muravchik, "The Strange Debate Over Bosnia," *Commentary,* November 1992, and Charles Krauthammer, "Sarajevo Burns. Will We Learn?" *Time,* June 15, 1992, p. 78.

16. Kristol interview, July 21, 1993. The leading proponent for a democracy-centered foreign policy is Joshua Muravchik. See Joshua Muravchik, *Exporting Democracy* (Washington: American Enterprise Institute, 1991).

17. Michael Novak, "Father of Neoconservatives," *National Review,* May 11, 1992, pp. 39-42; Kristol interview, July 21, 1993. For another celebration of Niebuhr's centennial, see Arthur M. Schlesinger, Jr., "Reinhold Niebuhr's Long Shadow," *New York Times,* June 22, 1992, p. A17.

18. For Jeane Kirkpatrick's increased sympathy for conservatism, see Jeane Kirkpatrick, "Welfare State Conservatism," interview by Adam Meyerson, *Policy Review,* Spring 1988.

19. Brigitte Berger and Peter L. Berger, "Our Conservatism and Theirs," *Commentary,* October 1986, p. 65; Dan Himmelfarb, "Conservative Splits," *Commentary,* May 1988, p. 56.

20. Kirk and Buchanan quoted in Jacob Weisberg, "Hunter Gatherers," *New Republic,* September 2, 1991, pp. 14, 15. For more of Kirk's thoughts on the neoconservatives, see Russell Kirk, review of *To the Right: The Transformation of American Conservatism* by Jerome L. Himmelstein, in *National Review,* March 19, 1990, pp. 46-50. For the Buchanan controversy, which also included charges against conservative columnist Joseph Sobran, see William F. Buckley, Jr., "In Search of Anti-Semitism," *National Review,* December 30, 1991, pp. 20-63. Responses to Buckley are in *National Review,* March 16, 1992. See also Norman Podhoretz, "What is Anti-Semitism? An Open Letter to William F. Buckley, Jr.," *Commentary,* February 1992, and Norman Podhoretz, "Buchanan and the Conservative Crackup," *Commentary,* May 1992. A more comprehensive critique of Buchanan is Irving Kristol, "From Perot to Buchanan," *Wall Street Journal,* November 24, 1993, p. A16. For a paleoconservative view of neoconservatism's role in the conservative movement, see Paul Gottfried, *The Conservative Movement,* revised edition, Twayne's Social Movement Series (Boston: Twayne Publishers, 1993).

21. For details of Clinton's appeal to the neoconservatives and their response, see the epilogue.

22. Arthur M. Schlesinger, Jr., "Democracy; What Does It Mean?" pp. 402, 401.

23. Aaron Wildavsky, "The Triumph of Ronald Reagan," *National Interest,* Winter 1988-1989, p. 7; Susan F. Rasky, "The Jackson Democrats, Updated," *New York Times,* August 27, 1987, p. B6. See also Robert W. Tucker, "Reagan's Foreign

Policy," *Foreign Affairs: America and the World, 1988/89* and Jay Winik, "The Neoconservative Reconstruction," *Foreign Policy*, Winter 1988-1989.

24. Daniel Patrick Moynihan, "Defining Deviancy Down," *American Scholar*, Winter 1993, p. 19. For an interesting analysis of and addition to Moynihan's argument, see Charles Krauthammer, "Defining Deviancy Up," *New Republic*, November 22, 1993. Moynihan also made headlines with a spring 1993 speech to the Association for a Better New York criticizing the city's (liberal democratic) government's failures. For the text, see Daniel Patrick Moynihan, "Toward a New Intolerance," *Public Interest*, Summer 1993.

Midge Decter is an intellectual who succeeded in moving beyond the cold war. In December 1990, she closed down the Committee for the Free World, declaring that "it's time to say: We've won, goodbye," and has since focused her writings on education and family issues (E. J. Dionne, Jr., "Cold Warrior Melt-down," *Washington Post*, December 19, 1990, C1).

25. On October 7, 1991, Abrams pleaded guilty to two counts of withholding infor-mation from Congress and was sentenced to two years' probation and 100 hours of community service. Abrams has since written a memoir of what he views as a political prosecution by independent counsel Lawrence Walsh; see Elliot Abrams, *Undue Process* (New York: The Free Press, 1993). Although reviewers have divided along partisan lines in their treatment of Abrams's complaint of persecu-tion, most have acknowledged the validity of one of his major points, that Walsh and his assistants turned political disputes into criminal charges and that inde-pendent counsels are not held to adequate standards of accountability. President Bush pardoned Abrams in December 1992.

Epilogue

1. "Excerpts From Interview with Clinton on Goals for Presidency," *New York Times*, June 28, 1992, p. 17.

2. "Excerpts From Clinton's Speech on Foreign Policy Leadership," *New York Times*, August 14, 1992, p. A15; "Excerpts From Speech by Clinton on U.S. Role," *New York Times*, October 2, 1992, P. A21.

3. "Excerpts From Interview with Clinton," p. 17; Gerald F. Seib, "Cold War's End Shuffles Foreign Policy Debate: Bush Urges Caution and Clinton Takes Hard Line," *Wall Street Journal*, October 22, 1992, p. A16; Don Oberdorfer, "On Global Matters, Two Candidates' Positions Are Mostly in Sync," *Washington Post*, Sep-tember 29, 1993, p. A7; Leon V. Sigal, "The Last Cold War Election," *Foreign Affairs*, Winter 1992/93, p. 4.

4. For information of the effects of the end of the cold war on Democratic strategy, see R. W. Apple, "Campaign Shifts to a New Turf," *New York Times*, July 29, 1992, p. A12.

5. Thomas L. Friedman, "Clinton's Foreign Policy Agenda Reaches Across Broad Spectrum," *New York Times*, October 4, 1992, p. 1; Jeffrey H. Birnbaum, "Aching for Approval," *Wall Street Journal*, September 21, 1992, p. R4; Elizabeth Kolbert, "An Early Loss Cast Clinton as a leader by Consensus," *New York Times*, Septem-ber 28, 1992, p. A12; "Clinton for President," *New Republic*, November 9, 1992, p. 7. For comments on Clinton's abilities as a politician, see Fred Barnes, "Cool Hand Bill," *New Republic*, November 16, 1992.

6. Angelo M. Codevilla, "Magnificent, But Was it War?" *Commentary*, April 1992, p. 20; Laurie Mylroie, "How We Helped Saddam Survive," *Commentary*, July 1991, p. 18. Not all neoconservatives saw the war as an incomplete success; see Daniel Pipes and Martin Peretz, "Bush, Clinton & the Jews," *Commentary*, October 1992.

7. "Same to You, Buddy," editorial, *New Republic*, March 30, 1992, p. 8.

   Foreign affairs were not the only areas of contention between Bush and the neoconservatives. For an example of their poor opinion of Bush's domestic policies, in this case affirmative action, see Chester E. Finn, Jr., "Quotas and the Bush Administration," *Commentary*, November 1991. For an angry neoconservative attack on Bush's overall performance as president, see John Podhoretz, *Hell of a Ride* (New York: Simon and Schuster, 1993).

8. Joshua Muravchik, "Conservatives for Clinton," *New Republic*, November 2, 1992, p. 22; Fred Barnes, "They're Back!" *New Republic*, August 3, 1992, p. 12. For neoconservative debates on Clinton, see Richard Schifter and Thomas Sowell, "Have the Democrats Really Changed?" *Commentary*, September 1992, and Daniel Pipes and Martin Peretz, "Bush, Clinton & the Jews," *Commentary*, October 1992. For a post-election analysis, see Joshua Muravchik, "Why the Democrats Finally Won," *Commentary*, January 1993.

9. Podhoretz, Abrams, and Kristol quoted in Barnes, "They're Back!" p. 14.

10. Warren Christopher, "Ceasefire Between the Branches: A Compact in Foreign Affairs," *Foreign Affairs*, Summer 1984, pp. 996, 999, 1003; "The Quiet Man," editorial, *New Republic*, January 18, 1993, p. 7.

11. Leslie H. Gelb and Anthony Lake, "Four More Years: Diplomacy Restored?" *Foreign Affairs: America and the World, 1984,* p. 469; Anthony Lake, *Somoza Falling* (1989; reprint, Amherst: The University of Massachusetts Press, 1990), p. 273 (page references are to reprint edition).

12. Lake, *Somoza Falling*, pp. 264, 279-80; Gelb and Lake, "Four More Years," p. 466; Anthony Lake, "Do the Doable," *Foreign Policy,* Spring 1984, pp. 121, 113.

13. Congress, Senate, Committee on Foreign Relations, *Nomination of Warren M. Christopher to be Secretary of State*, 103rd Cong., 1st sess., January 13 and 14, 1993, p. 20; Anthony Lake, "From Containment to Enlargement," *Vital Speeches,* October 15, 1993, p. 15; Warren Christopher, "U.S. Foreign Relations," *Vital Speeches*, April 15, 1993, p. 387.

14. The administration's economic foreign policy was based more on the writings of Secretary of Labor Robert Reich than it was on world order theory or Christopher's restatement of common assumptions about the changing global economy. See Robert B. Reich, *The Work of Nations* (New York: Alfred A. Knopf, 1991).

15. Thomas E. Ricks, "Defense Secretary Aspin Draws Heaviest Fire As Criticism Mounts Over U.S. Role in Somalia," *Wall Street Journal*, October 8, 1993, p. A16. Aspin resigned on December 15, 1993, in part because Clinton lost confidence in him after the Mogadishu debacle. See Thomas L. Friedman, "Others Tottered Earlier, but Aspin Fell," *New York Times*, December 17, 1993, p. B13.

16. George J. Church, "Anatomy of a Disaster," *Time,* November 22, 1993, p. 49.

   At the same time that the Somali situation erupted, problems with Haiti and North Korea also demonstrated the administration's difficulty in dealing effectively with regimes that defied American will. In Haiti, the military government went back on its agreement to allow the return of the country's democratically elected president, whom the army had overthrown, and prevented the agreed-to landing of lightly armed U.S. marines. The United Nations quickly placed Haiti under a strict economic embargo, which was enforced by the U.S. navy. North Korea, suspected to be developing nuclear weapons despite its obligations under the nuclear nonproliferation treaty not to do so, frustrated attempts to arrange an inspection of its nuclear facilities and threatened war if pushed too far. The United States began negotiations with North Korea in an effort to resolve the inspection deadlock. Under a compromise arrangement, Pyongyang allowed a one-time, limited inspection in March 1994. The inspection was unsatisfactory, however, and tensions continued to increase.

17. Fred Barnes, "Neoconned," *New Republic*, January 25, 1993, pp. 14, 15; "The Quiet Man," *New Republic*, January 18, 1993, p. 7; John M. Goshko, "Neoconservative Democrats Complain of Big Chill," *Washington Post*, March 15, 1993, p. A17. For Clinton's criteria for appointees, which emphasized racial, ethnic, and gender balances, see John B. Judis, "The Old Democrat," *New Republic*, February 22, 1993. For neoconservative disappointment with domestic policy appointees, see Michael Kelly, "'New Democrats' Say Clinton Has Veered Left and Left Them," *New York Times*, May 23, 1993, p. A20.

Like many deputy secretaries, and because of his inexperience, Wharton was given mostly administrative tasks and had virtually no role in policy making, which was dominated by Christopher, Lake, and Tarnoff. After the Somali and Haiti incidents, however, the administration faced calls to shake up its ranks and to fire whoever was to blame. Wharton was deemed expendable and forced to resign in early November. For the circumstances of his resignation, see "With Foreign Policies Under Fire, Top State Dept. Deputy is Ousted," *New York Times*, November 9, 1993, p. 1, and "The No-Guts, No-Glory Guys," *Time*, November 22, 1993.

18. Joshua Muravchik, "Lament of a Clinton Supporter," *Commentary*, August 1993, p. 16.

Clinton's problems in balancing his administration were not limited to appointments. Policy feuds, reflecting ideological differences among Democrats, were also endemic. See Thomas L. Friedman, "President Chides Centrist Council," *New York Times*, December 4, 1993, p. 10.

19. Irwin M. Stelzer, "Clintonism Unmasked," *Commentary*, May 1993; Muravchik, "Lament of a Clinton Supporter," p. 22.

20. Muravchik, "Lament of a Clinton Supporter," p. 20; Edward N. Luttwak, "If Bosnians Were Dolphins . . ." *Commentary*, October 1993, p. 32. For the growing importance of Bosnia to the neoconservatives, see the text of the open letter to Clinton, "What the West Must Do in Bosnia," *Wall Street Journal*, September 2, 1993, A12; signatories included Jeane Kirkpatrick, Paul Nitze, Joshua Muravchik, Richard Perle, and Norman Podhoretz.

21. Charles Krauthammer, "The Cost of Promises," *Washington Post*, October 22, 1993, p. A23; Charles Krauthammer, "Capitulation in Korea," *Washington Post*, January 7, 1994, p. A19.

22. Charles Krauthammer, "Paper Promises From Dictators," *Washington Post*, December 10, 1993, p. A31; Charles Krauthammer, "The Greatest Cold War Myth of All," *Time*, November 29, 1993, p. 86.

23. Joshua Muravchik, "Beyond Self-Defense," *Commentary*, December 1993, p. 24; Fareed Zakaria, "Is Realism Finished?" *National Interest*, Winter 1992–93, p. 30.

24. Zakaria, "Is Realism Finished?" pp. 30, 32 (italics in the original); Fareed Zakaria, "The Core vs. the Periphery," *Commentary*, December 1993, p. 29; Krauthammer, "The Cost of Promises"; Jeane J. Kirkpatrick, "'Clarifying' the Clinton Doctrine," *Washington Post*, October 4, 1993, p. A19.

25. Robert W. Tucker, "Realism and the New Consensus," *National Interest*, Winter 1992–93, p. 36; Muravchik, "Beyond Self-Defense," pp. 22, 23; Zakaria, "Is Realism Finished?" p. 30.

Index

Abrams, Elliott: 48, 138, 140, 141, 162,
171, 174, 185, 192, 197; joins Moynihan, 92; on neoconservatives, 122; on
Jews and Democrats, 129, 131; on
Moynihan, 135, 170; on Carter, 135–136;
and Reagan campaign, 139; assistant
secretary for IO, 149, 155–156; and
Kirkpatrick, 156; assistant secretary
for human rights, 156–161; on human
rights policy, 156–157; style, 157–158,
on human rights and democracy, 158–
160; and Chile, 160–161; on Reagan's
policies, 161; on U.S. role after cold war,
183; on neoconservative influence, 189
Adelman, Kenneth, 141, 151
After 20 Years (Barnet and Raskin), 25
Alsop, Joseph, 10
Alsop, Stewart, 10, 13
American-Russian Relations, 1781–1947
(Williams), 18
Americans for Democratic Action (ADA):
37, 41; 71; founding, 13; battle with
PCA, 13, 24

Arendt, Hannah, 115, 187
Aron, Raymond, 115, 140

Barnet, Richard J.: 26–27, 32, 104; on
cold war, 25; on U.S. imperialism, 26;
on Third World revolutions, 26; criti-
cisms of U.S., 27; influence of, 27
Bell, Daniel, 42, 47, 60
Bentsen, Lloyd, 191, 203
Berger, Brigitte, 185
Berger, Peter: 106, 109, 122; on authori-
tarianism and totalitarianism, 116; on
conservatism, 185
Between Two Ages (Brzezinski), 30
Beyond the Melting Pot (Glazer and
Moynihan), 67
Bloom, Alexander, 4, 35
Brown, H. Rap, 38, 40
Brzezinski, Zbigniew: 25, 30–32, 195; on
technetronic era, 30–31; and trilater-
alism, 31; on ideology, 31; influence of,
32; and Carter, 99
Buchanan, Patrick J., 174, 186, 192, 196

237